PABLO ESCOBAR'S STORY PART 2
NARCOS AT WAR

SHAUN ATTWOOD

First published in Great Britain by
Gadfly Press (Shaun Attwood) in 2019

Copyright © Shaun Attwood 2019

The right of Shaun Attwood to be identified as the author of this work has been asserted by him in accordance with the Copyright, Designs and Patents Act 1988. All rights reserved

No part of this book may be reproduced, stored in a retrieval system or transmitted in any form or by any means (electronic, mechanical, photocopying, recording or otherwise) without the prior written permission of the author, except in cases of brief quotations embodied in reviews or articles. It may not be edited, amended, lent, resold, hired out, distributed or otherwise circulated without the publisher's written permission

Permission can be obtained from attwood.shaun@hotmail.co.uk

This book is a work of non-fiction based on research by the author

A catalogue record of this book is available from the British Library

ISBN: 9781076176387

Typeset and cover design by Jane Dixon-Smith

ACKNOWLEDGEMENTS

A big thank you to Mark Swift (editing), Jane Dixon-Smith (cover design and typesetting)

SPELLING DIFFERENCES: UK V US

This book was written in British English, hence US readers may notice some spelling differences with American English: e.g. color = colour, meter = metre and = jewelry = jewellery

SHAUN'S BOOKS

English Shaun Trilogy
Party Time
Hard Time
Prison Time

War on Drugs Series
Pablo Escobar: Beyond Narcos
American Made: Who Killed Barry Seal? Pablo Escobar or George HW Bush
The Cali Cartel: Beyond Narcos
We Are Being Lied To: The War on Drugs (Expected 2020)
The War Against Weed (Expected 2020)

Un-Making a Murderer: The Framing of Steven Avery and Brendan Dassey
The Mafia Philosopher: Two Tonys
Life Lessons

Pablo Escobar's Story (4-Book Series)
T-Bone (Expected 2022)

SOCIAL-MEDIA LINKS

Email: attwood.shaun@hotmail.co.uk
YouTube: Shaun Attwood

Blog: Jon's Jail Journal
Website: shaunattwood.com
Instagram: @shaunattwood

Twitter: @shaunattwood
LinkedIn: Shaun Attwood
Goodreads: Shaun Attwood
Facebook: Shaun Attwood, Jon's Jail Journal, T-Bone Appreciation Society

Shaun welcomes feedback on any of
his books and YouTube videos.

Thank you for the Amazon and Goodreads
reviews and to all of the people who have
subscribed to Shaun's YouTube channel!

CONTENTS

Intro	1
Chapter 1 Shootout	3
Chapter 2 Guerrillas	5
Chapter 3 Reunited with Virginia	9
Chapter 4 Palace of Justice Attack	16
Chapter 5 The Extraditables	34
Chapter 6 Assassinations	42
Chapter 7 Plotting Evil	54
Chapter 8 Kidnapping Traffickers	66
Chapter 9 Cali Threat Grows	71
Chapter 10 Lehder's Downfall	84
Chapter 11 Home and Family Life	94
Chapter 12 Lehder's Trial	101
Chapter 13 Jorge Ochoa's Arrest	107
Chapter 14 War with Cali	110
Chapter 15 Early Elite Kidnappings	131
Chapter 16 Cali's Foreign Mercenaries	152
Chapter 17 Galán Assassination	167
Chapter 18 Elite Police	187
Chapter 19 Death of Mario Henao	194
Chapter 20 Avianca Airlines Flight 203	206

Chapter 21 Bombing Bogotá	212
Chapter 22 Death of Gacha	219
Chapter 23 Christmas Kidnappings	225
Chapter 24 Death of Pinina	231
Chapter 25 President Gaviria	242
Chapter 26 Apocalypse 2	251
Chapter 27 Death of Gustavo	262
Chapter 28 Attacking Cali	265
References	271
Get A Free Book	274
Join Shaun's Newsletter	274
Sign Up Page	274
Shaun's Books	275
Social-Media Links	276
Shaun's jail journey starts in Hard Time New Edition	277
Shaun's incarceration concludes in Prison Time	284
Other Books by Shaun Attwood	289
About Shaun Attwood	294

INTRO

Many authors have tried to dissect Pablo's character, with each only providing a few pieces of the puzzle. The first Escobar book I wrote was part of a series exposing the War on Drugs. Since its publication, I've received requests to write his biography in more detail and without the War on Drugs politics. This new series of books containing approximately 1,000 pages is my response.

After doing a talk about Pablo in London, I was approached by a Colombian. She said that there was far more information available about him in the Spanish-speaking world. On a mission, I ended up getting hundreds of thousands of words translated, which transformed my understanding of his story. Previously, I had viewed him through the filters of the English-speaking world – and many of those authors had an agenda such as portraying certain people or government agencies in particular ways.

This book also includes everything I have learned about El Patrón while researching information for my books on the Cali Cartel and Barry Seal. Since the explosion of interest in Pablo, far more up-to-date information has become available thanks to those closest to him who later became authors, including his ex-lover and TV celebrity, Virginia Vallejo (*Loving Pablo, Hating Escobar*); his son, Juan Pablo (*Pablo Escobar: My Father*); and his former hit man, Popeye (*The True Life of Pablo Escobar* and *Surviving Pablo Escobar*) – who was released and now has a popular YouTube channel. Two of the men chiefly responsible for his demise, Don Berna (*Killing the Boss*) and Carlos Castaño (*My Confession*), also published books about their roles, which contradicted the official story of the police killing Pablo. *In Secret* (*En Secreto*) by the journalist Germán Castro Caycedo and *The Words of Pablo* (*La Parábola de Pablo*) by Alonso Salazar also contain lots of information.

These combined accounts helped to revise my earlier versions of the big stories such as the absence of Los Pepes at Pablo's death, and the role of the state in the murder of the presidential candidate Galán, which had largely been overlooked. In 2017, Pablo's nemesis, General Maza, was sentenced to thirty years for conspiring to murder Galán, which had been squarely blamed on Pablo by most authors. This book also contains stories untold in the English-speaking world. It is my hope that I have provided the most detailed and up-to-date account.

CHAPTER 1
SHOOTOUT

Preparing for war, Pablo held a meeting in a farmhouse for seventy people, ranging from traffickers to priests, who arrived with 200 bodyguards. After warning about the humiliation of extradition and Colombian citizens rotting away in US prisons, he proposed the formation of an army to repel the government forces from Medellín. The city would be divided into zones, each protected by a different group of troops. Carlos Lehder – the Medellín Cartel leader whose power was declining – was assigned to oversee jungle operations and to maintain relations with the guerrillas.

After the meeting, a Mercedes-Benz arrived at the farmhouse after midnight. A well-dressed woman emerged and knocked on the door. "I have flowers for Dr Hernandez."

"You're at the wrong address," said Roberto, who warned his brother that he had never seen anyone in the flower delivery business arrive in a Mercedes-Benz. Pablo was unconcerned. Roberto instructed the men to shoot in the air if any strangers arrived.

Around 2 AM, a burst of gunfire alerted the brothers and their cousin, Gustavo, who dashed from the rear of the farmhouse. With shots whizzing by them, a bullet grazed Roberto's leg and pieces of brick ricocheted off his face. With blood streaming down his skin, he ran for his life.

Seven-year-old Juan Pablo awoke to a gun thrust into his stomach and asked, "Where's my father?" Holding Pablo's white poncho, a policeman said that Pablo had dropped it while escaping.

Fleeing from the scene, the bosses returned fire, hoping to

halt their pursuers. Spotting a bodyguard returning in a car, they waved at him to pull over and jumped inside.

"Go! Go! Go!" yelled the men as the car screeched away.

Pablo learned that a trafficker from Cali who had attended the meeting had tipped off the authorities, hoping for a guarantee against extradition. The colonel in charge of the raid had been paid $50,000 a month by Pablo, who sent him a message: "Now you are against me and you know what I think about that."

Perhaps things weren't as safe in Colombia as Pablo had thought. He went everywhere with bodyguards, moved around frequently and took extra precautions. His problems multiplied after ten of the co-conspirators in Lara Bonilla's assassination were arrested. Six, including Pinina, escaped and joined Pablo in hiding. On top of federal charges for importing cocaine into Florida, Pablo was indicted in Colombia for Lara's murder.

Outside a courthouse, one of Pablo's men approached Tulio, the judge who had indicted him for Lara's murder. "Ask for whatever you want," he said, offering a bribe for a dismissal of the charges, "and they'll put it wherever you want it, in Colombia or outside the country … Then you'll be able to relax. Neither your life nor the lives of your family will be in danger." Tulio declined, so Pablo began to plot his assassination.

On January 5, 1985, four Colombians were extradited to Miami, including the president of the Atlético Nacional soccer team on money-laundering charges. President Betancur and the new justice minister had signed their extradition orders. Pablo exploded at the injustice and the betrayal by a president whose campaign he had supported. After ranting about extradition, he instructed two of his men to bomb Betancur.

Shadowing Betancur, Pablo's men learned that his security coordinators changed his routes frequently. After finally positioning dynamite in a Mercedes-Benz on the correct road, they waited for the president to arrive. When his car approached, the remote control was pressed, but the bomb failed to explode. Pablo almost managed to kidnap Betancur's daughter, María Clara, who escaped by jumping from a car onto the lane divider of a large avenue.

CHAPTER 2
GUERRILLAS

After Pablo's death squad, the MAS, had started to annihilate the guerrillas responsible for kidnapping Marta Ochoa, he had met their leader, Iván Marino Ospina, a tall man from the peasant class with a thick moustache. Not only did each side agree not to attack the other, but as a show of good faith, Ospina gave Pablo the famous sword of the liberator Simón Bolívar, a Venezuelan military leader who had helped Colombia gain independence from Spain in 1810. A co-founder of the M-19, Jaime Bateman, had stolen the sword – a symbol of unfulfilled liberation – from a museum in 1974 and announced that it would not be returned until the government agreed to peace with the M-19. Initially, Pablo hung it on a wall.

Over time, Pablo and Ospina became friends, meeting regularly, engaging in animated discussions and railing against extradition. After receiving an arms shipment from Russia, Ospina gave Pablo a new AK-47. The majority of the traffickers, including the Ochoas, approved of the alliance with the M-19 because the group had gained such national importance. Only Fidel Castaño remained quiet, because he disapproved of any friendship with the guerrillas.

In February 1985, at a conference held by the M-19, Ospina was criticised for his hard-line approach, which was threatening negotiations with the government, and for publicly applauding in Mexico the traffickers' idea of responding to extradition by targeting US citizens in Colombia. The traffickers appreciated his commitment to the fight against extradition. Even Lehder said,

"I have returned to speak with commander Iván Marino Ospina because he is a nationalist man. He belongs to a movement that has made some positive changes and has spoken out against the extradition of Colombians to the United States."

As Ospina's actions appeared short-sighted in light of the August 1984 treaty with the government, he lost his leadership position to Álvaro Fayad, a co-founder of the M-19, and he was demoted to second-in-command. Negotiations fell apart on May 23, 1985, when a guerrilla leader barely survived a hand-grenade attack. Three weeks later, the M-19 announced its return to arms.

Despite the fluctuations in the relationship between the guerrillas and traffickers, the friendship between Pablo and Ospina lasted. He told Pablo that the new M-19 leader wanted to teach Betancur a lesson by peacefully occupying a public building and performing a mock trial with Betancur as the defendant, charged with violating the treaty he had signed with the M-19.

The first choice of building had been the National Capitol, but it was disregarded because of the difficulties of keeping an operation under control in such an enormous place. The second choice was the Palace of Justice in Bogotá, which would be easier to control due to its architecture and because it only had two entrances: the main door and an entrance in the basement. The Palace of Justice was adjacent to Bolívar Square, a huge area with a statue of Simón Bolívar in its centre, facing the Metropolitan Cathedral Basilica of the Immaculate Conception on the eastern side. The area also hosted the mayor's office, the Senate, and beyond the Senate, the presidential palace, protected by the Presidential Guard Battalion.

Impressed by the M-19's ability to commit spectacular attacks against the government, Pablo decided to exploit the plan to occupy the Palace of Justice. In the hope of repealing the extradition treaty, the traffickers had filed lawsuits, which nine Supreme Court justices were assessing. Now he had an opportunity to terrify them by targeting their building and the files on extradition. If he could destroy or intimidate the justice system in such a sensational way, maybe he could exercise his power over the entire country. He would do the unthinkable: go after the Supreme Court.

The M-19 assigned Ruiz to head the Palace of Justice occupation and to train the troops. At a safe house near Hacienda Nápoles, Ruiz, Ospina and other guerrilla leaders met Pablo. They were furious with the president for mocking them. Pablo said that the military owned the presidency, and that the military was unwilling to support the peace process. The guerrillas said that the attack would earn them respect and bargaining power. It required fifty troops.

"Twenty-eight guerrillas will enter by the basement, where our man will let them in. We'll have six already inside the palace, posing as lawyers. Around the exterior, we'll have ten more ready as backup."

After several hours of strategising, El Patrón asked how much they needed. "Pablo, we want you to finance the whole operation," Ospina said. "If it's successful, it can help with your fight against extradition. That's why we sought you out."

"We estimate we'll need about $1 million," Fayad said. "We'll need rifles and C4."

"I'll lend you a plane," Pablo said, "that can land here in order to move the weapons and explosives. You should bring the weapons in from Nicaragua. You should enter the building through the basement, go to the cafeteria and occupy the building floor by floor. You'll need radios inside and outside the building to check what's going on. To help you escape, you need to wear Colombia's civil defence uniforms, as they are the agency which will be assigned to respond to the disaster."

"Thank you, Pablo."

"But I'll make a more interesting proposal. We must take advantage of your infiltration of the palace to give extradition a strong blow. I'll give you $2 million, but there will be five more waiting for you when you finish. Two of my men will accompany you, and together you will burn the files for every person scheduled for extradition to America." He listed the justices he wanted dead for backing extradition.

"No," Ospina said. "It's not a good idea for people outside of the command to come with us. We have been training our people for several months for the operation, and it would be too risky to bring your men."

"Well," Pablo said, "you must ensure that this objective is accomplished. If all of the extradition files are destroyed, you'll receive a cash bonus. Then, you should think about occupying the Colombian Congress and getting rid of every corrupt politician. It would be a more effective and spectacular blow to the government, who would be forced to negotiate more easily and give into any demands."

CHAPTER 3
REUNITED WITH VIRGINIA

The TV show, *The Jobs of Man*, invited Virginia for a one-hour interview about her life. Wearing noticeable jewellery on the set, she denounced extradition. After the broadcast, Gacha and Gustavo called her on behalf of the Extraditables and thanked her for her bravery. The programme garnered record views, but she received no thanks from Pablo or the families of the two Mafia bosses incarcerated in Spain.

Fired from *Show of the Stars*, she started to date a tycoon in his 60s, but after he asked her to marry him and have children, she ended the relationship. Angrily, he yelled that he had heard that she hated children because having babies would ruin her figure. She replied that Pablo had $3 billion, not only $300 million like him; Pablo was the same age as her, 35, not 65 like him; he had a dozen planes, not only one like him. He said that the truth was that she didn't want to get married because she was still in love with the King of Coke.

A few days later, flowers started to arrive, including a batch of ten orchids with her favourite newspaper photo and a letter from Pablo which stated that he now had only one plane and could not spend the rest of his life without her face on his pillow. He called, but she hung up. Hearing her favourite tango music outside, she rushed to a window and saw a violinist, who played the tune three times and left.

Pablo called and said she had been spotted getting out of an Avianca plane with the airline owner. Although he wasn't an airline owner, he had owned a plane since he was 30 and they both needed to stop their foolishness because life was short and neither of them really gave a damn about Gilberto. He desperately wanted access to the mind behind her beautiful face, which no one else was allowed to have. If she didn't get on his last plane, she would have to buy an Avianca ticket, which would make the greedy owner $100 richer, plus he wanted to know why she was unemployed. She said she would come provided he were not waiting for her at the airport. If she found him there, she would take a wheelbarrow straight back to Bogotá.

Alone on a small plane with an inexperienced pilot, Virginia was alarmed when they entered torrential rain. With zero visibility and no radio, she braced herself to die like Jaime Bateman, the M-19 leader whose plane had crashed in the Panamanian jungle.

"Can you come and sit in the co-pilot's seat, because four eyes are better than one?" the pilot said.

She did as instructed. "Can we attempt to land after 6 PM," she said, "when the Medellín airport will be closed, which will reduce our chances of crashing into another aircraft?"

After the rain cleared, the plane landed and two bodyguards met Virginia. To check if they had been followed, they first stopped at Pablo's office, where Gustavo greeted her.

Pablo's cousin had been forced to enter a war not of his making. He once said, "I do not owe anything to the authorities, but my cousin's reflection comes to me." Even though he disapproved of some of Pablo's decisions, he dared never criticise him. Although he preferred a low profile, he was considered cruel. After a hair transplant had failed, he had decided to kill the surgeon but was talked out of it after he was reminded that the man was a family member. He spared his life, but exiled him from Colombia. Managing accounts and receipts down to the last penny had branded him as stingy. He was known to say, "Come see, there's this tiny bit missing. There are some coins missing." Whereas Pablo doled out money, instructed his underlings to spend as much as they needed and gave away his change. He would say, "Take that little bit for you. Let's leave it that way." As Pablo gave so much away, he was asked, "Is it true that Gustavo is a richer man than you?" He responded, "I don't know, but the day I need his money I will spend it."

Gustavo told Virginia that the business was as crazy as ever; half a dozen rented planes were presently flying with hundreds of kilos. Their business was feeding 100,000 people and one million indirectly. He was working like a slave trying to find enough planes to keep the business going, while his asshole cousin was a lucky man. She guessed that Pablo had sent her a little plane because all of the others were transporting cocaine.

She had been in a car for two hours when three other vehicles surrounded her. Bracing to be kidnapped, she was relieved to see that Pablo was one of the drivers. She got into his car, kissed him and headed for Hacienda Nápoles. He commended her for displaying bravery on the flight through the torrential rain. Her attitude had relaxed the pilot. With her unemployed, he hoped they could spend more time together. He wanted her to promise that she would forget what had happened in the past year and that they would never talk about it.

"I can't forget it, but I did stop thinking about it a long time ago." After making love at Hacienda Nápoles, she mentioned what had happened in a movie called *The Night Porter*: a Nazi raped a prisoner, and years after the war had ended – by which point the former prisoner was married – the two were coincidently staying at the same hotel, where they ended up having sex. Pablo protested that he was not a Nazi rapist and that she watched horrible movies. Yes, he was the devil, and that night he had been completely out of control, but if he took her to the most beautiful place in the world, she would start to heal.

He offered to have her boss rehire her, which she rejected because her career was built on her own talent, not through shady deals. She expected to be hired by a Miami TV station, which would help her leave Colombia before it was too late. He said he would die if she left, which was unlikely because the station would hire a Cuban. She was unable to drive, and with no chauffeur in

Miami, she would be stranded. If the station found out who her boyfriend was, she would be fired amid a scandal. He swore on his daughter's life to provide her with anything to make her happy.

The next day at noon, she got onto the back of a motorcyclist's bike and held onto Pablo in front of her. From a hilltop, she got off and admired a view of green planes punctuated by the sun reflecting off water for as far as the eye could see. Exploring the unspoiled land, she said, "Is this all your estate?"

"Nothing is really mine." He smiled. "God tasked me with taking care of it. To keep it intact and to protect its animals." He asked whether he was cursed or born evil like Judas or Hitler. He doubted that such an angel as her could be cursed.

"I can be a devil," she said. "I have my horns."

After lying on the ground, she rested her head on his chest. He said that provided they were condemned to be alive, they would be cursed because that was the inescapable destiny of humans. Absorbed by the beauty, she suggested that John Lennon must have written 'Imagine' in similar surroundings, which were worth dying for. He said that from now on, due to the war, he wouldn't be able to leave the estate much.

"With all your passports, you should leave the country. With a new identity, you could live like a king."

Why would he want to do that when he had the most profitable business in the world? He lived in and was in charge of his own paradise and he could corrupt almost anybody. Plus, he was loved by Colombia's most beautiful woman. At least in hell, he would have his memory of the present day with her.

With his words lifting her spirits, she said that she would one day write a book about him called *Heaven of the Damned*, but that sounded too much like a Greek tragedy for Pablo. She warned about other journalists writing his story and omitting how the country was truly manipulated by the most powerful. Knowing the history of the elites and the presidential families qualified her to write it. He said that she was a witness to a unique history, and that if he died before her, she could tell the truth.

Everything she could see for miles and beyond the horizon was his, but he was still vulnerable from the sky, which the government controlled, so he needed missiles. She chastised him for sounding like Genghis Khan. He should never discuss such things with anyone because they would think he was crazy. Even though he could afford missiles with which to destroy Colombia's air fleet, hundreds of American bombs would have been used in retaliation against such an action, disintegrating Hacienda Nápoles.

After contemplating her response, he said he needed worthwhile targets. She wanted him to stop the crazy ideas and bribe the poor to vote for him to become the president, so that he could remove extradition. While he gazed at the sky, she rested her head on his chest, convinced that she would take her memory of the day to heaven, but that it wouldn't quite be her definition of heaven if he were absent.

In the following months, they met regularly. She taught him about the Colombian power structure, controlled by people so cruel that they made him seem saintly. Their fortunes had been built on theft and mass murder, committed on a grand scale during The Violence. Their greed would have destroyed Colombia if it wasn't for their ineptitude and the resistance from the guerrillas. Pablo was still so young and talented; he could easily outwit them without war. She would help him.

Virginia was unaware that he had ordered the assassination of Tulio, the judge who had indicted him for Lara's assassination. Tulio had rejected bribery and signed arrest warrants for Pablo and Gacha. Getting into a taxi outside of the Saint Thomas University, he was shot.

Following his death, Cano, the senior editor at *The Spectator*, wrote on July 28, 1985: "The Mafia start by offering money and if the bribe is not accepted they proceed to threats, and if the threats go unheeded they proceed to execution at the hands of hit men armed with machine guns, pistols and grenades. This is the terrifying outlook for our judiciary these days, faced with blackmail and bribes, which if not accepted, are converted immediately into a death sentence without right of appeal."

"Another judge murdered has become almost daily news," Cano wrote. "The initial indignation and protest has unfortunately fallen to a certain indifference, understandable given this intolerable and monstrous situation."

At another rendezvous with Virginia, Pablo said that Santo was arriving the next day to request money for the 1986 presidential elections, ten months away. Would she hide her hatred of the politician and accompany him? With Santo claiming to everyone that he hadn't seen Pablo since 1983, he wanted her to witness his lies. Would she quietly observe the situation? She agreed, but refused to keep quiet.

While Pablo was attending business, Santo arrived in a red shirt, greeted Virginia and kissed her cheek. "When did you arrive?"

"Many days ago," she said.

"How come I haven't seen you on TV?"

"It's the high cost of my relationship with Pablo. Just like what you've experienced."

Pablo and Gustavo joined the conversation, which turned to the votes in the towns adjacent to Medellín. With Barco favoured to win the election, Virginia said that Galán might concede to Barco to prevent him from dividing the Liberal Party again. If he joined the official Liberal Party, his supporters would guarantee a landslide victory over the Conservatives. By doing so, he would be repaid by being the Liberals' sole contender for the 1990 presidency with the full support of the ex-presidents. Pablo and Santo objected that the Liberals would never forgive Galán, who was third in the polls, and Barco didn't need his votes. Virginia said that Galán was only down temporarily because he had gone against the whole party. By 1989, with the party's support, things would be different.

Pablo said he would rather finance Galán than the son of a

bitch Ernesto Samper. Santo warned that Galán would extradite Pablo the day after his inauguration, but if he were eliminated, the country would be brought to its knees. He urged Virginia to help Pablo to see it that way. She warned that they would both be extradited if Galán were assassinated. Why repeat the Lara Bonilla mistake? She urged them to back another candidate for 1990. Growing impatient, Pablo said that Galán was finished, and 1990 was five years away. It was imperative to back Barco now, hence Santo's visit.

Gustavo took Virginia to see his latest diamond purchases. He said that even though he was a Conservative, he hated politics. His priorities were running the business, racing cars and motorbikes, and investing in diamonds. She said she despised politicians, too, but unless extradition was abolished, she would be the only one remaining in Colombia. She prayed to God that if Barco won, he wouldn't make Galán the justice minister, because the inevitable war would be unthinkable. With hundreds of rings in velvet trays distracting her from politics, she wondered why Pablo had never told her to choose one if he loved her as much as he claimed.

By never giving herself completely to Pablo, she presented a constant challenge, which prevented him from taking her for granted and required constant seduction. Over time, she saw how Pablo attempted to seduce society in a similar way. She believed that he needed her because she was the only freethinking, educated and highly connected woman he trusted who was his own age. Despite his psychopathy, she viewed him as an overgrown child whose actions were creating increasing burdens.

CHAPTER 4
PALACE OF JUSTICE ATTACK

Pablo decided to introduce Virginia to the M-19 leaders who had helped him to get established in Nicaragua. He told her they were preparing something important together that he hoped would help them to live in peace and that he wanted her opinion of them. In August 1985, she arrived at Hacienda Nápoles, just as a white car was leaving with Álvaro Fayad Delgado, a.k.a. the Turk, the M-19 leader who had negotiated the peace agreement with President Betancur in 1983, signed in 1984. Hearing that Virginia was on her way, the Turk had fled rather than meet such a high-profile person who could have been tortured into revealing the location and nature of the meeting.

After walking outside to greet Virginia, Pablo said that the leaders of the M-19 had been his great friends since they had agreed to a non-aggression pact following the kidnapping of Marta Ochoa. The other co-founder, Iván Marino Ospina, was inside waiting to meet her. Having spent years in the jungle without a TV, Ospina didn't know who Virginia was and Pablo hadn't yet decided whether to tell him. He added that 43-year-old Iván Marino was completely fearless, even of the King of Cocaine. He asked her not to denounce anything Communist and to stick to local and national subjects. She protested, but he said to allow him to talk about Simón Bolívar and to avoid talking about Castro, as Pablo was relying on Iván Marino to remedy his problems. He didn't want her acting like a movie star in her silk dress and heels. She needed to be a simple, charming and discreet girl. He warned that Iván Marino was high, but they had both seen it all when it came to other people's weaknesses.

Proudly, he introduced Virginia to the lean commander, who was in casual clothes with short hair and a moustache. She noticed how his eyes, bulging from cocaine use, were roaming over her face and body. He said he had been in Libya for several months for combat training. Pablo changed the subject to the hardships of the jungle and the commander admitted to spending years in the Eastern Plains amid gigantic rivers where the main enemy was a spiny corkscrew worm that inserted itself into the orifices of the body and used pincers to slash flesh when removed.

"Do they get in through the mouth, nose or ears?" she asked.

They entered through the orifices of the sexual organs, which doubled the risk for women. They had to wear protective boots and clothing from the waist down, which added to their burden in the jungle. Repulsed by his continued ogling, she asked how many worms he had removed over his years of revolutionary struggle. Gazing at the wall as if reminiscing, he said a few. Pablo's glower urged her to visit the bathroom.

Returning, she halted by the door to listen. Iván Marino was demanding a woman just like her, who crossed and uncrossed her legs the same. He liked how she moved and smiled, and asked whether she was like that in bed. She was his dream woman, and he wanted not just one, but two exactly like her in a jacuzzi, and Pablo could deduct whatever he wanted from the $1 million.

El Patrón joked that he needed to think about it, including the $1 million, and added that there were two problems. Firstly, she was Colombia's most famous TV anchorwoman, which was like being a movie star in a country without any Hollywood; and secondly, she was his treasure, she knew about everything and he wouldn't surrender her in duplicate. He waved some of her magazine covers.

After apologising to his brother, Iván Marino said that Pablo should have told him, and come to think about it, he would prefer two Sophia Loren lookalikes, preferably mute as the dumber the better. While he cackled, Pablo offered to get a brunette and a blonde and even a redheaded Sophia Loren, provided that they all fitted into a jacuzzi. And for them, he wouldn't charge his brother anything.

Bored by their machismo, Virginia contemplated sleeping, but couldn't resist interrupting the conversation between the world's most wanted trafficker and Colombia's most wanted guerrilla. Surprised by her re-emergence, Pablo transmitted a shocked look to the commander to indicate that it was time to change the conversation. Ignoring Pablo's request to sit next to him, she sat at the table with their machine guns and watched the commander gazing at her on a magazine cover wearing a flesh-coloured bikini, which made her appear naked.

"Would you like me to sign it so you can keep it as a souvenir?" she asked.

Grabbing the magazines, Pablo yelled at her to not even think about it. After locking them in a drawer, he warned that if the Army found a signed magazine, she would be interrogated about their whereabouts.

"Why did you start the movement?" she asked.

The commander revealed that at the inception of The Violence, after the assassination of the presidential candidate Gaitan, the Conservative mob in the Valle del Cauca had butchered three of his uncles with machetes, including killing one in front of his eleven children.

Moved by his story, she said that her family had lost all of their land in Cartago due to the same Conservative butchers. Her Liberal minister grandfather had arrived home to discover his deceased administrator. His ears, tongue and genitals had been cut off and put in the belly of his young wife, who had been impaled and cut open. Foetuses had been removed from other pregnant peasant women and left in the mouths of their husbands' corpses. Her family's land had been sold for pennies to a multimillionaire sugar family who had financed the mob.

The commander grumbled that in her oligarch family only the

servants had been slaughtered, whereas in his, the adults had been tortured and killed in front of their children. After expressing more horror at his stories, she pointed out that all three of them had been affected by The Violence and that Pablo was now a bigger landowner than her family had been generations ago.

Asked why the M-19 had broken the ceasefire in June, he said that the extreme right had taken advantage of their demobilisation and amnesty and that numerous associates of his had been murdered. She asked whether the extreme right included the MAS. He said that thanks to Pablo they didn't mess with the MAS and vice versa. Their common enemy was the government, and the enemy of his enemy was his friend. The defence minister and the chairman of the Joint Chiefs of Staff were hell-bent on eliminating the left. During Turbay's presidency, they were jailed and tortured, but under Betancur, they were being systematically slaughtered. The Conservative mob of The Violence was still alive and well in modern-day Colombia with the goal of exterminating them like cockroaches.

Hopes for peace had been raised after Betancur had opened dialogue with three of the guerrilla groups. The ceasefire agreement signed with the FARC had led to those guerrillas forming a political party called the Patriotic Union. The president had allowed the M-19 and the EPL (Popular Liberation Army) to form peace camps in the big cities. With the state having never listened to the guerrillas before, the dialogue was a first in Colombia. It captured the attention of the public, which expressed its euphoria by painting doves across the country. But even as the dialogue continued, both sides accused the other of breaches, guerrilla leaders were ambushed and towns were seized in return by the guerrillas. In Cali, the guerrilla leader and spokesman in the peace process for the M-19, Antonio Navarro, and other militants were seriously wounded when men recruited by the secret service of the Army threw a grenade inside a restaurant during breakfast time.

Virginia said she had lost the highest-paid job in television for refusing to refer to the M-19 as a band of criminals. Now reduced to little, she had nothing to lose. Pablo added that she was fired from another programme for supporting the formation of a technicians' union and that she had just declined TV work in Miami because he had convinced her to stay in Colombia, where her enemies had schemed to make her unemployed. She was braver than both he and the commander combined, and that's why he had wanted them to meet. The commander gazed at her with a new-found respect before departing for dinner.

Asked what she thought of him, she said that although Iván Marino was fearless and dedicated to his mission, he had a suicidal personality and lacked greatness. Neither Lenin nor Mao would have requested two prostitutes in the presence of a journalist. She wanted to know why Pablo was paying him $1 million.

El Patrón admitted that they were going to steal and destroy his criminal records. If the paperwork didn't exist, he could never be extradited. She said that he could never get his innocence back and his records would easily be restored by the Justice Department and the DEA. She asked whether the commander had given him the idea. He said nobody had put anything in his head. It was the only plan he had. It would work because it would take years to rebuild the cases. How would they find anyone to testify against him? They would have to be members of Suicide Anonymous.

In a matter of weeks, the Constitutional Court was scheduled to start evaluating their cases to meet the US requirements for extradition. His warnings to the justices had gone unheeded, so the only option was to destroy the paperwork in the Palace of Justice. She asked why destroying the paperwork would cost $1 million. He said there were 60,000 files. She said she thought his record was a few phone books, not crates of them. He warned her not to underestimate him; she was in the arms of the world's biggest criminal, who, after the mission, would have no criminal history. She laughed and they kissed.

While he put on sneakers, intending to order prostitutes for the commander, Virginia objected to the plan on the grounds that the Palace of Justice was not the Dominican Embassy, which the M-19 had struck successfully. The embassy had been a soft target in a quiet area with easy access and exit roads, whereas the Palace of Justice oversaw Bolívar Square – a large open space – its two narrow exits were always busy and the Presidential Guard Battalion was nearby. Getting in might be simple, but taking the paperwork out would be hard. She had no idea how it could be done, and perhaps it was best if she didn't find out.

Sitting on the bed, he held her face, while silently gazing into her eyes. He said she should never talk to anyone about what had happened that night, nor who she had met or seen leaving, and to deny that she had seen Pablo again. Many people had been tortured to death in the hope of extracting information about the M-19 leaders. Those who knew nothing suffered the most because they were tortured slowly, whereas those who had information provided it within ten minutes. The brave commander was an excellent strategist who would perform an efficient and fast strike. Pablo knew how to choose people, including her out of ten million women. He had wanted her to meet the commander because he was in a unique position to do him this favour and he wanted to expose her to a different viewpoint from the one that existed in her superficial high society. There were some other reasons, which he couldn't talk about.

Sensing her sadness, he hugged and kissed her and said that in two weeks they would be celebrating the success of the mission with champagne. Due to his ever-increasing enemies, she needed to constantly keep a gun in her pocket. He opened the door and blew her a kiss. She said that the M-19 had always brought them bad luck and his plan was crazy. As he left with a group of bodyguards, she wondered whether he was taking advantage of the commander or if it was the other way around.

On the morning of August 28, 1985, the Army surrounded a house in Cali. Trapped inside, Iván Marino Ospina engaged in a shootout for over an hour, but was killed along with his bodyguard. The president had never forgiven him for calling for the murder of a US citizen for every Colombian extradited.

"Iván died as a man," Pablo told his bodyguards.

Virginia hoped that Pablo's plan to strike the Palace of Justice had died with the commander, and she fretted about his safety. Upset by the loss of his friend, he feared that the M-19 would cancel the Palace of Justice mission. Instead, the loss of Ospina increased the guerrillas' resolve to put President Betancur on trial. The Iván Marino Ospina Commando Unit was delegated the Antonio Nariño Operation for the Rights of Man, and would be run by Luis Otero and Andrés Almarales.

In the mountains of Cauca, the plan was discussed with Commander Carlos Pizarro, who told the guerrillas, "The difficult thing is not the seizure. The decisive thing is the defence, for which the building should be thought of as a mountain." He imposed the military requirements to carry out the operation. Some objected that such a big operation was too risky and would provoke massive retaliation by the government. The majority believed that they would be shielded by the important hostages, the justices and judges, which would restrain the Army.

Backed up by the extradition order signed by the president, Colonel Ramírez closed in on Lehder. On August 5, 1985, Lehder only just managed to slip away by fleeing towards a river in red underwear, carrying a machine gun. The police found a letter from one of his lawyers: "All your problems began when you started with the politics. The trick is to make yourself dead, the phantom – no publicity so the gringos and Colombians forget you … The important thing is not to die rich. The important thing is to live rich – like before."

By September 1985, six Colombians out of 105 on the US list had been extradited, nine were in jail and the US had activated 105 Requests for Provisional Arrests. The justice minister announced that the US and Colombia were cooperating beautifully. It was the perfect time for Pablo to strike the Supreme Court.

PABLO ESCOBAR'S STORY

Since his early arrests, Pablo had refined his intimidation tactics against judges. A judge assigned to a narcotics case would be visited by a bright, young, well-dressed lawyer carrying a briefcase. On the judge's desk, he'd place a brown envelope and say something like, "You have a choice. You can have lead, bullet in your head, or silver, some money as a pay-off. It's your call." If the judge prevaricated, the lawyer would reach inside his briefcase and take out an album containing pictures of the closest family members and friends of the judge: their children leaving home in the morning, going to school, playing in the playground, talking to friends … The threat of their entire family being wiped out persuaded most judges.

Pablo was about to refine his tactics again. The traffickers sent letters to the Supreme Court justices, demanding that they declare the extradition treaty illegal. The letters were designed not to give any evidence to the police. Block letters were used. They were signed by the Extraditables or with a first name such as Manuel. When Pablo wasn't writing on behalf of the Extraditables and he wanted people to know that he'd authored a letter, he wrote in his own handwriting, signed his name and added his thumbprint.

In October, Pablo called Virginia for an update on Italian interest in a movie about his life. If they hadn't made any progress, he could finance it himself. The Supreme Court decision to approve his extradition was imminent, so he might have to flee the country. If she came with him, she would be endangered.

Pablo divulged information about the M-19 mission to a trafficker, who alerted his army general friends. Due to increased security at the building, the M-19 was forced to postpone the operation. After nothing happened, the security was reduced, and the M-19 set a date for the occupation: November 6.

The traffickers obtained the justices' private phone numbers and threatened them. With the extradition ruling due, the justices were afraid. More letters came for the justices stating that the Extraditables knew everything happening in their lives.

"We declare war against you. We declare war against the

members of your family. As you may suppose, we know exactly where they are – we will do away with your entire family. We have no compassion whatsoever – we are capable of anything, absolutely anything."

Some letters included taped recordings of private conversations they'd had. A voice on a tape recorder warned a justice called Alfonso that his wife wouldn't be alive to make an upcoming trip.

"I'm having a little trouble," Alfonso told his wife. "You should change your travel routes during the day. Don't talk to me over the phone about your plans and, really, be very careful." After Alfonso reported the intimidation tactics, he was assigned four DAS bodyguards, and his wife got one.

Alfonso learned that all of the justices were suffering the same treatment. One had taken his daughter to a hospital for an operation and was about to leave her there when he was paged to the reception. A nurse handed him a phone. A voice said, "We know where she is." A judge with a heart condition received a miniature coffin with his name on it, which brought on panic attacks.

Even though Alfonso had four bodyguards, the pressure increased. Numerous letters arrived on one day, including one for his wife: "You must convince your husband to abrogate the treaty. Remember, we are the same people who dealt with Rodrigo Lara Bonilla. Your bodyguards won't save you, no matter how many you have." An accompanying cassette contained recordings of his wife on the phone in her office in the Foreign Ministry.

The couple stopped taking walks and going out at night. They gave relatives numbers to decode to ascertain their whereabouts. Alfonso insisted that they no longer drive to work together. "That way, you'll save yourself."

The night before the decision about extradition, the couple couldn't sleep. Before leaving for work, Alfonso kissed his wife. Heading for the Palace of Justice on November 6, 1985, he had an upset stomach.

Due to visiting foreign dignitaries, pomp and circumstance was in full swing in the Protocol Salon of the National Palace.

National anthems were played. Armed grenadiers were marching in the courtyard. By 11:30 AM, Betancur had received the Indonesian ambassador and had moved on to the Mexican official. At first, the gunfire was difficult to hear over the noise, but the sound of marching boots drew the public's attention. Informed about gunfire in Plaza Bolívar, the president hastily resumed the ceremony.

Just before 11:40 AM, a few small covered trucks had diverted from a narrow, congested road and assaulted the basement door of the Palace of Justice. Thirty-five guerrillas, including ten women, stormed inside with rifles, machine guns and grenades. They fired at security guards, killing two of them and the palace administrator, and joined a smaller group of comrades who had entered through the main door in civilian clothes. They rapidly trapped over 300 hostages, including Alfonso and most of the justices. Others included visitors, lawyers, secretaries, shopkeepers and shoeshine people. The guerrillas blocked stairwells with furniture and mounted machine guns on top. During the initial raid, they lost one member and a nurse.

Having arrived to work early to participate in a hearing, Enrique Low Murtra, a balding, foreign-looking jurist, had been on the verge of leaving the palace when machine guns started firing. Seeking sanctuary in an office where other people were also hiding, he threw metal filing cabinets to the floor in the hope of protecting himself from the explosions, while gun smoke seeped into the room.

On the fourth floor, the guerrillas held ten magistrates of the Supreme Court and the Council of the State. They told the president of the court to request a ceasefire from the president. The incoming call was not passed to the president even though the hostages included his brother, Jaime Betancur.

The media received a cassette recording of the guerrillas' demands. They wanted to put the president on trial for treason at the palace, for failing to keep his promise to establish peace with all of the disarmed insurgent groups. They wanted a radio broadcast condemning the atrocities committed against their members who had accepted the government's amnesty agreement, and the systematic aerial bombardment of their forces. They wanted their programme published in the newspapers for four consecutive days, a government guarantee of daily radio time for the opposition, and the Supreme Court to uphold their constitutional right to make the president or his representative answer them in court. They also sought an official announcement against extradition. They had hoped to negotiate a settlement, but the president decided to liberate the Palace of Justice at any cost. Foreign governments offered to mediate, but the president refused to listen. He wanted to make an example out of the M-19 for withdrawing from the peace process, which had been the backbone of his campaign.

In the lobby of the Cartagena Hilton Hotel, Virginia was doing a radio broadcast on the Miss Colombia Beauty Pageant when all transmissions were interrupted. Convinced that Pablo was overseas, she assumed that he had no involvement in the M-19 operation.

The police extracted some hostages, but gunfire repelled them. By noon, the Army had arrived with tanks, grenade launchers, helicopters and hundreds of troops with hard helmets and rifles, who positioned themselves in rows against walls for cover. Rockets blasted the building's masonry facade, leaving craters in the walls and littering the pavement with debris. Tank fire and rockets pounded the entrance door. Helicopters from GOES – Operative Group Against Extortion and Kidnapping – dropped troops onto the roof, where they dodged sniper fire which shattered the skylights. Tanks entered the basement. One demolished the palace gates and headed inside, followed by others with members of the Presidential Guard Battalion. Blocked stairwells and machine-gun fire prevented the troops from advancing. Although completely surrounded, the guerrillas had enough riflemen to cover every window and entrance, and their heavy machine guns had been positioned to wipe out any entrants.

Around 3 PM, over 100 people were evacuated from the lower three floors. Before 5 PM, more were released, including Betancur's brother. Coughing and caked in soot, they emerged in small groups holding hands and walked into a security alley formed by the Armed Forces stationed opposite the palace.

Amid a cacophony of gunfire and explosions, Alfonso was trapped on the fourth floor with his bodyguards. With no guerrillas there, they felt relatively safe until a secretary screamed, "They're coming through the wall!" When the guerrillas arrived, the hostages put up no resistance. Alfonso's phone rang. Guerrilla commander Luis Otero snatched the phone and yelled at Alfonso's son to tell the police and soldiers to stop shooting. He gave the phone to Alfonso.

"I'm all right," Alfonso said, "but see if the DAS and the police will stop shooting."

With gunfire in the background, Otero got on the phone. "If they don't stop shooting in fifteen minutes, we're all going to die!" When Alfonso's son called back, the distraught Otero was prophesying doom because the government was refusing to negotiate.

"The shooting must stop," Alfonso told his son, who was so frustrated that he gave a radio station his father's telephone number.

With the televised attack shocking the nation – Pablo was watching, too, as happy as a child at Christmas – Radio Caracol called Alfonso. Across the country, Colombians heard him request a ceasefire and negotiations. An hour later, he spoke to his son. "The guerrillas want to negotiate." Shortly after 5 PM, the line died.

Luis Carlos Galán, the leader of New Liberalism, was surprised by what he called the demented action of the M-19 and an excessive official reaction. He approved of the presidential decision not to negotiate, but asked to try humanitarian dialogue to save the lives of the hostages.

Around 7 PM, smoke started filtering through the building. Burning files ignited a fire, which spread to the wooden building dividers. Gagging and coughing, some of the people hiding on the top floor went downstairs and were captured. The scorching heat forced the guerrillas and hostages to flee to the bathrooms and the fourth floor. Traumatised by the possibility of imminent death, some were bleeding, others were having breathing difficulties and some died. The room stank of sweat and bodily fluids. Commander Andrés Almarales ordered the evacuation of the women and the wounded.

At a hideout, Pablo was gripped by developments on the TV. Delighted by the fire, he imagined the extradition files burning. Also on fire were the records for 1,800 human rights cases against branches of the government, including the Army.

The jurist, Low Murtra, had been carrying the wounded until his legs had grown numb. Around 10 PM, he spotted a rescue group. From the offices, magistrates, assistants and other workers emerged. Low Murtra urged them to help him drag the wounded towards the Army personnel. Searching for an exit, they encountered shootings, devastation and corpses, until fresh air guided them outside to a view of the palace in flames, an image the public watched throughout the night, amid explosions and small groups of escapees. Requests to surrender were rejected by the M-19.

In the morning, Galán broadcast by radio a demand for a humanitarian dialogue and a ceasefire. The director of the Red Cross arrived to open negotiations, but the Army denied him access and detained him in the Casa del Florero, with approximately 200 hostages who had been freed or rescued, including the president's brother. The 200 thought their troubles were over until military intelligence and F-2 police began to interrogate them. Anyone who gave a reason for suspicion was put on a truck and sent to a military school in northern Bogotá, never to be seen again except for two law students found on a highway showing signs of torture. Some of those selected for torture and murder were saved by their colleagues, who begged the Army not to take them.

In the afternoon, troops braced to storm the building. Betancur had authorised an assault that would wipe out everybody.

After a tank rammed the front door, troops charged in. A tank blasted the fourth floor, blowing a hole in the wall where the last of the guerrillas and hostages were hiding. Sharpshooters on the surrounding roofs unleashed hellfire onto the palace. Grenades thrown inside knocked down people, leaving them injured and bleeding or dead.

With people dying indiscriminately, the guerrillas sifted through the corpses to find the living, whom they ordered to get up. They threw corpses down the stairwell, including Justice Humberto Murcia Ballén, who only appeared dead but was still alive, his artificial leg shattered by a bullet. After they left that area, the injured justice crawled to the cellar and up a flight of stairs. Mustering energy, he raised himself and his arms, shouting, "Don't shoot!"

Approximately 100 died in the bloodbath. Alfonso didn't make it. He was one of the eleven justices – half of the Supreme Court – shot dead. All of the guerrillas died, as well as eleven police and soldiers. To prevent any evidence of wrongdoing, the defence minister stopped members of Forensic Medicine from retrieving any corpses and he ordered all of the dead to be stripped and washed. Firefighters were ordered to hose the corpses, which were moved by the military to destroy the evidence. Afterwards, misidentified bodies were given to the wrong families, including a charred female body given to the family of a male victim. The communications minister – a cousin of Jorge Ochoa's wife – deflected the public's attention from the aftermath by telling the TV channels to only broadcast the beauty pageant and soccer games. At 2:30 PM, the generals informed the president that the palace had been recovered.

Despite the censorship of the media, TV cameras had filmed a dozen cafe workers and two female guerrillas getting extracted from the palace by the Army. When the families asked for their whereabouts, they were told they were being temporarily held in army barracks. The authorities refused to provide the exact location of the barracks or to give any reason for their detention.

The women were destined to join a group that would be known as the disappeared. The sister of a victim asked the military about her sister's whereabouts only to be told to "leave things as they are and stop asking so many questions." The father and wife of a male victim were told, "Stop bothering us about people who aren't worth the trouble because they were guerrillas and murderers."

According to information obtained from military sources by Pablo and Virginia, as stated in her book *Loving Pablo, Hating Escobar*, the women rescued from the palace were tortured, including gang-rape and strangulation, and some had their fingernails removed. The bodies were placed in baths of sulphuric acid or disposed of at garbage sites.

Conveniently for the government, the news quickly switched to the death of over 20,000 people in Tolima. After sixty-nine years of dormancy, a volcano had erupted, causing glaciers to melt and huge mudslides full of rocks and debris to descend at 30 mph, which wiped out an entire town and the surrounding area. The government had been forewarned months before the eruption, but had chosen not to incur the cost of evacuating approximately 50,000 people. A funeral banner read, "The volcano didn't kill 22,000 people. The government killed them." By sending soldiers to the disaster zone, the government converted them from Palace of Justice murderers into heroes.

In June 2010, Colonel Alfonso Plazas Vega was sentenced to thirty years in prison for actions that led to the deaths of eleven Palace survivors. In 2015, on the thirtieth anniversary of the siege, President Santos apologised for the disappearance of the people, mostly café workers. He vowed to find their remains.

At first, the cartel's role in the M-19's action was hidden. Many blamed the guerrillas and the government's overreaction. Controversy remains, with some researchers claiming that the fire that torched the extradition files was due to the Army's response. Roberto Escobar stated that the Extraditables had financed the operation for the destruction of the records – not mass murder

– and that the traffickers had offered to double the guerrillas' fee if the government negotiations had succeeded.

Justice Minister Enrique Parejo was one of the first to link the act to the traffickers: "Everything indicates that there is a close connection between the criminal acts that were registered against the Supreme Court of Justice and the activities of the drug traffickers, about that I do not have the slightest doubt."

Survivors, including the justice who'd been thrown down the stairs with the corpses, criticised the government for not negotiating. When the president eulogised in a church for the dead justices, the survivors didn't attend. Afterwards, some people quit working for Pablo, others for the government, including many judges.

Alejo of the M-19 admitted the group's intention and mistakes:

"We made a miscalculation in evaluating the enemy and we naively believed that power worked with three branches in balance. In the middle of the twentieth century, we made a political move with the liberal doctrine of the French Revolution. We knew that with the seizure there would be shootings and people killed, but we did not suspect that the state had evolved towards a presidentialist state, otherwise we would not have taken this action. Some people have asked us, 'Why did you not get into congress where the corrupt political class was?' The answer is simple: because we were going to establish an armed demand to the President of the Republic for his wrongdoings and the competent authority to judge him, according to the constitution, was the Court. In that we were extremely legalistic.

"For the operation some weapons were moved from Cali, and other things like rifles and plastic explosives, the C4 that we bought in Nicaragua, we embarked in Panama and unloaded them in Antioquia. We could not get the grenades for the RPG2s. That would have allowed us to stop the tanks. But it does not matter. [Regardless of] the weapons that we would have obtained, the political will of the Army was to devastate us. They would have done it whether there were rocket launchers or not. We could have had 1,000 men and 1,000 men would have died. We never thought of surrender, but the truth is that there was no space to consider it either. The president was not able to contain the military, who massacred even the people who came out alive. There are testimonies that Jackim, Almarales and other militants of the M-19 were left alive, but they disappeared. The monument to naivety is the courthouse.

"Since the files got burned, the myth was created that we did the operation for drug trafficking. But the argument is silly: there are always legal reserve files. We were the only revolutionary organisation that set a clear position about drug trafficking. We proposed legalisation of capitals, no extradition, trials of drug traffickers within the country and legalisation of drugs as a definitive solution.

"After the courthouse, Pablo and those who moved around him – they looked at us with great respect. The level of heroism moved them. Pablo felt that the guys who were there were brothers and, despite their operational capacity and their thugishness, from that moment he looked at us with such respect that his habit of not proposing to us anything different from his political [solutions] was accentuated."

The holocaust at the Palace of Justice ruined the image of the M-19. Commander Pizarro distanced the guerrillas from the traffickers, whom he defined as a new oligarchy. In 1988, the M-19 released a slogan: "War to the oligarchy, peace to the nation and truce to the Armed Forces." The group sought to negotiate with the government, which led to it surrendering its weapons and becoming a legal political force in 1990.

When Virginia learned about Pablo's role, she decided that her brave lover was really a monster. Believing that she was no longer in love with him, she changed her number in the hope of never seeing him again. She began dating a wealthy 34-year-old ecologist who lived on his family's tiny island. In the middle of 1986, upon visiting her apartment in Bogotá, she opened an envelope that contained photos of sixteen dismembered corpses accompanied by a letter which accused Pablo and Gacha of committing atrocities, and threatened that she would pay with every inch of her skin and drop of her blood.

CHAPTER 5
THE EXTRADITABLES

In January 1986, at Hacienda Nápoles, Pablo was admiring exotic birds in a cage. As his son walked by the pool, El Patrón yelled that he had something to show him and pointed at a sword in-between his thighs. What is it? His father replied that it was the sword of our liberator, Simón Bolívar, referring to the gift he had received from Ospina. Unimpressed, Juan Pablo asked what he was going to do with it. He wanted his son to store it in his room and take care of it due to its historical importance. With his 9th birthday approaching, Juan Pablo had hoped to receive a motorbike or toys, not a sword. Pretending to be grateful, he swung it at a bush, disappointed by its inability to slash branches. In his room, he stashed it among his toys.

Things were relatively calm until February 1986, when Barry Seal was assassinated. Mired in legal problems, the ace pilot had sought help from George HW Bush. Rebuffed by the vice president, he had threatened to expose their CIA dealings. The federal court system had stripped Barry of his right to bear arms or to have armed bodyguards, and sentenced him to spend time at a Salvation Army halfway house. Unarmed and at a fixed address, he was an easy target for his many enemies. On February 19, 1986, Colombian hit men cornered Barry in his white Cadillac outside of the halfway house. Sat in the driver's seat, he was shot to death. Federal agents immediately confiscated his belongings, including files he stored in his car that pertained to his work for George HW Bush and multiple federal agencies.

A month later, President Ronald Reagan went on TV with

grainy photos of Pablo in Nicaragua loading drugs onto Barry's plane. "I know every American parent concerned about the drug problem will be outraged to learn that top Nicaraguan government officials are deeply involved in drug trafficking. This picture, secretly taken at a military airfield outside Managua, shows Federico Vaughan, a top aide to one of the nine commandants who rule Nicaragua, loading an aircraft with illegal narcotics bound for the United States." Reagan was attempting to drum up support for the Nicaraguan rebels on the basis that the Nicaraguan government was trafficking cocaine. The photo evidence and Barry Seal's testimony enabled the DEA to finally issue indictments for Pablo, Gacha and Jorge Ochoa.

With the Reagan-Bush administration hyping up the crack epidemic to ramp up the War on Drugs, the US authorities increased their efforts to extradite Pablo. Eight different agencies were pursuing him, including the DEA, US Customs, the Coast Guard, federal police, state police and the military, none of which put a dent in the supply of cocaine to America, which tumbled in price from $40,000 a kilo to $10,000.

In April 1986, Reagan signed National Security Decision Directive 221, which classified drug trafficking as a threat to national security. In retaliation, traffickers targeted the staff at the US Embassy in Bogotá, and a $350,000 contract was put out on the head of the DEA. Car bombers repeatedly attacked the buildings occupied by Americans. Family members of diplomats and DEA agents fled Colombia.

In August 1986, the Liberal candidate Barco became president, supported by Galán. Having campaigned on reducing poverty and promoting human rights, he got more than 58 per cent of the votes, one of the biggest margins ever in Colombia. With the elections distorted by drug money, many politicians had obtained their seats thanks to the Mafia. Barco had a strong relationship with the US. His wife was American, and he had lived there as the Colombian director of the World Bank. Like his predecessor, he had the difficult task of keeping America satisfied to obtain foreign aid, including fighting the War on Drugs, while not upsetting those who had financed his campaign, including the traffickers.

Alberto Villamizar was an ally of Galán in politics, they were related through marriage and were even neighbours. They had married sisters: Maruja Pachón and Gloria Pachón (Galán's wife). In 1985, Villamizar had helped to introduce the National Narcotics Statute, which created legislation against drug trafficking. The traffickers had schemed to have the parliamentarian José Elías Náder introduce a bill to neutralise extradition, which would be discussed in the constitutional committees of the Senate and the Chamber. With Santo president of the Commission and Jairo Ortega Ramírez nominated in the Chamber, the bill seemed sure to pass. Under advice from Galán, Villamizar had pulled numerous strings to become the President of the Commission, and he had stopped the passage of the bill. In return, Pablo had put a hit on him in 1986.

Outside of his home, Villamizar braced to die as what seemed like an earthquake rocked his Mercedes-Benz. Incredibly, the hail of bullets missed him. Noticing a hit man in sports clothes, he yelled at his driver to accelerate. In shock, the driver abandoned the car, raised his arms and repeatedly yelled at the hit man, "Don't kill me!"

The politician braced for another explosion of shots, but the hit man's gun had jammed. A second hit man was approaching to finish the job, but a doorman emerged and pretended to have a gun, which confused the hit men. Having heard gunshots, DAS agents, who just happened to be in the area, chased the hit men. While one fled on a motorbike, a motorised patrol killed the other a few blocks away. Gazing in a mirror, Villamizar noticed that the blood had drained from his face. Finding ammunition in his coat, he realised that a ricocheting bullet had caused a minor wound at the base of his spine.

In Congress, Galán, gesticulating wildly in a business suit, said: "The despicable attack against Alberto Villamizar is nothing but the latest attempt of drug trafficking and its allies to put an end to the New Liberalism, its policies of change and its constant accusations. But they won't kill or silence us! We won't rest until our country is in peace and free from the corruption of the drug trade and its political allies. How much longer will these criminals and their allies walk freely? How much longer are we going to let them threaten honest Colombian citizens?"

The politician who had introduced the bill, José Elías Náder, was reputed to have said, "Why did they involve Villamizar, when they should have killed Galán?"

Upon hearing this, Galán confronted Náder in Congress: "Be a man. If you want me dead, do it yourself!"

"They are very upset because we are going to see who ends up winning the game," Pablo said.

At all times, up to fifteen bodyguards accompanied Villamizar, who no longer discussed the draft law. Convinced by Galán to leave Colombia, he was appointed the ambassador to Indonesia. A year later, US security forces captured a Colombian hit man in Singapore, who was travelling to Indonesia, most likely sent by Pablo to finish the job.

Pablo turned his attention to Judge Serna, who had issued an arrest warrant for his role in the murder of the two DAS agents who had held him and Gustavo at gunpoint. The ancient judge with an expressionless face worked in Medellín and drove without taking any precautions. Due to a problem with his right foot, he used a crutch to walk.

On October 30, 1986, Serna left the rebuilt Palace of Justice at 12:30 PM, and headed for his old orange Renault 12 station wagon. After resting his crutch on a seat, he got in the driver's side and started the engine. In a Renault 18, Pinina and La Yuca followed the judge to the Pontifical Bolivarian University, maintaining a distance in heavy traffic. As the congestion thinned, the Renault 18 approached until the cars were next to each other, with the judge oblivious until two shots were fired. The station wagon swerved and crashed into the sidewalk.

After Betancur's presidency ended in August 1986, Pablo planned to kidnap and keep him captive in a small windowless hut deep in the jungle. For three weeks, a hut was constructed by men who received supplies by helicopter. After indigenous people discovered the hut, he ordered another to be built further away from civilisation. Two months later, the second hut was built, but the two men assigned to kidnap Betancur kept failing and the plan was abandoned.

After having a nightmare that he was captured and extradited, Pablo came up with a counter strategy. If he were incarcerated, his men would board a school bus in Washington DC and threaten to blow it up unless he were released.

By November 1986, he was ready to announce the existence of the Extraditables. To ensure that he had the correct words and spellings, he consulted a dictionary. Although he was the prime mover of the group, he wanted his press releases to give the impression that it was a large organisation. He settled on the motto: "Better a grave in Colombia than a jail cell in the US." Making a blood pact, the traffickers agreed that faced with extradition they would commit suicide instead of rotting in an American prison. Their preferred method was to shoot themselves behind the ear, which allowed a bullet easy access to the brain by circumventing the skull. They pledged to pay monthly contributions to finance the war. Traffickers who didn't contribute received menacing calls from Pablo. The war against extradition was fought on multiple fronts. A team of lawyers worked around the clock, led by Guido Parra and Humberto Buitrago. Pressure was exerted by Santo.

Popeye was dispatched to Bogotá with $2 million in cash to bribe the justice in charge of extradition. "Be calm," Pablo told Popeye. "The appointment with the justice is set. He is aware that the Extraditables are sending him a message. In Bogotá, Gacha's security team will take care of you."

A convoy of sixty bodyguards in armoured vehicles escorted Popeye and the money to the law office. He went inside accompanied by the contact who had set up the meeting. After formalities were exchanged, Popeye placed the bag on a desk. "There is $2 million inside the bag sent by Pablo Escobar Gaviria and Gonzalo Rodríguez Gacha. They will not accept the return of the money. You already know what you have to do, and what they will do if you don't." The justice's mouth opened but no words emerged. Popeye hurriedly departed.

On December 12, 1986, the Supreme Court of Justice ruled that the 1979 extradition treaty was illegal because a government minister had signed it and not the president.

To celebrate, Jorge Ochoa hosted a party for thirty traffickers at his ranch in Bolombolo, Antioquia. Pablo and Gacha arrived with bodyguards. High on their success, the men hugged, yelled and congratulated each other. By a pool and an artificial waterfall, women in bikinis moved to music played by a mariachi band. Endless food and drink were served, but Pablo's men limited their alcohol intake to remain vigilant.

Known as the head of the Bogotá Cartel, Gacha was now one of Colombia's wealthiest. His houses were adorned with gold taps and toilet paper featuring Botticelli figures. Millions of dollars had been buried under his properties. He loved listening to ranch songs, and one of his favourite guests was the Mexican singer Vicente Fernández, for whom he had a special reserved chair. Gacha built churches, financed social projects and gave awards to beauty queens. He owned the soccer team Millonarios FC, and played games with the stars of his team on the pitch in his estate. Passionate about horses, he refused $2 million for his favourite steed, Túpac Amaru, which he rode adorned with cheetah-skin shawls and reins. Fabio Ochoa Sr praised Gacha for possessing such a fine horse because the Ochoa patriarch believed that the Liberator Simón Bolívar had succeeded due to his horse, Palomo, and Alexander the Great thanks to his horse, Bucephalus. Ochoa wrote to Gacha: "A man with a horse like Túpac Amaru deserves to be president." In his hometown, Pacho, Gacha's hit men roamed with the zeal of fanatics. He employed ancient torture techniques such as tying a person to a tree occupied by dangerous ants or throwing someone into a lake with crocodiles.

Smoking cannabis, Pablo was sitting with Gacha. From a freezer, Gacha extracted a plastic snake and threw it at a trafficker. Taken by surprise with a cold snake on his neck, the man jumped and yelled hysterically. He extracted his gun and aimed it at the snake. Realising that it was only rubber, everybody laughed.

Gacha offered Pablo a horse to give to Manuela. "How much is it worth?" Pablo asked.

"Fifty million pesos."

"With that I could arm many bandits."

"Then I give it you as a gift."

Jorge Ochoa told the story of another party he had hosted with the same mariachi band. "The police surrounded the main house, so I grabbed a hat and an instrument from a mariachi. In the living room, the police ordered the men and women to separate from the musicians. They said they were looking for Jorge Ochoa Vasquez. Everyone was asked for ID except for women and musicians. After three hours of searching, the police left. I quickly escaped before anyone could rat me out." Everyone praised his quick thinking.

By 3 PM, most of the traffickers had women on their laps. Accompanied by four women, Gacha and Pablo were still chatting. Around 6:30 PM, a bodyguard whispered bad news to Pablo: President Barco had pledged to use an older treaty that permitted extradition without judicial approval. He had overturned the decision by the Supreme Court of Justice, which he had ruled lacked any grounds. He had promoted General Maza from the head of the Central Directorate of the Judicial Police and Intelligence, a.k.a. the DIJIN, to now running the DAS.

As word spread, the mariachis stopped playing, the women retreated to their rooms, the men stopped drinking and gazed forlornly at each other, and the waiters began to remove glasses. The bosses hurriedly said goodbye and headed for their hideouts.

For his return journey, Pablo sent two cars ahead. Holding a gun, he was preoccupied as he prepared to escalate the war.

The Spectator proclaimed the president's announcement a major victory against the traffickers. Its headline read: "The party is spoiled for the mobsters." Cano wrote: "These sinister men have managed to create an empire of immorality, tricking and making fools of the complacent, doling out crumbs and bribes upon them while a cowardly and often entranced populous stand idly by, content with their illusions and entertained by their jet-set lives."

It was the same newspaper that had published Pablo's mugshot, which had helped to destroy his political goals. Cano had pushed his luck too far. It was time for him to go.

CHAPTER 6
ASSASSINATIONS

In late January 1986, an informant told the police that Pablo had issued a contract worth $150,000 on a police colonel, which had gone to the Medellín chapter of the Ricardo Franco Brigade. On a quest to purge any police infiltrators, the guerrilla group had recently butchered a few hundred of its own members. The Brigade had delegated the hit to its chief of executions, Foxy, who had taken a $12,000 down payment from Pablo, which he spent on a MAC-10, four pistols and a revolver. The weapons were outside one of Pablo's safe houses in North Bogotá, stashed in a Renault 18, with one hit man overseeing it.

The informant said that Pablo had accumulated a file on the colonel, which he had shared with Foxy. El Patrón had paid $30,000 for the information to a lieutenant whom the colonel trusted. They were aware that the colonel was starting a course at generals' school, and they had details of his going away party. They knew where he lived, his mother's address, the car he owned and that he drove an armoured Mercedes-Benz on loan from the DEA. The informant gave all of the specific details.

A hit scheduled for outside of a club had been called off due to the colonel's large escort. A hit at his mother's house had also failed because too many relatives had accompanied the colonel, and Pablo wanted a clean kill without numerous casualties. The hit team had picked three potential locations: his mother's house, a highway overpass by a police academy and across the street from a bakery. In regular contact with Foxy, the informant pledged to give further information for the right price.

Police intelligence believed that Colonel Ramírez – who had been relieved of duty at the end of 1985 – was the target due to the enormous losses caused by his raids, especially on the jungle labs. Despite refusing the offer made by the men who had menaced his brother, he had survived his tenure as Anti-Narcotics Unit police chief, during which his men had made almost 8,000 arrests and confiscated more than half of the cocaine seized in the world in 1985, as well as countless vehicles, boats and planes. In 1985, he had overseen the destruction of 90 per cent of Colombia's cannabis crop, which had been decimated by crop dusters spraying chemicals provided by the DEA. Following up on the information from the informant, the police watched the safe house with the weapons in the car outside. Neighbours spotted the undercover agents taking photos and called the police.

Ramírez returned to work in February 1986 in high spirits. He had won awards, was ready for a promotion to general and his advice on drug eradication was being sought worldwide. With his family, he relocated to the General Santander National Police Academy in Bogotá, which offered extra protection. Although safe at the base, he had to drive to the war college daily. The bosses wanted him dead, but would they dare go after him? Watching the safe house with the Renault parked outside produced no evidence.

Ramírez grew more concerned after questioning the informant, who described two previously planned hits that had been cancelled. The thought of assassins staking out his parents' Christmas Eve party disturbed him. When the interview ended, the informant promised to provide more information. Ramírez told his family that the informant was truthful.

The threat had come at an awkward time because he was no longer in command of an armed force that could retaliate against Pablo. Unable to apply his motto of constantly booting the traffickers in the nuts, he started to worry. For eight months, he only left the base to drive to police headquarters in an armoured Ford LTD provided by the DEA, wearing a bulletproof vest, armed with a revolver and a MAC-10 and protected by a chauffeur with a gun. Mindful of the details provided by the informant, the driver always varied the route. Before he set off, the route was checked by police on motorbikes.

The threat made his wife ill. His father dreamt that his son was dead. He urged his brother to minimise any descriptions of the danger to his father. His two boys travelled to school in an armoured bus. The family rarely ate out, and if they did, they wore bulletproof vests. One of his sons had become proficient in the use of a MAC-10, which accompanied them on journeys.

Prior to Easter Sunday, his brother invited him and his family to stay at a cabin. Ramírez was desperate to unwind. "I've always been the pursuer, and now they're pursuing me. I'm the one who puts people against the wall, not the other way around."

The information from the informant stopped after he revealed that the hit team had acquired nine vehicles, explosives and rocket-propelled grenades and launchers. Security around Ramírez increased. Investigators were unable to find any new leads or the identity of the lieutenant alleged to have leaked information.

Due to his previous successes against the traffickers, Captain Ernesto Mora of the Anti-Narcotics Unit was assigned to infiltrate the cartel and issue reports to Ramírez with any updates on the threat. Ernesto ascertained that the contract with Foxy was still active and that other cartel leaders had shares in the contract. New information revealed that Pablo was considering cancelling the contract, but it was unconfirmed.

Pablo requested a meeting with the colonel to talk things over. Not wanting to fall into a trap, he declined. Maybe he wouldn't be killed, but secret photos would be taken of him with El Patrón, and his career ruined. Captain Ernesto Mora delivered a message from Ramírez: Pablo would be treated fairly if he turned himself in.

In May 1986, four strangers – who had arrived in a red Renault – were noticed lurking around the ranch belonging to Ramírez in Granada. Their leader had curly hair and a solid build. For a few days, they walked around, staking out the house. The caretaker took a bus to Ramírez. At the police academy, the caretaker identified the leader of the strangers from a photo.

In August, Ramírez and his classmates went to Europe for a month, where they visited other law enforcement and did workshops. With his luggage crammed with tons of information and reports, he returned excited to apply the knowledge in the hope of enhancing and modernising the police force. While awaiting his new career, scheduled for the year's end, he did jobs at police headquarters and also worked as a consultant with foreign governments fighting the War on Drugs. In Bolivia, as part of the DEA's Operation Blast Furnace, he was finally able to strike back at Pablo by helping to find some of his labs, which the authorities burned down. Returning to the thick of the action lifted his spirits, but the threat – particularly to his family – gnawed away at him.

On October 21, 1986, Foxy was killed in a gunfight in Medellín, so Captain Ernesto Mora told Ramírez that Pablo had probably cancelled the contract. It was unlikely that anyone would attempt to kill the colonel in the wake of Foxy's death, as a new hit team would have to start from scratch, gathering information and staking out locations. The safe house with the Renault outside had been repeatedly raided, with no leads produced. No further sightings of the strangers led by the curly haired man had occurred. Feeling safer, he gave up his bodyguards. Daily, he spoke to Ernesto, but there were no new developments, so he relaxed more.

On Thursday, November 13, 1986, Ramírez was invited to a family dinner scheduled for Monday. Even though the thirty-mile drive seemed low-risk, he said he needed to give it more thought. On Friday, he received a ten-minute call from Ernesto. After hanging up, he turned to his wife. With his face relaxed in a way unseen for a long time, he said, "They've suspended the contract." With the threat gone, the family rejoiced, excited to attend the upcoming get-together. It was the kind of occasion that they would appreciate after their ordeal. Finally, things were back to normal.

On Sunday afternoon, they left the armoured vehicle in the garage and set off in a Toyota minivan with a MAC-10 on the floor by one of Ramírez's sons. With so much holiday traffic, it would be difficult for any pursuers to set a trap. After stopping to eat at a ranch near Bogotá, they drove for another hour to a friend's house, where they stayed overnight.

At 10 AM on Monday, they drove in high spirits for the ranch belonging to the colonel's brother. The four family members hadn't taken such a trip in a long time. The ranch was packed with people in a celebratory mood, anticipating a feast. In-between eating pigs' knuckles, Ramírez told stories to everyone sat on the lawn. He was proud of his imminent promotion. He would probably become the police's chief of personnel. Excitedly, he said he was going to employ many of his former men in his new department, and encourage everyone to keep fighting the traffickers. It would be just like old times.

After 4 PM, he said it was a good time to leave in order to beat the holiday traffic returning to Bogotá. As they set off, multiple cars – which had been parked in the area for hours – followed the minivan.

At 5:43 PM, the minivan encountered heavy traffic on a highway bridge. Failing to notice their pursuers, they crept along in the right-hand lane. Ramírez and his wife discussed how they were getting on in years, and the ways in which they'd like to spend the rest of their lives together. When they were halfway over the bridge, a red Renault 18 approached their left side as if overtaking. It slowed down with its occupants observing the colonel. One raised a MAC-10.

"Get down!"

An explosion of shots ripped into the colonel, forcing him forward. He slumped as if dead. His two sons had been shot, one in the hand. The one bleeding from the thigh scrambled to find the MAC-10. His wife – hit in the knee – reached for the steering wheel. Veering towards the side of the bridge, the minivan stopped at a curb. The Renault halted in front of the van. Three smartly dressed passengers in their 20s got out, brandishing MAC-10s. While two guarded the Renault, the third approached the van.

Bleeding from the leg, Ramírez's wife was crawling across the bridge, hoping to get to the other side of the van to help her husband. She looked up at an assassin. "Please don't kill me." Leaving her unharmed, the hit man opened the driver's door and blasted Ramírez. He got in the Renault, which sped away.

The next day, the US authorities announced a super indictment of the top traffickers – the Ochoa brothers, Pablo, Lehder and Gacha – which included charging them with producing fifty-eight tons of cocaine from 1978 to 1985:

"From as early as 1978 to the date of the return of this indictment there existed an international criminal narcotics enterprise based in Medellín, Colombia, South America, known by various names, including 'the Medellín Cartel' (hereinafter 'cartel'), which consisted of controlling members of major international cocaine manufacturing and distributing organizations … Through the cartel, major cocaine organizations were able to pool resources, including raw materials, clandestine cocaine conversion laboratories, aircraft, vessels, transportation facilities, distribution networks, and cocaine to facilitate international narcotics trafficking."

The indictment made more headlines in Colombia than America, especially with *The Spectator*, which published multiple stories. Cano wrote:

"Legalise drug trafficking? That would be like legalising and justifying all the collateral activities: money laundering, the assassination of Supreme Court justices, of Cabinet ministers, of judges, and of so many other persons who, by doing their duty have fallen victim to the narcotics traffickers and their hired killers."

On December 17, 1986, Cano returned to his office from a lunch break, laden with Christmas gifts. At 6:45 PM, two of Pablo's men parked a motorbike nearby in an industrial area on train tracks that crossed Avenue 68 in west Bogotá. They kept the engine running. Busses full of people passed by in busy traffic.

After working late, Cano left the building in the evening. With the gifts on the back seat, he started his station wagon and attempted to leave the car park. Recognising the elderly journalist with white hair and glasses, the bus drivers stopped to allow him to enter the flow of traffic. Smiling, Cano waved at them.

Watching him, the hit men slowly approached his vehicle from behind. They came to the side of his car, until they were by his window with the gun inches from Cano's head. It fired, splattering blood on the windshield. The motorbike roared away.

Just like after Lara's assassination, Cano's death provoked demands for retribution and public opinion turned against the cartel. The investigation units of the leading newspapers formed a team called the United Front, which lambasted the traffickers. Joint reports denounced the acts of terrorism and the Mafia that had infiltrated politics. Cano's widow and members of the board of directors of the Circle of Journalists of Bogotá called for a silent march to demand freedom of the press and expression. Spokespeople, trade unionists, students, businessmen and workers rallied to the cause.

The people running the news systems for Caracol Radio, RCN, and Sutatenza led a "chain of solidarity" – a joint transmission on the repercussions of the assassination. The radio stations linked up and at 11 PM on Thursday, December 18, one hour before the start of the Day of Silence, RCN, Caracol, Todelar, Colombian Radio Group, Super, Sutatenza and Melodía jointly broadcast a special programme, which started with Colombia's national anthem. Extinct, through one of its channels, joined the initiative and presented an interview that Cano had recorded just twenty-four hours before his murder: "You know when you leave the house, but you do not know whether you will arrive." The presenters paid tribute to the life and work of Cano. Five minutes before midnight on Friday, December 19, the networks stopped broadcasting. The last sentence heard was: "The homeland we are looking for is a good homeland."

On Friday, journalists marched in silence. Speeches were given, praising almost two-dozen journalists killed. Thousands attended the funeral, including the president, whose car led a convoy past mourners waving Colombian flags.

The Spectator lost ten staff members. A truck containing 700 pounds of dynamite exploded outside of its head office in Bogotá. The cartel went after investigative reporters, political columnists, editors and anyone who opposed them. Pablo's men set fire to newspaper delivery vehicles and threatened newspaper vendors until *The Spectator* vanished from Medellín.

After Pablo learned that the justice department had evidence of him ordering Cano's murder, he ordered the assassination of the lawyer representing Cano's family. Amid the chaos, Pablo and his family hid at the El Peñol reservoir east of Medellín. Months later, three hours after signing the warrant for Pablo and Gacha for Cano's murder, the judge was killed.

Lara's successor, who had signed Pablo's arrest warrant and the extradition order for Lehder plus a dozen other Colombians, ended up in Hungary. Working in the well-protected Colombian Embassy, he assumed he was safe because Hungary was difficult to smuggle weapons into and it restricted tourist visas. Even though his men doubted the possibility of an attack, Pablo was undeterred.

Death threats arrived: "You can run, but you can't hide." Men trailed him for weeks and learned his routine, including when he drove to the embassy or took the bus.

January 13, 1987 in Budapest commenced with a blizzard in weather twenty-two degrees below zero. The ambassador left his house in the hills above the capital and examined his car. As the roads were iced over, he decided to walk to a bus stop. Going down a hill, he spotted a man.

"You, Enrique Parejo?" the stranger yelled.

"Yes."

Instantly, a gun was drawn. The first shot entered his neck. With a bullet lodged in his spine, he collapsed. Unable to move, he watched the man stand over him, take aim at his head and shoot him in the mouth, cheek and arms. Miraculously, he survived thanks to doctors who removed the bullets in two operations.

Travelling from Hacienda Nápoles in the early afternoon, Pablo was driving a Toyota SUV with his family and Lehder. Men in two cars were scouting the route ahead and communicating with Pablo by radio-telephone. If they spotted the authorities, El Patrón would be over two miles away.

"We've just passed through the tollbooth in Cocorná." The scout added that there were some police in uniforms.

As the SUV approached the tollbooth, Lehder asked Pablo what the plan was and pointed out that it was a bad idea to approach it with his family in the same vehicle. Pablo said he intended to pull over on a hill to observe the booth. After parking by a restaurant, he surveyed the booth without leaving the SUV and radioed Otto to bring his car to the restaurant to collect him and Lehder. Otto helped him move his belongings to the new car. Lehder transferred a rifle and a crossbow. Pablo kept his SIG Sauer pistol on his waist and a submachine gun hanging from his shoulder. In the SUV, Victoria drove her family towards the tollbooth.

Having watched Pablo transfer to a new car, two undercover DAS agents ran from the restaurant towards the booth, waving handkerchiefs. "Armed men are approaching!" one yelled.

Stuck behind two cars at the tollbooth, Victoria craned her head to see Pablo's car charging towards her on the wrong side of the road. As it reached the booth, Lehder's head and a submachine gun emerged. Lehder yelled that they were F-2 agents and not to shoot. Firing erupted from both sides. People screamed. Bullets hit the SUV transporting Pablo's family. Juan Pablo dove onto Manuela. Aiming at Pablo's head, an agent fired a bullet which went through the back windscreen. Otto pointed a gun at a policeman, who jumped into a ten-foot deep sewage pipe, where he remained trapped. With an AK-47 firing into the sky, Pablo's car roared away.

"Drive on," a policeman told Victoria. "You don't need to pay the toll."

"Wait there!" yelled an agent who had witnessed Pablo and Lehder transfer cars. Agents surrounded the SUV and trained their guns on the occupants. "Get out of the vehicle!"

After their belongings were searched, the family members were crammed into a hut with over twenty people the authorities had rounded up from the tollbooth. Manuela sobbed. Accusing them of being murderous narco bastards, the police taunted them through the windows and refused to give Victoria her baby supplies.

After five hours, Colonel Quintero arrived to transport them to the Antioquia police headquarters. As the incorruptible commander of the Antioquia police, he was on a mission to find any police on Pablo's payroll. "Why would you want to raise children with a criminal?" Quintero said, while driving the SUV. Holding Manuela in a blanket, Victoria remained quiet.

After the colonel arrived at Medellín, the family got out. As Victoria reached for her baby supplies, Quintero grabbed them and the blanket, causing Victoria to almost drop her child. While Manuela cried, Quintero yelled at his men to incarcerate the goddam woman and her bastard child. Victoria begged for food and water for Manuela, but the colonel marched away. After midnight, a policeman came to the jail cell with a bottle for Manuela, who was still crying. The policeman was subsequently fired by the colonel.

After Pablo heard that a general from Bogotá had shown up to interrogate his wife and kids, he exploded and picked up the phone. "I demand to speak to Colonel Quintero." After getting rebuffed by a police commando, he yelled, "This is Pablo Escobar Gaviria. You need to tell that son of a bitch colonel that he better leave my innocent family out of this immediately. If not, there will be consequences." He hung up, enraged. He made enquiries about bribing policemen at the headquarters, but none were willing to take money because they were afraid of Quintero.

Interrogating Victoria, the general received no useful information, so he changed his strategy. Addressing Manuela, he said, "When you go to where your father is, is it hot or cold?" Manuela continued to cry. "Have you seen your father? You are now at his location, are you not?"

A lawyer sent by Pablo entered the building, yelled at the guards because they didn't have a warrant and secured the release of the family members, whom he took to an office occupied by Pablo, Lehder and bodyguards. One of Pablo's men said that day was the only time he had seen his boss cry. It was during a rant about the injustice his innocent wife and children had suffered at the hands of the police.

In his lavish offices on the outskirts of El Poblado and Envigado, Pablo rose from a massive desk of thick glass on stone pillars and kissed Manuela's forehead. After hugging Juan Pablo, he said, "Colonel Franklin is dead. I swear." He asked his son to stay and eat with him. He pledged to retaliate against the man who had refused to give Manuela her bottle. He told Pinina to make it a dramatic assassination with a car bomb.

While his men went to shadow the colonel, Pablo coached Manuela on what to say in future police interrogations. "Manuelita, if a policeman asks for me, how will you answer?"

"Ask my papa!" Manuela chuckled.

Pinina found that the colonel lived in one of Medellín's residential districts, and he took regular routes to work in an official Mercedes-Benz. On July 28, 1989, the Mercedes-Benz was spotted approaching a roadside bomb, surrounded by police motorbikes. Upon activation, 100 kilos of dynamite exploded in a white Mazda, destroying the Mercedes-Benz and launching two motorbikes to the height of a third-floor balcony. The explosion shook the city.

Returning to inform Pablo about their success, Pablo's men listened to the radio announce, "The beloved Governor of Antioquia was killed in a terrorist attack today." Aware that the Liberal governor was a friend of Pablo's, the men exchanged shocked expressions. By the time they arrived, Pablo had already heard the news.

"What happened, Pinina?"

"Our man saw the police escort with the Mercedes-Benz in front. The time matched with the colonel's routine, so he pressed the button. Never before had we seen a convoy other than the colonel's pass by that location."

Remaining calm, Pablo accepted their mistake, which he gave them the opportunity to fix by assassinating Quintero. Just in case, he made the contract eligible to other assassins, so that several groups were competing. He paid a man to appear in court and testify that the Cali godfather, Chepe, was behind the bombing. After reflecting on having murdered innocent people, Pablo said, "Terrorism is the atomic bomb of the poor. I have to use it even if it goes against my principles."

Holding a press conference, Quintero announced that he was the intended victim of the bomb. "Pablo Escobar is responsible for this attack. I shall move with fewer bodyguards to avoid more unnecessary police deaths." He assumed he would be harder to target without a police convoy. "If they are going to kill me, they can kill me on my own." Not wanting his bodyguards to die with him, he said, "I do not want them to kill humble people."

CHAPTER 7
PLOTTING EVIL

After receiving an envelope with photos of sixteen dismembered corpses accompanied by a threatening letter, Virginia feared that someone had learned about her meeting with the M-19 leaders. After deciding to inform Pablo, she called a real-estate agent to put her apartment on the market, and flew to Medellín with a million-dollar diamond she hoped to sell to Gustavo to earn a $100,000 fee from the seller.

Greeting Gustavo, she sensed an embittered mood in his eyes. She claimed that the diamond had come from European royalty. After examining it, he said it was one of the biggest he'd ever seen and probably stolen judging by the price of it. He disliked its colour and carbon flaws. She protested that flawless it would be five times more expensive.

Pablo knocked, entered and remarked on how tanned the Little Mermaid was. Since she had seen him, he had turned 36, but appeared to have aged five years. He was less agile, more overweight and the hair at his temples had greyed. Displaying the diamond, Gustavo said that she needed the commission money because all of his advertising contracts had been cancelled. Taking the diamond with his arm extended, Pablo puckered and gestured as if to throw it away. He said they were in the drug business, and if she wanted money, she should ask him. After sighing, Gustavo said the diamond was too big to convert to cash if an emergency arose. She asked how the billionaires had ended up with liquidity problems and couldn't raise a million. "The rich cry, too," Gustavo said, and abandoned her to Pablo.

Handing Pablo the envelope, she demanded to know who he had told about their meeting with the M-19. In stunned silence, he gazed at the photos and letter. He sat down, picked up tweezers and examined each photo, while reading aloud some of the letter. He said they needed to talk and asked whether she was married. She said she was still single, and the seller of the diamond was expecting her that night. He said to return the diamond and give her friend the impression that she was going to travel, and to wait for Pablo, because their lives depended upon what he needed to say. She should tell her boyfriend that she had missed the plane and would fly tomorrow. She needed to relax because he wouldn't let anybody hurt her nor would he touch her himself. Immediately, the photos would be analysed for fingerprints and the culprits traced. They must be suicidal to accuse him of atrocities.

She protested that she had already contaminated the photos with her fingerprints. She didn't want him to find out why they had been taken. She was happy on her tiny island with an angelic boyfriend, but exasperated for taking the blame for Pablo's crimes. Sobbing, she attempted to grab the photos.

Attempting to calm her, he stood and reached an arm around her shoulders. He returned the photos to the envelope and promised to burn them after he had ascertained whether the faces of the victims matched the disappeared people who had escaped from the Palace of Justice. It would be hard work because there wasn't much left of their faces due to the sulphuric acid. After she agreed to stay overnight in Medellín, he left.

After following his instructions, she arrived at his apartment, where she found a gold bracelet too small for her arm. Imagining that only a child could fit into it, she guessed that he had been having sex with young girls. Indeed, Pablo craved young flesh. He had organised an event with the contestants from Miss Teenager International. The outfits ranged from swimsuits to gala dresses, and the girls received cash in excess of the prizes at Miss Teenager International. It was customary for him to have installed secret cameras behind polarised glass in the changing rooms and bathrooms. After the girls had left, Pablo enjoyed watching the movies.

Pablo appeared, exhausted, downcast. "You look ten years younger than me and like a gold statue." She thanked him and explained why she had changed her telephone number. After gazing down in silence, he said it was great to see her. He threw himself onto the bed, rested his hands behind his neck and revealed what he had learned about the disappeared.

Gacha's military contacts had revealed everything. Soldiers had attempted to take a secretary with third-degree burns from a hospital. The director attempted to stop them, but he backed down after they accused him of collaborating with the guerrillas and threatened to take him to the barracks. In the Army cavalry school, the woman was flayed for hours. They were removing strips of flesh when she died. In an army truck, a woman gave birth and was tortured and killed. A baby was removed from a pregnant woman and thrown onto a dump. In the military garrison, a café worker was raped for four days and then bathed in sulphuric acid. Other corpses were buried at the cavalry school amid many more who had disappeared dating back to Turbay's presidency.

Pablo believed that the colonel in charge was torturing people to extract information about the $7 million he believed Pablo had paid the M-19 to bribe the military and security forces. He said he had only paid $1 million in cash for the M-19 to occupy the building and demand an explanation from the president, but everything had deteriorated fast. The military hellfire had started the blaze and killed the justices, who had witnessed the atrocities.

Rumours that he and Gacha had paid the military to assassinate the leaders of the M-19 were nonsense because he had always been friends with Fayad and Ospina, who were his connection to General Noriega, Nicaragua and Cuba. He had introduced her to them because he knew they would demand TV coverage from the government, which she could have facilitated. Only his most trusted men knew about the meeting with Fayad and Ospina, and her presence was only known by the two bodyguards who had transported her.

She said he had a traitor working for him or maybe he had mentioned the meeting to one of his girlfriends, who informed the intelligence services. Maybe he and Gacha had paid to have the justices and guerrillas slaughtered so that he wouldn't have to pay the M-19 the balance of what he owed. Pablo said that would have put him in the pockets of the military and intelligence organisations, which would have cost far more than the debt to the M-19.

She advised him to increase his protection. If she were killed, he would be blamed and all of his little whores would go running. After throwing the bracelet at him, she said it was too big to belong to his daughter. She called him a pothead and a pervert. By de-virginising girls, he was trying to replicate how he felt when he fell in love with his 13-year-old wife.

Pouncing on her, he yelled that nobody dared to talk to him like that. Who did she think she was? While he shook her, she yelled that she was his only real friend. She had never demanded anything from him such as leaving his wife and kids. She was the only iconic woman who had ever loved him or ever would. She threw her career away for him, which she had worked her entire life to build. He should be ashamed. Just when she had moved on, she received photos of the disappeared women, a consequence of his mission against extradition. She wasn't afraid of him and she had a conscience. She would rather die at his hands than be tortured. Since he had personally killed 200 people, he should quickly do her a favour with his famous expert strangulation techniques. He said that he only killed criminals, not angels. After spending so many months apart, he didn't want to hear this. As she pounded him with her fists, he hugged her until she cried and rested her head on his shoulder.

He kissed her hair. "Do you still care about me a little?"

"I stopped loving you a while back, but I'll care about you till the day I die because you're the only man who was ever good to me and took care of the poorest people." She sobbed in his arms.

He suggested she stay on her island, which was safer than Bogotá. But soon she would be bored and in need of a real man, not a kid. Jane needs a Tarzan. She said anything was possible after her Tarzan of the Zoo and laughed. He dried her face and asked whether she would include the truth about the Palace of Justice in his movie script. If the Italians wouldn't give her $100,000 for the film rights, then he would as an advance.

She said the Italians didn't have that much money, plus she would have to move to Italy and say goodbye to her boyfriend and the island. In writing the movie, she didn't want to turn into an apologist for Pablo, who asked if she now viewed him as just a rich criminal. She said he was the man she had loved the most, and if he were just a wealthy criminal, what would that make her? She believed that the blood of the Palace of Justice massacre was not entirely on his hands, but she would not congratulate him on fighting extradition that way. The unanticipated results of his actions terrified her. The country was on its knees, so why did he insist on killing more people? He needed to stop boasting about victory, to deny his involvement in the massacre for the rest of his life, to emerge from the hell he lived in and to allow peace for everyone. She pledged to keep everything secret, which he would have to carry in his conscience. The authorities who had butchered the disappeared would have to answer to God.

Asked why she had lost her advertising contacts, she said that she had received adverse publicity about her relationship with him in *The Spectator* and the Kaplan family had terminated her contract on the grounds that a celebrity was too expensive. He said that *The Spectator* was behind many of the dirty tricks to sabotage her job. Media people now viewed her as easy prey because she was no longer with Pablo. *The Spectator* was printing lies about him, so her enemies were his enemies, and if she sat in the doorway of her house, she would watch the corpses of their enemies go by.

Sitting on the bed by Pablo's feet, she said that if he removed extradition he should concentrate on building his life and forget about the media, being out of which relieved her. She hoped he would return to being the man with the charitable spirit whom she had fallen in love with. After silently studying her face, he said that she had foolishly fled to an island to escape from him and the pain caused by people. Stroking her cheek, he said he found it odd that she had such a clean soul, uncontaminated by the years spent with him, whose soul was blacker than coal. He jumped up, kissed her forehead, and thanked her for bringing the photos. He said he would always be there for her and insisted that she kept him updated on her phone numbers. He hoped she would never completely leave his life. She said she would only stop their contact after she were married.

Weeks later, Pablo enticed her back to Medellín with a job offer that he could only tell her in person. While he smoked cannabis for the first time in front of her, she said that the only drug she would like to try was LSD. After reading about Huxley, she too would like to do some on her deathbed. Due to her affinity for hallucinogenics, but dislike of cocaine and heroin, Pablo called her Cleansoul, a nickname he would often tease her with. Sitting on the chair where she had once been blindfolded and prodded with a loaded gun, she watched him lying contentedly on the bed. After discussing love, he got up, held her face and admired her beauty. Wriggling out of his grasp, she asked why he had summoned her to Medellín.

He said he had an idea to extract money from Colombia's wealthiest families by kidnapping their richest men. If she helped, she would earn 20 per cent of hundreds of millions of dollars. She could not understand why a billionaire would kidnap people worth less than him. Perhaps he had smoked too much cannabis. He said he had only taken three hits, and she would be excluded from his offer if she didn't change her tone. With the majority of his assets overseas, money-laundering laws had turned his life into hell due to illiquidity.

He expected to be indicted in America and rewards for his

capture to follow. Escalating the war would be expensive. The M-19 had taught him the art of kidnapping. She had insider knowledge of Colombia's four richest men. Was she in or was she choosing to be Cleansoul? Feigning interest to get more information, she asked what he had in mind.

He detailed his potential victims, including two bottlers from the Santo Domingo family, who would be kidnapped in New York, and Carlos Ardila, an easy target in a wheelchair. The next was Luis Carlos Sarmiento, who answered her calls and would grant her an appointment. Then Carlos Jaime, who owned oil and soap interests and was a friend of Betancur. As the fourth was one of her neighbours, he needed to use her apartment as a launch point.

She said the four richest men had private armies trained in America and Israel to prevent the guerrillas from kidnapping them or their family members. Presently, he wasn't at war with the superrich, some of whom secretly appreciated the MAS. If he kidnapped any of them, they would forget their quarrels and unite against him. Asked why she felt that way, as they had all abandoned her to unemployment, she said that hating them was different from hurting them. As an expert in banking, Carlos Sarmiento could help get his money into Colombia. He should arrange a business meeting with him, not kidnap him. When his daughter had been kidnapped, Sarmiento appreciated Pablo offering help. Since Pablo had been listening to her conversations, he must be aware that Sarmiento had no problem granting an appointment to Gilberto.

Pablo said that he preferred cash to the methods employed by the Cali godfather. If she didn't want to help him kidnap her ex-boyfriends, then how about the Echavarrías or the flower exporters of the Bogotá savannah, the sugar manufacturers of the Valle del Cauca or the wealthiest in the Jewish community? Due to her relationship with him, their wives had disowned her. Didn't she want to get revenge?

She said that he presently had enough enemies, including

PABLO ESCOBAR'S STORY

the American and Colombian governments, and the media. He needed to leave kidnapping to the guerrillas. How would he feel if the leader of the FARC attempted to replace him as the King of Cocaine? He said he would destroy him the next day and that the FARC were richer than him due to kidnapping. As the biggest outlaw in Latin America, his value system differed from that of tycoons. Exasperated by his suicidal thinking, she said that her heart would be broken if he died. She had loved him more than all of her exes combined.

After touching her face and hugging her, he said he had been testing Cleansoul. He now knew that even if she ever stopped loving him completely, she would never betray him for any price offered by the Americans. He liked to test a person's loyalty by revealing something that only he knew, true or untrue, and if the secret came out, he knew why. He urged her to never forget that lesson because he cared about her.

She said that if she ever told anyone about their conversations she would end up with no friends and in an asylum. With his creativity, he could easily find a way to increase his liquidity without kidnapping anyone. She wished him peace and no more sins like the Palace of Justice. He said he always knew what was going to happen before everybody else. She would not have kids with the man on the island. Within three months, she would be back with Pablo, whose face she was destined to see and whose name she was going to hear for the rest of her life.

Flying back, she knew that he hadn't been testing her and that he would become the most notorious kidnapper Colombia had ever seen. She believed he would risk his life in a carefully planned way for reasons beyond his cocaine empire and fight against extradition.

While swimming at the island, she wondered whether he would ever stop killing. The newspapers had reported the deaths of Guillermo Cano and Colonel Ramírez. Pablo was right about her always seeing his face: his evil expression was all over the news. His latest round of assassinations meant more death threats on her answering machine. Swimming against the tide for hours, she suffered fatigue and almost drowned, but was rescued by a passing yacht. Her boyfriend's father expelled her from the island because she was suicidal and a risk to everybody. In a small boat, her boyfriend silently steered her to Cartagena. She denied him a goodbye kiss.

With the media circulating rumours about her, Pablo called and mockingly asked if it were true that she had syphilis, AIDS, had attempted suicide and was on the run from the police. Rather than speak on the phone, he would send a plane because he was going to wipe out all of her enemies. A night-time serenade from a mariachi softened her towards him. When she felt vulnerable, he always made her feel protected in his arms. Aware that she always lost her ability to reason around him, she returned to him and they swore undying love.

He wanted to murder the family that had expelled her from the island. He was about to employ a Basque explosives expert, so bombing them would be good practise. Ramping up the war with explosives, he would have to fight the Americans. A missile attack on the Pentagon would knock out the US defence headquarters.

She said he obviously hadn't watched enough *Pink Panther* movies in which expensive jewels were protected by lasers only visible with special glasses. Miles of airspace above the Pentagon were similarly protected, otherwise the Russians would have attacked it. Perhaps he had watched too much James Bond, because he was committed to becoming a movie super-villain. Was extradition worth wiping out humankind for?

Grimacing, he yelled that extradition was worth everything and more. If she repeated that, he would throw her out of the window. No rays were protecting the Pentagon. The conceited Americans were vulnerable. He had already outsmarted their ability to defend themselves by exporting so much cocaine that the kilo price had fallen from $50,000 to $10,000. The Reagan presidency was obsessed with him. That's why Nancy Reagan had invented the phrase "Just say no!"

Virginia said she had watched a movie in which a missile fired at the Pentagon had turned around at the limits of US airspace and ultimately exploded on its sender. Pablo would convert Medellín into Hiroshima.

He mocked her for believing Hollywood movies financed by Republican Jews with President Reagan's perspective. Had she turned as cowardly as other women? What had happened to her being his other half? She wasn't just Cleansoul, but also a moralist and an imperialist. Recalling that she had mentioned Hiroshima, he thanked her for a sudden idea. He danced and spun her around, while singing a love ballad.

Scared, she said he would end up in a madhouse. They used to talk about current events and history, but now he was stuck on terrorism. He should think about his children or something constructive. Tired of receiving threats, she wanted to rest. He said she should travel to Miami, but always return to him because he went crazy every time she disappeared.

After she returned from Miami, Pablo said he had everything in place to bomb her ex-boyfriend's family and boat. Realising that he wanted to deter anyone else from dating her, she said exploding the boat would kill dozens of tourists and workers.

"That's precisely my idea." He said he was tired of Cleansoul. His favourite thing was making mischief and he would terrify the people threatening her. She needed to demand respect. For an hour, she tried to convince him not to bomb anyone. After a few hits of cannabis, he said, "Can I rest my head on your lap?"

"Of course," she said, stroking his forehead while he gazed at nothing.

He protested that their enemies were trying to detach her from him, his only true friend that he shared things with besides Gustavo, Roberto and Gacha. He needed someone with a different value system to care about him and challenge him non-judgmentally. She had prevented many mistakes, so he could not allow her to leave again.

To stop him from bombing them, she convinced him to

verbally threaten her ex-boyfriend's family. She asked why he never killed with his fists. Recently, a famous boxer had asked for her phone number, and she had given him a fake one. He said he would win such a fight.

He wanted to use Cuba to smuggle drugs into America. Perhaps Gabriel García Márquez could arrange a meeting with Castro. She advised against having the Nobel Laureate facilitate a drug deal. Using Cuba would threaten America, which had stationed Guantánamo Bay Naval Base there. His foray into Nicaragua had failed miserably. He protested that the US had used the proceeds from seized cocaine to finance the Nicaraguan Contras, which had spawned the crack epidemic. Crack was so addictive and destructive, he had tried to prevent its use from his merchandise, but had been unsuccessful. He chastised Nancy Reagan for not holding Oliver North accountable for dealing with cocaine traffickers to finance the war against Communism. From Mexico, he had learned that it was sometimes easier to bribe the generals than the country's leader. In Cuba, the generals were desperate for his money. She said Castro would execute them for dealing with Pablo just to boost his image. Wars and political mistakes would render him poorer than when he had started. He would go down in history as an idealist. He yelled that she had no idea what he was planning.

Gustavo asked Virginia into his office for a private chat. He said he was exhausted from being on the run. With Jorge Ochoa incarcerated and Carlos Lehder in hiding, his workload had multiplied. Whenever she disappeared, Pablo's behaviour spiralled out of control as no one dared to restrain him. Smoking cannabis, surrounded by hit men and teenage girls, he was ill-advised. His family couldn't intervene because they viewed him as godlike. Only when she returned was he more reasonable. Having secured his future generations, Gustavo realised happiness meant having a beautiful woman who loved you. There was a TV actress he adored whom he wanted to marry, but he was terrified of rejection. Would Virginia approach her in Medellín?

She refused to even hear her name, because she wouldn't want her to suffer like she had for years with Pablo. Gustavo was married, and she was no matchmaker. Pablo's crazy ideas were hard enough for her to deal with. Asked what she wanted in life that was unobtainable, she said just for the threats to stop. She hoped to study translation in Geneva and to start a cosmetics company, but Pablo wanted her to stay in Colombia to witness and document his life, which was getting more dangerous every day.

Gustavo named the TV actress and promised to help Virginia get out of the country and start a new life in exchange for an introduction. She didn't deserve to be suffering, and what Pablo now planned would bring untold consequences. Would she promise to try, so that the uncertainty that kept him awake would go away? Unlike Pablo, he was not promiscuous. He would make her happy. Moved by his plea, she promised to consider it.

CHAPTER 8
KIDNAPPING TRAFFICKERS

In one of Pablo's houses called La Cascada, on a hill in eastern Medellín, the boss waited for Pablo Correa, one of the region's wealthiest traffickers. After Lara's death, most traffickers had fled. Staying behind as the only remaining exporter, Correa had capitalised on the spike in prices, which had upset some of his competitors. Correa parked and emerged with an air of arrogance.

"Let's walk alone to a pavilion on the edge of the pool," Pablo said.

Walking along, Correa said, "Will you get rid of one of my associates, Frank Gutiérrez?"

As he would be paid well and it would reinforce his power, Pablo was going to take care of the hit, but he chose to probe further. "What's your problem with this guy? Can't this be resolved with a friendly agreement?" After receiving answers, he agreed to the hit.

The next day, he called La Yuca: "The deal is this: 100 million pesos for you and 100 million for me. As a warm-up, throw a coffin from a helicopter over Gutiérrez's estate in the San Jerónimo resort."

Shot at the Kokoriko restaurant near the Medellín airport, Frank Gutiérrez was hospitalised.

"To this clinic," Pablo told La Yuca, "they bring wounded policemen and they are kept under surveillance. Gutiérrez's bodyguards are there. Let's wait and think about it."

La Yuca and his men painted a stolen car like a police vehicle. Two hit men pretended to be injured policemen. After entering the clinic unchallenged, they found Gutiérrez without any bodyguards. Using guns with silencers, they shot him.

Without asking permission, La Yuca brought his own bodyguards to Pablo's office. While paying his men their share from the assassination, he complained about Pablo: "The boss does nothing and gets a lot of money." During a fit of rage, he broke a billiard cue.

"Go and calm down," Pablo said, "and then we will talk." After La Yuca left, Pablo called Big Gun: "I haven't slept for several days. I lie down with the submachine gun at my side because I'm worried about La Yuca. I have to finish him before he gets ahead."

Days later, La Yuca returned to the office with some of his men, where Big Gun and another hit man accused him of stealing. After five minutes of arguing, he was shot 500 times. With weapons trained on them, his men were told, "Be quiet. The boss will explain everything."

Pablo emerged from his office. "I ordered him killed for his defiance. I do not want war with any of you guys. I'm going to give you fifty million [pesos] each to go in peace." They all took the money. Some swore allegiance to Pablo and stayed to work for him. La Yuca's corpse was thrown on a road for the authorities to take credit for his death.

The trafficker Pablo Correa asked the boss for another favour. Aware that the DEA had misidentified him as Correa Ramos, a sports leader, he believed that he could fake his own death if Escobar would assassinate Correa Ramos. Intrigued by the misidentification plot, Pablo arranged the hit, but then started to scheme against Pablo Correa.

One of Virginia's friends was owed $2 million for jewellery by a Cali trafficker called Hugo Valencia, so she called him on her friend's behalf. Enraged, he yelled at her for collecting another's debts. The shameless old bitch should be calling her lovers instead, including schizo Pablo and inmate Rodríguez. How dare she talk to him like that!

Remaining calm, she said if he didn't want to be talked to like that, he needed to pay his debts like honourable wealthy people. Also, she was never Gilberto's lover. He said Gilberto's wife was paying the media to say that she was. She listened to him rant about her and Pablo until he hung up. Within a few days, $1 million had been repaid. The friend thanked Virginia, who told her about the insults. The friend said to disregard his behaviour because he was going through hard times.

Valencia was a friend of Mauricio Restrepo, a trafficker who had rallied to the cause of the kidnapped Marta Ochoa. An expert in transporting cocaine to America, Restrepo was admired by Pablo because he was a sailor and a diver, who spoke English and was a master of radio communications. El Patrón even gave him a nickname: Youth.

In early 1987, Valencia arrived in Medellín for a cycling event and stayed with Restrepo. After leaving the house, Valencia was kidnapped. Worried about his friend and also considering the possibility that he had been the intended victim, Restrepo consulted the Ochoas, who knew nothing.

"I don't know anything about Valencia's kidnapping," Pablo said, "or any threats against you."

"I'll start looking for my friend," Restrepo said.

"Do it, Youth, and when you need backup, let me know," Pablo said.

With American equipment, Restrepo triangulated a vast area, including Antioquia and the north of the Caldas section. The kidnappers allowed Valencia to talk to his girlfriend long enough for the phone's signal to be detected, originating from near a dam east of Medellín. Combing the area, Restrepo encountered the familiar faces of some of Pablo's men. Greeting them, he instinctively felt they were involved in the kidnapping. Fearing that Valencia would immediately be moved, Restrepo ordered his men to search the local houses.

While they were smashing doors open, Pablo called, "Youth,

leave that business alone. Valencia is mixed up with powerful people. Do not get involved because they will kill you."

After suspending operations, Restrepo suspected Pablo, but did not report anything to Valencia's family. He told the negotiator not to pay anything: "They will kill him anyway." After $4 million was paid, his body was found. Restrepo learned that the Cali Cartel had offered Pablo 100 million pesos to kill Valencia. Pablo had responded, "I'm ready, but I'll do it my way."

Further investigation revealed that Pablo was behind the kidnapping and murder of other wealthy traffickers, including Pablo Correa, who had killed some of his own associates to fake his death to mislead the DEA. Some of Pablo's men had urged the boss to kill Correa due to his arrogance and selfishness. Sentenced to death by hanging, Correa was held hostage, while a ransom was demanded, including transferring his properties into Pablo's name. But Correa died instantly when a gun accidentally misfired and the bullet entered his forehead.

To convince the family to pay the ransom, Pablo's men gave the corpse a makeover to remove its pallor of death, propped its eyes open with sticks and photographed him holding the latest newspaper. Believing he was alive, his family deposited $2 million. Buried without lime, his corpse was discovered by a dog, and his family refused any further payments.

Restrepo learned that Pablo was behind the abductions of Rodrigo Murillo and the Ochoas' brother-in-law, Alonso Cárdenas, another friend of Restrepo. Tracking Cárdenas, the signal suddenly failed.

"Who else knows about my investigation?" Restrepo asked the Ochoas.

"We've only told Pablo."

The radio announced the discovery of Murillo, buried from the torso, with his legs sticking out. After hearing the broadcast, Cárdenas, aware of his fate, used his own blood to write on a wall MURDERERS BASTARDS and committed suicide. Angry over Cárdenas outsmarting them in death, Pablo's men abused the corpse. A medical examiner found over fifty wounds.

Restrepo warned the Ochoas that Pablo was, "A man who wanted to live on what others earned … He's going to kill us all. We have to kill him." Remaining silent, they departed. Pablo put a $10 million contract on Restrepo, who was pursued by killers ranging from hit men to soldiers. He later stated that he had to dig a hole in the earth to hide.

CHAPTER 9
CALI THREAT GROWS

In Cali, Virginia visited a friend, who displayed an emerald and diamond necklace and earrings set. With accusation, she said that Pablo had ordered Hugo Valencia to be chopped into pieces, and that he had ordered jewellery worth $250,000 for a weekend with a whore in a tin crown. He had done nothing for her, other than cause her to lose her job and to receive death threats. He preferred whores from his own social class rather than a high-society beauty who only dated royalty and multimillionaires.

Her friend's words punctured her dreamworld. She decided to ask Gilberto, recently transferred from a Spanish to a Colombian prison, to invest in her cosmetics idea. Without being searched, she waltzed inside the prison to salsa music and lawyers in suits, all smiling at her. The Cali godfather had converted his living quarters into an office. After exclaiming that she was a vision from heaven, he hugged her. She said she would like to spend six months at his hotel if she ever had his illegal wealth.

He laughed sadly. "You haven't changed at all." Sitting opposite one another, they chatted over a long table. After years in terrible conditions, he was fortunate to be back. Overseas, he had lived in a perpetual nightmare of the possibility of extradition to America. His presidential connections had pulled strings to open minor cases as grounds for him and Jorge Ochoa to be sent to Colombia instead of America. Now he had food home-cooked or from his favourite restaurants, whereas in Spain he had scraped by on unsalted spaghetti. The internal noise and clinking of bars had never stopped, and all the while he suspected that his woman was cheating on him.

She said his wife cheating was unimaginable. He said he was talking about Virginia or had she forgotten their Paris agreement? Rather than reveal that Pablo had raped her upon learning about Paris, for which she had made him pay and considered the debt settled, she ignored that Gilberto considered her his woman and pointed out that he had only written to her once. "When will you be released?"

"In a couple of months, and I'd like to see you. With hair like yours, you should launch a shampoo."

"Thanks, but I'd like to launch a line of make-up and skincare products. I just need capital."

"When I'm free, we'll talk about that." Asked about the murder of Hugo, he said that Valencia hadn't paid his bills, which had created dangerous enemies in Medellín. At least the Valle del Cauca lacked such atrocities. As he was retired, he didn't know exactly what had happened. Did she believe that he had retired?

She said he was in forced retirement. "You should consider yourself the luckiest man in the world." He said years of incarceration had scarred him and everything had changed. His children would suffer from his notoriety. She said they would be grateful for his sacrifices, the price of inheriting $1 billion.

"I can never leave Colombia, otherwise I'd be arrested on an American warrant and extradited. I'll never see Paris again." They discussed what he had read in Spain, including Conrad's *Heart of Darkness* and his favourite author Stefan Zweig. "I would like to have been an orchestra conductor." After chatting for a few hours, he promised to visit her within days of his release.

Contemplating the jewellery Pablo had bought for his latest fling, she rejoiced at her accomplishments in the past twenty-four hours. With Gilberto's support, she would launch her own cosmetics empire. After two weeks of research, she met Gilberto again.

On the verge of war with Pablo, Gilberto was in a sour mood. He reemphasised that he wanted to retire, but Pablo had threatened the Cali godfathers because they had refused to do him a favour. He said Pablo had gone insane and might even have her killed.

She said that Pablo would never kill her because they were best friends and he truly cared about her. She would try to broker peace, because with Galán in the official Liberal Party he would become the next president and both bosses would be extradited unless they formed a united front. If they tried to kill each other, her heart would break. Although in agreement, Gilberto feared that things had spiralled out of control.

Free from jail, Gilberto arrived at Virginia's apartment in Bogotá, accompanied by Santo. They could only stay for one hour because they were about to visit the home of ex-president López to celebrate Gilberto's freedom with Ernesto Samper. While hiding her disdain for Santo, she greeted an ecstatic Gilberto with a gift of the only book by Zweig that he hadn't read. After they had gone, she felt that the strength of Gilberto's political alliances would accelerate Pablo's fall, and the only beneficiary of their war would be the establishment, who would liquidate the godfathers and maintain the status quo.

After asking herself which boss she would choose if they were the only two people left on the planet, she selected Pablo because she knew what to expect from him, even though he was cruel. She and Pablo were carved from one piece. She called him and announced that they needed to meet urgently to speak about Cali and that she would board a commercial plane, while omitting that she intended to say goodbye to him and Gustavo forever. She sensed that Gilberto was too preoccupied to finance her cosmetics idea, so for the first time ever, she was going to ask Pablo for money to finance a stay in Europe to study languages.

Pablo was in a meeting when she arrived in a figure-hugging red designer dress, chosen from 150 European outfits to give him a final memory of her. While she waited, a hit man commented on her famous legs from the stockings commercial. She was glad she was saying goodbye to a sleazy community of criminals with killers' eyes. Pablo emerged from an office with an attractive woman in her late 20s whom he introduced as his girlfriend. Contemplating the woman in a red sweater with a gold Virgin Mary necklace, she imagined her working at a sales counter in a beauty store.

"Congratulations on having such a pretty girl at your side." After small talk, Virginia asked to see him alone to deliver a message from Cali. She entered his office, followed by Pablo who closed the door, sat at a desk and yelled that he only had a few minutes to spare because his girlfriend was waiting.

She said that Gilberto and Ernesto Samper wanted to annihilate him. Explaining how would take longer than a few minutes, because finishing him off would be complex. He needed to respect her or she would board a plane. After gazing down, he said he would meet her at 10 AM the next day and that he now rose at 9 AM to attend meetings, so she shouldn't be alarmed by the time. He said Gustavo was waiting to see her.

By prioritising his girlfriend over the prospect of discussing peace with Cali, he had displayed a vulnerability to Virginia. Hardly anybody could outwit him under normal circumstances, but when he surrendered to his passions, he lost his sense of proportion. She feared that Gilberto – with the ice-cold soul of a banker combined with the vast resources of the four Cali godfathers – would outwit Pablo, who tended to be impatient, arrogant and stubborn. Taking on Cali was one thing, but waging war simultaneously with so many enemies – including the US and Colombian governments – was suicidal.

Chatting on a sofa, Gustavo wanted to know whether she had arranged the meeting with the actress he secretly loved. She said the mention of his name and him being a cousin of Pablo Escobar was enough to send her running. She couldn't understand why she was getting asked by Virginia, whose own career had been ruined by her association with Pablo. The actress only felt contempt for Gustavo and she would never meet him even for all the gold in the world. She would rather die than date a narco!

In shock and disbelief, he insisted on hearing more. While he gazed silently out of the window, Virginia reminded him of the wicked rumours circulated by the media about her, including traffickers having kidnapped and assaulted her; how her face had been shredded by a knife on the orders of a female enemy; how doctors had treated her for AIDS and syphilis; and how the police had raided her house for drugs and weapons.

She unloaded on Gustavo the pent-up frustrations she had never bothered Pablo with, including the price she had paid for supporting extradition. She added that millionaires bought beautiful women for the illusion of love. Pablo only deserved the love of his high-priced prostitutes. Mistakenly, she hadn't set a price at the beginning when he had offered her anything she wanted. As an iconic woman, she believed that love meant making a partner happy and protecting him from the world.

"It's obvious that a woman of your education level," Gustavo said, "should be with an important man and not the lover of a bandit. All of us have wives who love and care for us with or without riches."

"Those women trade public humiliation for diamonds and furs, without which they would leave." She mentioned the $250,000 emerald jewellery Pablo had ordered, and asked him to help her convince Pablo to give her $100,000, so she could advertise her apartment for sale and go overseas to escape the hostility. In Europe, she would get a job utilising the six languages she spoke.

"With the cartel war that's coming, we're going to need a lot of cash," Gustavo said. "You should be prepared for my cousin to say no to an amount that years ago he would have given you without thinking twice. He isn't going to accept that you are leaving for good because he needs you to discuss things that he can't discuss with his family or any other woman." Gustavo opened a safe and put a tray containing hundreds of diamond rings on a coffee table, mostly ranging from 1 to 2 carats. "I'd like to give you one as a souvenir. We're grateful for everything you've done."

Initially, she refused, but changed her mind and asked for

the biggest one. After laughing, he said that she should take the purest. She said purity was for saints, and she would like the fattest one with the least defects. She placed an oval one on her finger, and the door opened.

El Patrón burst in and demanded an explanation as to why she was still there. He thought she had left. Was she getting engaged to Gilberto? Gustavo's mouth dropped. She laughed. Pablo yelled not to give her any diamonds because she was different and disinterested in them. Gustavo asked whether she was different because she had a moustache like him. He said that he had never met a woman who didn't like diamonds and asked her whether that was true.

She said she adored them, but for five years she had pretended she didn't like them to demonstrate that she wasn't dating Pablo for money. She said Pablo also believed that she had been deceiving him for years with Gilberto, and now she had come to broker peace before they castrated each other and all womankind was left mourning.

While Pablo yelled about her being allied to Cali, she admired the diamond. Pablo shouted that diamonds were only for beauty queens on the correct side of the war. Gustavo said she wouldn't be there if she were with Cali. Everybody was trying to starve her, so he wanted to give her something valuable, for which he didn't need anybody's permission including Pablo's. The only real queen Pablo had ever had was Virginia, who had chosen him over millions of admirers.

Pablo said that she should be writing instead of posing for photos, working on books instead of being a chatterbox. Gustavo urged her not to write about them and said she had come to say goodbye forever. In a threatening voice, Pablo demanded an explanation. Was she getting married? Why didn't he know what was going on?

Ignoring him, she promised to wear the diamond until death. Pablo said he thought she was different from the rest. She said he had been wrong. She had just discovered a love of diamonds.

Gustavo laughed. Disappointed, Pablo said they would meet tomorrow and he left.

The next day, his men transported her to a small white house in the country adorned with flowers, where the cleaning lady recognised her. Pablo arrived and said he had only twenty minutes to spare. He knew she was there on her lover Gilberto's behalf and she was going to ask for money. He was going to destroy Gilberto and not give her a single cent.

She said she was there on Pablo's behalf and how could she be Gilberto's lover if he had just spent three years in prison. She wanted Pablo to help her get out of the country and away from his enemies. Gazing at her hand with the diamond, she said calmly that the Rodríguez brothers and Ernesto Samper would finish him. If he wanted to know how, she would explain the details in front of the cleaning lady.

After ordering the lady to leave, he sat on a bamboo sofa opposite Virginia, who detailed the meeting with Gilberto and Santo and how they had gone to the house of ex-president López to celebrate Gilberto's freedom. She urged him not to trust Santo, especially if he were at war with Cali. Gilberto's daughter had married Santo's cousin. Santo's partner in Chrysler was a powerful influence over the Barco presidency. She said that Machiavelli had recommended the strategy of divide and conquer. War between the two biggest bosses would only benefit the Americans, including the DEA. It would deplete their fortunes, fortify extradition and casualties would skyrocket.

He said that Gilberto would run out of money first. She said that if Pablo were so rich, he wouldn't be plotting to kidnap wealthy people. He had over 1,000 bodyguards to support, which meant 6,000 people including their families, whereas Gilberto had no such overhead. He said Gilberto's army were politicians and journalists who cost more than all of his bodyguards combined. Even if their costs were equal, he had the advantage because he had invested in people's affection – the world's best investment. None of Gilberto's senators would die for him.

She said that Gilberto was a personal friend of several ex-presidents and protected by every level of government in his territory. He had thousands of taxi drivers and telephone workers as his eyes and ears, and had even cultivated a relationship with the M-19. His silver was more effective at winning people's affection than Pablo's lead. War would fracture the guild that supported him into smaller bloodthirsty gangs looking to acquire territory. If he joined Gilberto, they could halve their costs, double their strengths and defeat extradition. The day after Galán becomes president, extradition would be enforced. With Gilberto's contacts and the respect Pablo commanded, they would be unbeatable. Rather than spend millions on war, he needed to allow her to prevent it by extending his hand to Gilberto as a demonstration of true greatness. With peace accomplished, she would leave Colombia the next day.

He said that Gilberto needed to take the first step. The Cali godfather knew why, so there was no reason for Pablo to explain the situation. She said that the causes of the conflict were irrelevant. He needed to focus on the benefits of an alliance. He said that if she held Gilberto's wealth and power in such high esteem, she should ask him for money to leave the country. The insult provoked her to attack like a panther. She protested that she was incapable of asking anyone for money other than him, who had been her lover for five years and for whom she had sacrificed her career. Outside of their five-minute fling, she had never spent a night with Gilberto. She said that they had been arguing for over an hour with no progress and reminded him how busy he was.

He rose from the sofa, rested his hands on a balcony railing, gazed outside and asked why she wanted to leave him forever. To study translation in Geneva to become an interpreter, she needed a loan of $100,000. A multilingual translator would be of great benefit to him, especially with confidential documents and recorded conversations. He said that wouldn't happen with his money. She might end up married to a fat Swiss banker, while he endured hell in Colombia. Whether she loved or hated him, she was staying put to live through what was coming and document it all.

She said that he was selfishly condemning her to his enemies and starvation in Colombia, which only offered daily terror. "Where have you buried your greatness?"

"In the same place that your career is buried." He said neither of them could choose their fates. You get to choose one half, whereas the other you're born with.

She said a billionaire such as him had no right to claim he was a victim of fate. She should have known he would someday turn his cruelty on her. He said she would eventually understand the reasons for his decision, which he couldn't presently explain. They knew each other better than anyone. Whether she loved him or not, she would be a noble judge who would never betray his memory. Due to the time they had spent conversing about everything, she was best equipped to write his story, unlike his family or workers with whom he had never shared his soul. He needed to know that whatever her relationship status, she would be observing the mayhem that was about to unfold. She said that they were experts in inflating each other's egos when they were down. His diatribe was an excuse not to give her a cent. With his wife and any woman he wanted, he didn't need her for anything. If she had ever been important to him, she couldn't fathom why he wouldn't help her like when he had taken over her debt-ridden company five years ago.

"War is imminent," Pablo said. She laughed and mentioned the jewellery worth $250,000 she had seen for a woman he had probably already forgotten. He grabbed her chin and in a menacing tone stated that she had visited Gilberto the next day in jail. He released her chin. "What do you think of my new girlfriend?"

"I'm happy you have such a sweet and pretty woman to take care of and love you." His girlfriend would soon want a baby and under Colombian law each of his children would be worth $1 billion. She had never tried to possess him or enrichen herself through him.

While Pablo gazed sadly, she assumed that he was thinking of Wendy Chavarriaga, whose baby had been removed by a vet. He approached her, put an arm around her shoulder and drew her closer. He said her love was unique because it had really mattered. She was his intelligent love with the entire universe inside her head and heart. Combined with her voice and skin, he had been so happy that he suspected she would be the last woman he would ever love so intensely. He said she would marry a better man than him, but he would find her irreplaceable.

Touched, she said she would treasure his words in a corner of her heart. He said he had decided to leave her with nothing so that when she wrote his story, people wouldn't say it was an apology because he had bought her. Devastated, she said his decision was jealous revenge. He said he had never been jealous, and she would someday be grateful and understand because he knew everything that was going to happen. Wanting to sob alone, she said they had been talking for two hours and there were people waiting for him.

Resting on the balcony, gazing at the distance, he said his war against the state might be fatal, but he would at least destroy the Cali Cartel and his other enemies. There would be no more lead because he had graduated to dynamite, which was necessary even if the innocent paid for the guilty. Crying, she couldn't fathom how a wealthy man who had been so generous now harboured such hatred, ferocity and desperation that he wanted to punish everybody. She suspected that his rage was rooted in his inability to change Colombia due to the status quo maintained by people as ruthless as him. He told her to stop blubbering, as she would never be his widow.

She said she couldn't cry for somebody like him. She was crying for herself, her country and the fortune that would go to his widow, who wouldn't know what to do with it. What was the point in having so much wealth if he had to live on the run? He was evil and selfish to dynamite people in such a poor country. Strengthening his own security would protect him adequately rather than going to such extremes. Soldiers lacked the courage to come for him.

He said she was wrong. Whole armies were coming for him. That's why he needed dynamite and missiles. She said if anyone heard him say these things, he would be committed to an asylum. He should thank God he had listened to her so far instead of unleashing his crazy ideas. She predicted he wouldn't last five years. He called her a lecturing old wife. She said old wives were often right in the face of stubborn, brutish old husbands. They were equally old, but she looked ten years younger with her twenty-four-inch waist, whereas Pablo had turned as plump as the politician, Santo, from eating excessive amounts of beans. She said they had been conversing for three hours, and Gilberto had warned that Pablo would have her killed for collaborating with the enemy.

He said he would never kill his love and Gilberto was more miserable than he had calculated. He prayed that Virginia was not with Gilberto on the day he ended his life. Seeing her in the morgue next to him would make him want to shoot himself. He asked whether Gilberto had promised her anything. She said to produce a shampoo with her name.

Asked why he hadn't sent a hit man to kill her, he said he couldn't bear to see such a beautiful corpse with a twenty-four-inch waist. Hugging her from behind, he kissed her hair and said that he didn't want to create a tragedy worse than Romeo and Juliet.

"If you send someone to kill me with one shot, I won't feel a thing. You can throw my remains in a whirlpool with wildflowers. I can watch over you better from heaven than Bogotá. I'll even do some PR with everyone you've sent there."

Breathing her perfume, he remained silent for a minute. "I've never been so insulted." He promised to get a luxurious stolen headstone for Cleansoul the Beauty from Blacksoul the Beast. She chastised his dark mind. He said he was in the habit of writing daily death threats, which he signed with his fingerprints.

"Can I keep the Beretta handgun at least for a while?"

He said she should always have it, even in the shower. He stroked her cheeks. "As long as I'm alive, no one will touch even a hair on your head." If they did, he would cut off their hands with a chainsaw, and do the same to the culprit's entire family. At 2 PM, he said he needed to take her to her hotel so that his men could pick her up at 3 PM, but with her nose strawberry red from crying, she needed to apply some make-up otherwise the hotel staff would whisper that he had beaten her.

"Why am I the only woman you never gave jewellery or furs?"

He kissed her on the lips. "To show that I never had to buy the most beautiful woman, the bravest and most loyal, but somewhat unfaithful." They smirked at each other. She powdered her nose. Gazing proudly, he said, "Make-up is a marvel. It's a shame I only have cocaine labs, not cosmetics."

"When are you going to come up with some legal businesses?"

He said it would never happen in the life of the world's greatest outlaw. Before they parted for the last time, he had a surprise for her: a month in Miami to get away from all of the threats and danger. His men in Miami – including El Mugre – would take care of her. When she returned, he wanted to speak to her on the phone. Followed by a car with only two bodyguards, Pablo drove Virginia through Medellín.

"I'm surprised by your lack of bodyguards."

"I now have so much respect in Medellín, no one would dare touch me."

"By respect, do you mean terror? Who are you going to assassinate next while I'm gone?"

He pinched her cheek. "I don't like to be spoken about like that." They reminisced about the times they had shared, and he said he would miss her advice and stories. She said that when he died, she would want to shoot herself. At a red light, the couple were recognised by a woman to whom Pablo blew a kiss.

"You're on your way to becoming a sex symbol." He laughed, kissed her hand and promised to eat less beans.

She urged him to make peace with Gilberto before Galán became the president and reinstated extradition. He said that if he were elected, he wouldn't take his oath, and was she suggesting that he should buy him. She didn't think that Galán could be bought, but he would appreciate a peace accord. Pablo could stop Gacha from killing Communists and guerrillas. The Medellín and Cali Cartels could unite. If he killed Galán, he would die, and all of the poor he supported would be left to their fates.

He complained that with the DAS and the police against him and Gacha, they needed the Army and Santo's contacts in the security and military elites. He was aware that Santo was doing business with Cali because politicians have no loyalty. There was going to be an explosion of violence and nothing could change it. She warned that they would be useful idiots for the establishment by killing the enemies of the presidential families and financial conglomerates. Exasperated by her advice, he stiffened his expression. "I don't like to be talked to this way."

"The problem with all of you is that you have no one willing to tell you the truth. Behind every wealthy man is a great accomplice or slave."

He gazed at her. "What do you mean?"

Wanting to depart with advice he would never forget, she said that his wife was a saint and Gilberto was a viper. They would both be his perdition. She would carry Pablo in her heart forever and she hoped that God would protect him. Parked by the hotel, they said goodbye forever. He placed a hand behind her neck and kissed her forehead. In silence, they touched each other's faces. In his sad black eyes, she saw tragedy and danger. Fighting tears, she kissed him and forced a big smile. They would never see each other again.

CHAPTER 10
LEHDER'S DOWNFALL

Before his murder, Colonel Ramírez had pursued Lehder so aggressively that his empire had collapsed. With the government liquidating his assets, the former billionaire was almost bankrupt. He claimed that the guerrillas, with whom he had trained as a freedom fighter, "had kept part of my money," and "the representatives of the law took from me a cardboard box tied with a rope and inside was the last two million dollars I had in this life."

While on the run for over a year in the Orinoquía and Amazon jungles, Lehder had caught malaria. Pablo sent him a helicopter and he was treated in Medellín, where he began a slow recovery. Pablo purchased his Mercedes-Benz limo, an obvious red flag for the authorities, which ended up in El Patrón's antique car showroom. Jorge Ochoa gave him camouflage dyed binoculars, and his only other belongings were a Heckler & Koch G3 rifle, a massive ranger knife, green cloth boots with hard Vietnam-style soles, canting trousers, a sleeveless green flannel and a red scarf which he tied to his forehead. Pablo called him "commander" – which was a combination of affection and ridicule – and assigned him work, including the assassination of Judge Zuluaga, a magistrate of the Superior Court of Antioquia. Zuluaga had been pursuing Pablo ever since he had issued a detention order and lifted his parliamentary immunity.

The bosses met at Kevin's Disco. Even though the police had been bribed, Pablo's men secured the area and prepared a quick escape route. Staying by El Patrón's side, Lehder usually had his hand by his gun. Until dawn, they flirted with beautiful women.

Aware that his friend had an estranged daughter in Medellín, Pablo insisted on Lehder visiting her. After he agreed, Pablo's men located the 12-year-old, whom Pinina took to a hideout. Lehder's indifference towards his daughter surprised the men. After two hours, Lehder introduced her to Pablo, and said goodbye to his daughter with a kiss on the cheek. The bosses spent time together, travelling across the country, staying at ranches. Protected and feeling safe, Lehder hoped to remake his fortune.

In January 1987, the journalist Germán Castro Caycedo arrived at Nápoles to discuss writing a book about Pablo. Sat by the pool, they were greeted by a waiter in white jacket, bowtie, sash and black trousers. "How about a guava juice or a glass of champagne or whatever you want?"

Having noticed the plane over the entrance to Nápoles, Germán asked, "Was that the first plane that you sent with your stuff to the US?"

"No. It's a recreation," Pablo said. "The first one was lost at sea when it was flying five metres above the surface, with the pilot and seventy kilos of coca. About the book that you propose to me: it seems that there is no problem for me to tell you about my life or for you to write it down, but this is going to be a long process. That's why I want you to know me a little before." The journalist was distracted by a long-haired man and a sallow, indigenous woman frolicking in the pool. "It's Carlos Lehder. He left the mountains and is convalescing from a malaria attack that almost killed him, but he seems to have recovered."

At dinnertime with Pablo and Jorge Ochoa, Lehder reached into the waistband of his trousers, extracted his massive knife and carved meat. He praised Chairman Mao and the need to bring the revolution of the countryside to the city. He spoke of Adolf Hitler, Joseph Stalin, Betancur, the barbarian priest Pérez, guerrilla warfare, the FARC, one of its leaders called Jacobo Arenas and the theories of the French philosopher Régis Debray. He told stories from the jungles of Catatumbo, Carare, Opón, the Amazon rainforest and the Darién Gap. After Lehder retired with his female companion, Jorge Ochoa left and Pablo invited the journalist to the second floor to finish watching a movie about Al Capone.

"I've seen it a few times," Pablo said, "and I always learn something new because I always discover mistakes that the man made."

"So, that Ford 38 full of bullets that I saw in a shed near the house, has something to do with your admiration for Al Capone?"

"Yes, but I did not buy it in Chicago, as they say, but in Medellín, and it was here that I filled it with bullets to acclimate it."

"Was Al Capone the best?"

"No. For me, the very best was Machine Gun Kelly. Look, the first time I went to the US, I went straight to Chicago, to the Al Capone museum. It was like arriving … like arriving to …"

"Mecca?"

"No. To the Vatican. I'm Catholic."

Pablo decided not to watch the movie. As the night was warm, they settled on a poolside table. Around 3 AM, Pablo smoked a joint. "Those big rubber trees placed against the house are transplanted Japanese trees that were massive already. I like houses with shade and lots of green outside and inside."

Pablo hosted a party at Hacienda Nápoles. Many of the guests were high on cocaine when Lehder appeared dressed in khaki army gear, armed with two pistols, a machine gun, a crossbow, his knife and grenades on his chest. With a blonde prostitute, he started snorting cocaine.

Rollo, one of Pablo's most beloved men who led a group of bodyguards, and who was handsome, asked Lehder for cocaine. Pointing at the prostitute, Lehder nodded at her to give Rollo a line. Sharing the cocaine, she flirted with Rollo. Lehder noticed their chemistry. Rollo and the prostitute continued to flirt. Without Lehder's permission, Rollo began to take cocaine from the woman. He lifted the entire bag to his nose and snorted some. Excessively high on cocaine and alcohol, Lehder remained quiet.

At night, Lehder retired to his room with the woman. By

an artificially lit pool, Pablo was smoking cannabis. Music was playing and the parrots were squawking. Abandoning the woman he had been talking to, Rollo searched for Lehder and the blonde prostitute to get more cocaine. With another bodyguard, they knocked on Lehder's door for ten minutes. Exasperated, Lehder answered without his shirt or weapons. His rifle was on the floor. He chastised the men for bothering him.

Inebriated, the man with Rollo ignored Lehder's warning and put his head into the bedroom. "Blondie, can you give a line to Rollo?"

On the bed in her underwear, she replied, "Yes, honey." She grabbed a book from a nightstand, ripped a page into four pieces and filled a piece with cocaine.

Lehder watched angrily as the man entered the room to get the cocaine, while ogling the blonde's breasts. After laughing, the woman invited Lehder back to bed. After the man had departed, Lehder closed the door.

Around 2 AM, Rollo ran out of cocaine and sought out his friend again. The friend knocked on Lehder's door. Instead of allowing him in, Lehder opened the door partially, tossed out a bag of cocaine and quickly shut the door. After picking up the drugs, the friend laughed and returned to Rollo. Other than the bodyguards, most of the guests were asleep.

In the morning, waitresses brought lemonade to the guests in their rooms. At 8:30 AM, two gunshots pierced the tranquillity. Toting rifles, bodyguards scrambled to address the threat. They found Pablo on the second floor and everything in order in his room.

"Everybody hide until I find out what's going on!" El Patrón yelled.

The bodyguards found Rollo in his room in a pool of blood, his right shoulder ripped open and his head split in two, with Lehder stood over him, still pointing his rifle.

"What happened?" Popeye asked.

After remaining silent for a few moments, Lehder said,

"Popeye, tell the general that the colonel had to kill a soldier who had disrespected him."

Popeye went to get Pablo, who came down the stairs putting on a shirt, wearing jeans and sneakers. "What happened, Popeye?"

"Lehder killed Rollo," Popeye said. The two men approached the corpse.

"I killed the son of a bitch," Lehder said.

Lehder had pierced the inner circle of bodyguards, the foundation of Pablo's strength. If he didn't go unpunished, El Patrón's men would be disgruntled. Stifling his anger in a calculated way, Pablo said, "It's OK. You did the right thing." Instructing his men, he said, "Take Rollo to the Puerto Triunfo funeral home, where they'll fix him up before giving him to his family." He told Lehder to leave and ordered his men to clean up the mess.

Without saying goodbye or looking back, the blonde departed with the rest of the women. Pablo sent Lehder to a farm in eastern Antioquia. Protected by his own men, he refused Pablo's bodyguards.

Popeye was assigned to return Rollo's corpse to his family. The journey from the funeral home took almost four hours. With the hearse parked, Popeye approached the door. Rollo's mother and two sisters were chatting with neighbours. His mother spotted Popeye and started yelling no. After Popeye nodded, she passed out and collapsed. The daughters revived her. Popeye signalled for the hearse to pull up and he left in a taxi.

The high-profile assassinations had been followed by demands from the media and the public to arrest Pablo and the traffickers. The authorities clamped down with the usual raids, destruction of labs and seizures of property, cash, weapons and drugs that didn't impact the flow of cocaine. Something more needed to be done. The government made a secret list of the 128 most wanted traffickers, including fifty-six on the extradition list, and managed to arrest eight of them. Pressure was placed on the Medellín police to arrest one of the big four: Pablo, Jorge Ochoa, Gacha or Lehder. If no progress was made, the Medellín police director whom Pablo had bribed would be replaced.

Lemus, the police chief of Rionegro, started to receive information that Lehder was in a safe house in the area, hoping to rebuild his fortune by soliciting Pablo to invest in a joint cocaine venture. In the wake of the high-profile assassinations, Lemus had been granted special powers to search anywhere, but he had found nothing. He believed that Pablo had put Lehder in a mountainside chalet, but he didn't know which forest area to search.

On February 3, 1987, Lemus was introduced to an informant who had noticed some noisy men at a chalet in the woods. Upset with the mess they were making, the caretaker of the chalet had complained to the informant.

Around 4 PM, Lemus, accompanied by two policemen – who were under the impression that they were searching for guerrillas, not cartel leaders who could have their entire families slaughtered – located a two-storey chalet disguised by vegetation. It had a lawn upfront, an outbuilding at the side and behind it was a canyon with a stream. Three armed bodyguards protected the front and each side. For two hours, the police hid among the trees, observing sixteen occupants going in and out of the yard. At 6 PM, Lehder emerged with a canvas chair.

Taken aback, Lemus whispered to a colleague, "Do you know that guy?"

"No."

Realising he was about to reveal the nature of the operation, which would have spooked his colleagues, Lemus hushed and sent one of his men for reinforcements. Thirty-six police arrived, including a special-weapons team, which surrounded the chalet. Lemus stationed a dozen men at the back. Others blocked the escape routes. Even with his special powers, Lemus couldn't raid the house before 6 AM without a warrant. He sent a constable for one, who returned at 4 AM, by which time cold fog had descended. Unable to find anyone to sign the warrant, the constable had signed it himself.

At 6:30 AM, a bodyguard who fired at a police sniper was shot. Shots exploded between bodyguards on the second floor and the police behind the chalet in the woods. Fearful of Lehder escaping, Lemus charged for the front door, clutching his gun with both hands, ready to blast someone in the face. On the other side of the door, Lehder was racing towards it as the assault from the rear had convinced him to escape through the front.

When the door opened, Lehder almost ran into the gun of Lemus. "Little chief, don't shoot me."

"We aren't killers," Lemus said. "Put your hands on your head and get down on the floor."

Lehder complied. As he dropped, he fished a wad out of a pocket and threw it on the floor. "That's a million pesos."

"Pick it up, señor," Lemus said. "You're going to need it for soft drinks."

"Do you want green instead? How much?"

"No. I'm just doing my duty."

"Oh, little chief, what a hot number you are. You're the most famous man in the world. You know those gringo sons of bitches want to hang me by the balls, and now you've got me. Too bad we didn't meet earlier."

In the front room, the captives were searched and lined up. "Gentlemen, I'd like to introduce you to Carlos Lehder." The remark from Lemus was met with silence. Out in the yard, captives were photographed by Lemus. "Where's the soccer ball? We're taking the team picture." Everybody laughed. At 10 AM, vans collected the captives. Taking no chances, Lemus transported Lehder in his car. A dishevelled Lehder chatted with Lemus and women along the road.

At a telephone booth, Lemus called his boss. "We got him!"

"Yes. Calm down. You got who?"

"The Virgin has smiled on us. We have captured Carlos Lehder."

While reporters mobbed the police vans containing the captives, Lemus sneaked Lehder into the police station, where he gave him lunch. The telephone rang continuously and death threats were issued. Lemus was ordered to immediately gather his family and belongings, so that the US Embassy could relocate them out of the country.

At 2 PM, an army helicopter landed to take Lehder to the Rionegro airport, where he boarded a military plane to Bogotá. Having been told that they could have Lehder right away if they had a plane available, the US Embassy advised the Colombian government that a DEA plane was being rerouted to Bogotá. Lehder was rushed aboard a DEA Aero Commander. On the runway, a camera was filming. Fearing reprisals from the cartel, every soldier had his face covered with a black shroud. On February 4, 1987, at 5:15 PM, the Aero Commander took off. The DEA issued a worldwide alert for cartel retaliation.

"You got me now," Lehder told the DEA agents aboard. The plane stopped to refuel in Cuba, where the Army base was locked down due to Lehder's notoriety. The DEA agents offered Lehder a cigarette. "No, that's all right. I only smoke cannabis."

On February 5, 1987, at 2 AM, the Aero Commander landed at Tampa International airport, where it was immediately surrounded by agents with shotguns and automatic weapons. Lehder was rushed into a car. A convoy of armed agents escorted him to a federal courthouse. His mugshot was taken.

In the morning, he appeared in court, smiling. "I don't have any money."

"Is the information true?" a magistrate said.

"Yes, Your Honour. Most of my assets were frozen by the government of Colombia."

Facing a maximum sentence of life without parole plus 135 years, Lehder was assigned a public defender. The US Attorney demanded that no bail be set because there had been death threats made against judges.

"That's a lie!" Lehder yelled.

"He has said if he were caught, he'd kill a federal judge a week until he's freed," said the US Assistant Attorney.

At a hearing on February 9, Lehder claimed to have no access to any money.

"Are you aware that your watch is worth approximately $6,000?" the US Attorney asked.

"No."

"Your Honour," Lehder's public defender said, "we understand that he [Lehder] was turned into the police by an underworld figure: Pablo Escobar." No evidence was offered to substantiate her claim.

Bail was refused. On the basis that he had earned $300 million in 1979 and 1980, the IRS gave him a $70 million lien.

In a response mailed to Colombian newspapers, Pablo conceded that he had engaged in "personal quarrels with Lehder on several occasions, but these would not lead me to perform such a low and cowardly act as to betray him to the authorities." Pablo believed that Lehder's public defender had initiated a "plan to attack my moral and personal integrity."

In Marion, Illinois, Lehder was housed in the highest-security federal prison in the country. Then he was transferred to Talladega, Alabama. Although in isolation, he was disturbed by a neighbour who "spent much of the night and day yelling and emitting unintelligible guttural sounds." His lawyers complained that he "was unable to sleep day or night because of the incessant noise." He ended up in Atlanta on a maximum-security floor with empty cells. On the floors below him, 1,800 Cubans from the Mariel Boatlift disturbed his sleep. "Primal screams punctuate the air minute by minute, from time to time the din is so pervasive that one cannot hear himself think."

Eventually, he hired two expensive lawyers. Without his lawyers' consent, he sent a letter to George HW Bush about which the *Miami Herald* reported: "Accused Colombian Drug Chief's Offer To Cooperate Described As Frivolous."

His lawyers issued a statement: "It is absolutely false beyond any doubt that Carlos Lehder is cooperating. This letter [to

George HW Bush] is to some degree the product of his solitary confinement."

Despite the authorities bracing for a violent response to his extradition, none came, leading them to wonder what the cartel was up to. Behind the scenes, cartel lawyers were busy battling the legality of extradition. On June 25, 1987, the Supreme Court ruled that the president had acted unconstitutionally by re-signing the extradition legislation. Without going on a murderous rampage, the cartel had won. The US authorities were appalled. The new justice minister was forced to cancel all of the outstanding extradition warrants, including against Pablo.

In custody, Lehder described the day of extradition reversal as the happiest of his life. He blamed his extradition on "the burial of a Supreme Court that had sold out to imperialist interests." Mistakenly, he believed he would be returned to Colombia.

On July 22, 1987, three requests for the provisional arrest of Pablo were dismissed as unenforceable. Citing a lack of evidence, a judge withdrew orders for the arrest of Pablo and Gacha for the murder of Cano. Citing improper methods of obtaining evidence, a judge dismissed Pablo's indictment for Lara's murder. Now his only outstanding cases dated back to the 1970s, and all of the witnesses were dead. With their legal difficulties behind them, the remaining big three of the Medellín Cartel started to regain their strength.

CHAPTER 11
HOME AND FAMILY LIFE

Due to the relative calm, Pablo spent several months in late 1987 with his family in a 16,000-square-foot, two-storey penthouse at the Monaco Building. Reinforced steel protected the white, eight-storey structure, surrounded by palm trees and with a swimming pool at its rear. By the entrance was a work by the Antioquian sculptor Rodrigo Arenas. A walk-in safe the size of a room contained a mountain of cash for bribery. According to Juan Pablo in *Pablo Escobar: My Father*, the family ate at a twenty-four-seat dining table in the penthouse to music played by a live violinist. The large linen tablecloths – manufactured by Venetian artisans – had taken four years to embroider. The silver dishware had been crafted by Georg Jensen, a Danish silversmith. It included a monogram combining Pablo's and his wife's surnames. Flown from Bogotá to Medellín, fresh flowers were delivered twice a week. Pablo told Victoria that if Aristotle Onassis could send for warm bread in Paris for Jacqueline Kennedy Onassis, then he could at least fly flowers in for his wife. The boss hosted a private tennis tournament at the building. The winner received a car, which wealthy winners donated to a poor family.

The upper tier of the Medellín Cartel strived to demonstrate that they had superior taste in decor than their predecessors, who gravitated towards thoughtless marble, Doric columns, common mirrors, golden taps on a bath filled with champagne, gilded edges, dollhouses, paintings of orange sunsets and birds in flight, and a million dollars framed and hung on a wall. The two towers built by Kiko Moncada in Medellín's Loma de los Balsos had six apartments with marble from Carrara and a pool. Fidel Castaño's taste was esteemed by his colleagues. He dealt in art, collected the works of Botero and had an apartment and a driver in Paris. He appreciated luxury but did not overindulge. One time, he invited Pablo, the Ochoas and Gacha to a gallery to offer them paintings by Botero.

"They're not going to get dollars from me for those ugly fatties," Gacha said, provoking laughter.

Despite the millions invested in art, Pablo's dress style remained low-key, with him preferring new but simple shirts, jeans and sneakers. When challenged about his look, he said it was because he always had to be ready to flee. His family bought him designer shoes, which he never wore. He preferred Victoria's home-cooked food to eating in fancy restaurants. His favourite remained roasted meat, beans, rice and soup, but over time he branched out into seafood. If he didn't arrive home by 7 PM, Victoria left the food in the oven.

Often, he stayed out having affairs. Waiting for her husband to return, Victoria endured long hours, during which she sometimes listened to the songs of Helenita Vargas with lyrics of love and hate. Previously, when banned from the household, he had sent flowers and written love letters. Her years of exploding when he came home and ostracising him from the house for days ended after she decided to accept his infidelity. After her sisters complained that they were being cheated on, she told them, "That's what men are like. It's not worth suffering over."

In her darkest hours of loneliness, she distracted herself by studying languages and art history. Worried about the dangers of Pablo's business stunting Juan Pablo's personal growth, she focused on his home-schooling. Her other distraction was arranging parties. For her sister Claudia's 15th birthday, the theme was red. At a party that was themed green and pink, the food included giant prawns and hanging pheasants, and famous singers performed. For Juan Pablo's 12th birthday, the theme was black, a colour that Pablo refused to wear. As a compromise, he put on black shorts and appeared in the living room – amid everybody dressed completely in black – wearing a white shirt with blue stripes and sneakers. Victoria frowned. "What have you done, Pablo?" She was upset for days.

At home, Pablo's interests included watching gangster and James Bond movies, and reading *Playboy* magazine, *The Colombian* newspaper and books by Mario Puzo. He adopted traits from the characters in Puzo's books. From *The Godfather*, he absorbed Don Corleone's mantra of never being angry or threatening but rather to reason with people, to remain cold and calculating, refining the ability to not react to insults or threats, and instead to quietly wait for revenge. People who speak a lot create problems for themselves, so it is wiser to be silent. From *The Sicilian*, he related to the generous-warrior protagonist. Popular in the 1940s, the bandit Salvatore Giuliano walked through Italian mountain villages, doling out cash to old people starving to death, the sick who couldn't afford medical treatment and peasants on the verge of losing their farms. The children prayed for Salvatore's safety against his enemies.

Pablo's love of *The Godfather* saved one of the actors' lives. Gianni Russo played Carlo Rizzo, the first husband of Connie Corleone. In a 2019 interview on the YouTube channel Valuetainment, Russo described an incident at his nightclub in Las Vegas. An associate of Pablo's was in Nevada, looking to expand cartel business. Drunk at the club, he stabbed a woman and Russo intervened, only to have his throat slit with a broken bottle. With a weapon he carried legally, Russo shot the Colombian twice in the head. Although the killing was ruled a justifiable homicide, the brother of the deceased was close to Pablo and sought revenge. Upon learning that his whole family was scheduled to be tortured and wiped out, the actor decided to fly to Colombia to speak face-to-face with Pablo. The meeting was arranged by John Gotti, the boss of the Gambino crime family.

In his book, *Hollywood Godfather*, Russo described approaching a church on a deserted street outside of Bogotá. Entering, he noticed a man kneeling before candles by the altar. Walking forward, he smelled burning flesh. Bodyguards with guns rose from the aisles. Pablo turned around and greeted the American. The last thing Russo saw was a burst of light as he was knocked out.

Tied to a seatless chair, he awoke in a windowless basement, with pain in his head, lower back and testicles. On the floor were human remains and body bags in the corner. Three men entered, yelling in Spanish. One swung a nightstick under the chair, crushing Russo's testicles. Some of his projectile vomit hit one of the torturers. The nightstick launched again and Russo lost consciousness. After two days, he awoke to El Patrón in the room, dressed in light clothes, his shark-like gaze suggesting that the actor was going to die.

Smiling, Pablo displayed a hardback copy of *The Making of the Godfather*. He asked why Russo had not revealed that he had played Carlo in his favourite movie ever. The actor croaked that he had not been given an opportunity. Pablo summoned two of the torturers to free the actor and promised that he would be cleaned up, fed and given painkillers.

With a cloth over his head, he was transported for an hour to an air-conditioned house and pushed onto a bed. With the hood removed, he was told he had the room, which included clothes and a vial with blue pills for his pain. He admired the view of the mountains and fog. After examining his swollen testicles, he took a pill, had a shower and fell asleep.

Summoned downstairs to meet the boss, he walked delicately to a massive dining room, where he thanked Pablo for his hospitality. The boss apologised and suggested that they talk after dinner. After eating and drinking some coffee, he detailed how the shooting in his club had transpired because he wanted Pablo to hear his side of the story.

After pondering for a minute, Pablo said that he believed Russo and the behaviour of the deceased was out of line, so he had gotten what was coming. After apologising again for the torture, he asked for a final favour: a re-enactment of the scene from *The Godfather* when Michael Corleone challenged Carlo Rizzi for the betrayal that had enabled the assassination of Sonny Corleone, Michael's brother.

The offer to write Carlo's dialogue was refused by Pablo, who had memorised every word. Using chairs to recreate the scene, they practised the dialogue several times. During the final acting, Pablo handed Russo an envelope with a plane ticket, just like what had happened in the movie before Carlo had died. Drawing on instructions from Marlon Brando during the original filming, the actor looked in the envelope at two tickets: one to Miami and a connection to Vegas. Still fearful that he might die, Russo mustered his strength to give the performance of a lifetime.

In a car with Pablo outside, the torturers addressed him as Carlo, the last words the character had heard before getting choked to death in the film. Bracing to die, Russo thought of his daughter. Everyone laughed, and the men slapped Russo's back. Pablo wished him a safe trip. In Miami, on the connecting flight and unable to walk properly, the actor was handcuffed by DEA agents, in pain but glad to be alive.

Pablo's favourite sport was soccer and his favourite team Deportivo Independiente Medellín. He joked that, "Girls from the middle class are fans of Atlético Nacional, and of [Deportivo Independiente] Medellín, the tough ones from the town, from the neighbourhood." In 2016, Juan Pablo released a list of twenty-eight things that the Narcos Netflix series got wrong, including stating that his father was a fan of Atlético Nacional.

He was proud of his classic car collection. The James Bond car he had attempted to impress Virginia with had been a gift from his brother. Having flown in a James Bond aviation show, Roberto produced a photo of himself in 007's plane.

"How did you do it?" Pablo asked, incredulous.

"Well, here's the picture so that you can believe me. This is Bond and this is his pilot."

Despite Pablo's portrayal as a simple man of the people, his family caught glimpses into his vanity. If he didn't like the way he looked in a photo, he would burn it.

After he received a large photo with Santo and other high officials, Hermilda asked, "Pablo, what did you think of that picture?"

"Oh, I keep it stored somewhere, Mom. It's beautiful."

Juan Pablo intervened: "Granny, he's lying. My dad destroyed that photo because he looked ugly."

Sometimes Pablo asked Hermilda to destroy photos, but she kept some, including a black and white of him at 35 years old with black hair, a moustache and sideburns. Years later, she said, "What would have happened if I hadn't kept them? They are the only ones left to me by the police officers who carried away everything they found."

In a convoy of ten SUVs, Pablo travelled around Medellín with up to five bodyguards armed with AR-15 rifles in each vehicle. One day, they were pulled over by police on motorbikes.

"Show us your identity papers and letters of transit," a policeman said. The bodyguards got out and started to give their weapons to the police.

Victoria's brother, Mario, emerged with a submachine gun, and shook his head at the men submitting to the police. Pointing his gun at the officers, he asked Pablo why fifty chicken-shit bodyguards were surrendering their weapons to four cops. "If these are the kind of lions you've got protecting you, then you're fucked. Officers, do me a favour and give those weapons back right now or you can have an even bigger problem." Petrified of Mario, the police backed down and allowed the convoy to continue.

Over the years, Mario had transitioned from a university leftist activist into a gangster. Growing rich, he became known for lavish spending on trips to Europe and America, and his dancing at rumba parties. After listening to a concert performed by an impoverished pianist, he was so moved that he purchased a piano which he sent anonymously to the pianist's apartment.

He maintained a passion for books and philosophy. In Medellín, he supported an editorial that published the words of important thinkers, whom he talked with at length. In the early years of the war, the biggest threat to Mario was himself. On a plane, he overdosed on drugs and his heart almost quit. Due to drugs and alcohol, his heart pumped abnormally.

In October 1987, the leader of the Patriotic Union was assassinated, which triggered a backlash from the government against the traffickers. Pablo hid at La Isla.

On October 5, 1987, Pablo was listed as one of the richest people in the world in *Forbes* magazine, with a net worth of $3 billion. The next person on the list was Jorge Ochoa. Gacha was added in 1988. The article described Pablo's humble origins and how he had shrewdly reinvested his cash flow into cocaine. It mentioned how he had helped the poor and his foray into politics. It mistakenly claimed that he had offered to pay off the national debt in return for an amnesty, when the actual offer of the traffickers had been to repatriate their overseas wealth into the domestic banking system. For the next seven years, he would be included in the billionaires list.

In November 1987, now one of the most wanted men in the world, Pablo decided to play in the Peace Soccer Tournament in Envigado. In a convoy of ten Mitsubishi SUVs, he arrived in a Renault 18, guarded by the Envigado police and agents of the Department of Security and Control of the municipality, all on his payroll. Pinina's man Chiruza paid and coordinated law enforcement. When performing killings, Chiruza was known to hand his victims a cannabis joint. "Enjoy that before I kill you," he would say, and start pacing until the trigger was pulled.

The sun was out for the soccer game, and the attendees filled the bleachers. As the teams emerged onto the pitch, the stadium shook as noise erupted from trumpets, drums, gunpowder and war cries. Pablo hosted surprise contests, including for the woman who best narrated the goals.

CHAPTER 12
LEHDER'S TRIAL

On November 17, 1987, 38-year-old Lehder's trial commenced. Sporting a tailored suit and a new haircut, he grinned at reporters. During the proceedings, with three armed marshals sat behind him, he took notes and ate sweets.

"This case will take you back in time to 1974," a prosecutor said, "and forward over the course of many years in which Carlos Lehder pursued a singular dream, a singular vision, to be the king of cocaine transportation … He was to cocaine transportation what Henry Ford was to automobiles … He saw America as a decadent society. He saw cocaine as the wave of the future in the US, reeling from Watergate and Vietnam, particularly susceptible to the seductive allure of cocaine."

He said that Lehder dreamed of buying his own nation. To achieve his goal, he used violence and bribed Prime Minister Lynden Pindling of the Bahamas, with substantial sums "to preserve the integrity of the continuing criminal enterprise … Lehder's plan was to develop sufficient income from the sale of cocaine to literally buy his own … haven from international drug laws."

He added that while in Danbury, Connecticut's federal prison in 1974 serving a two-year marijuana-smuggling sentence, Lehder met George Jung, who was in prison on marijuana distribution charges. Lehder explained to Jung that he had access to unlimited supplies of cocaine but had no US distribution network. The prosecutor said that Jung would testify that "Lehder saw cocaine as the wave of the future in the United States," and that it was "a product that created and captured its users."

"'Evidence will show Lehder is a man of considerable intellect. Evidence will show Lehder is a man of considerable charm who is able to work his will on other people." The prosecutor said that Lehder's first cocaine shipments into the US were carried by women, hidden in the linings of their suitcases. He bought cocaine in Colombia for $2,000 to $5,000 a kilogram and sold it in the US for up to $45,000. "It was worth more than its weight in gold."

He said that Lehder made contacts in California, Massachusetts and Florida to establish a distribution network, and met a lawyer and pilot in Massachusetts, who suggested that the best smuggling route was through the Bahamas due to the prolific private aircraft traffic from the US, which would make a small plane smuggling cocaine almost undetectable.

Lehder's lawyers portrayed him as a Colombian whom American smugglers – now turned informants against him – had preyed on. "Lehder was his own worst enemy. He was a young, wealthy, brash Colombian, flamboyant, to say the least … He confronted the DEA with his mouth."

Numerous of Lehder's cohorts testified against him. Even the TV personality, Walter Cronkite, described getting threatened at Norman's Cay. Lehder's early business partner and former cellmate in federal prison, Carl Jung, took the stand, a small man with long brown hair. While he detailed his story, his wizened face lit up. He smiled often, as if savouring his revenge. The cross-examination was structured to discredit Jung.

"Knowing that you have used people before when it fits your interest, would you be using Mr Lehder in this case in order to lower your prison sentence, maybe?"

"Do you really believe that?" Jung asked.

"I'm asking the questions."

"Then, no …"

"And when you wrote down that you had been to Pablo Escobar's farm numerous times, weren't you trying to sort of puff up your importance in this case, to see if you can get a better deal, a better letter from the government, to see if they will reduce your parole and your sentence? Were you trying to do that, knowing Pablo Escobar to be somebody who has been publicised?"

"No. I didn't have to expand my role. I was married into a Colombian family that is tied in to people down there. That was well known. I didn't have to exaggerate my role. I mean, I was arrested in 1985 with 660 pounds of cocaine and, in essence, they suddenly confiscated more on the airstrip, close to 3,000 pounds of cocaine. I don't believe that I had to exaggerate my role with 3,000 pounds of cocaine."

After the testimonies of 115 witnesses, the jury heard more damning evidence: recordings from some of Lehder's interviews over the years, in which he described himself as a poor Colombian peasant who had made something of himself.

From June 28, 1983: "This was our obligation, to bring the dollars back to our people however we could. So then, that is it. It can be called Mafia. It can be called syndicate. It can be called a bonanza. It can be called whatever you like, but the truth is that it is a fact, and it is out in the open. In other words, Colombia would not be able to deny that it was the world's foremost producer of cannabis and cocaine." At fault was the US, "where there are forty-million cannabis smokers and twenty-five-million cocaine consumers ... What I ask that they do is help the Colombian drug addict that they themselves corrupted."

From another recording: "I have never transported drugs. It is just that my lands, the flexibility afforded by their location being 200 miles from the US, provided the opportunity for the Colombians, who were being trapped like flies over there with little suitcases and with little boxes, of going in there, by means of a different system, a different means, a different platform."

Speaking loudly, one of Lehder's lawyers expressed outrage. "This is a case in which the government brought into this courtroom twenty-nine bought witnesses."

Holding up a MAC-10 that had been found on Norman's Cay, the prosecutor attacked Lehder's businessman defence. "You have seen tragedy upon tragedy come into this courtroom. They were at war with society, together with Mr Lehder. He's still at war. He hasn't stopped … A trail of bribery, corruption, violence and personal debasement has been created and fostered by Mr Lehder with the help of those witnesses, and that wreckage exists in Colombia, the Bahamas and the US. That wreckage is the legacy of Mr Lehder's children. That wreckage in Colombia and the Bahamas and the US is an open wound, and that wound will not be healed by vengeance. That wound will only be healed by justice and truth and reconciliation." Holding up a spoon, he said it held one thirtieth of a gram of cocaine, and that Lehder was responsible for bringing in eighteen million grams or one billion snorts.

"Mr Lehder was an opportunity waiting to meet another opportunity: the US demand for drugs … His strength, ladies and gentlemen, was he was able to capitalise on the weakness of others … the disenchanted, the rogues, the crippled. He bought, charmed or pushed aside all obstacles. He's finally come to a situation where he can't do that."

In his final rebuttal to Lehder's lawyers, the US Attorney said, "The striking story in this case is that America, a substantial portion of America, has been an active partner with Mr Lehder. While it is true, as Mr Lehder told you on his own tapes, tragically, that his acts were motivated by hatred and bitterness against the US, it is also true that all of Mr Lehder's money and all of his guns and all of his power could not force American pilots to fly for him, could not force American businessmen to sell property to him, could not force aircraft salesmen to sell planes for cash, could not force victims of Mr Lehder's crimes to inject cocaine into their arms … or to snort it up their noses. The story of this case is the story of an absence of love, an absence of responsibility, a fleeing from responsibility by the witnesses in this case and by Mr Lehder. So your verdict is an act of reconciliation with truth, an act of reconciliation with the past. You have a duty and you have a privilege of returning a true verdict in this case, a duty which you must not shirk and you must not fear. Thank you."

After the jury left to deliberate, Lehder held up a sign to the journalists and other attendees: "Just Say No to Racism."

Over seven days, the jury deliberated for forty-two hours. In the packed courtroom, the anticipation of the verdict was palpable. While three women on the jury cried, the judge announced that Lehder was guilty on all counts. With a blank expression, Lehder gazed at the floor.

Both legal teams made announcements to the press. "Until we take the problem out of the schoolyard," one of Lehder's lawyers said, "you can put all of the Carlos Lehders you want in prison, but the problem is it doesn't work. What have we accomplished? Do we have one gram of drugs less available to us because of this prosecution?"

The prosecutor claimed it was a victory for the good guys and the American people. It "reflects to people in other nations that we are a nation of laws and will not tolerate the violence of drug traffickers." As if challenging Pablo directly, he said that the cartel had "nowhere to run, nowhere to hide … I think their days are numbered."

A journalist asked about the effect on the drug trade. "The War on Drugs is not measured in terms of the amount of drugs that's seized. It's a war of the human spirit … the real issue is will. The will of the American people versus the will of the cartel." The prosecutor said that the violent nature of the Medellín Cartel would be its downfall. "The Carlos Lehders of the world are going to have a narrower and narrower opportunity to wreak their crimes on this country."

Lehder had grown a beard by the time of his sentencing hearing. He spoke for almost half an hour. "I feel like an Indian in a white man's court." He said he was a political prisoner, a victim of an overambitious prosecutor, and it had been a case of "twenty-nine confessed criminals against one Latin … Witnesses that lacked a spare pair of underwear claimed they made millions from Lehder … I was kidnapped from my own country with the complicity of some Colombian police officers … I was flown against my will to this country. It's a far worse crime than any of these allegations. I am also against drug abuse. But I am also against kidnapping and extradition. This trial is illegal."

"The truth of the matter," the judge said, "is your main goal was to make money, and you did so at the expense of others. Your conspiracy burned a path of destruction and despair from the coca fields of South America to the streets and byways of this country. Accordingly, Mr Lehder, the sentence I impose on you today is meant to be a message for drug smugglers who control large organisations and for importers of cocaine and for street pushers. This sentence is a signal that our country will do everything in its power and within the laws to battle the drug problem that threatens the very fabric of our society."

With the US government wanting to send a message to Pablo and the other traffickers, the judge sentenced Lehder to life plus 135 years without any possibility of parole.

CHAPTER 13
JORGE OCHOA'S ARREST

On the afternoon of November 21, 1987, thirty miles east of Cali, a white Porsche worth $250,000 – with its own surveillance helicopter flying above it – slowed down for a tollbooth and was instructed to pull over by two policemen. They approached the driver's side and requested to see ID. After the driver gave an unsatisfactory response, the policemen said that the car, the driver and his female passenger would have to go with them to Palmira police headquarters. The driver offered $12 to let him go, which they refused. He increased his offer. They refused $200 and $48,000 and $400,000. There was no way around it: Jorge Ochoa was going to Palmira instead of a meeting that Pablo had convened to discuss the formation of a super cartel, which Pablo would lead.

Ochoa had an arrest warrant for a bull-smuggling conviction and for violating parole. Getting booked into the jail, he was hugged by a female lawyer, who promised to sort everything out. Attempting to get an official to sign his release, she made some calls, but was unsuccessful.

From a holding cell, Ochoa was transferred to an army prison, where he spent the night. On Sunday, a military plane took him to Bogotá, where policemen on motorbikes awaited him. By armoured van with a motorbike escort, he was transported to a military complex. There was no way for him to bribe his way out of the maximum-security prison.

The DEA issued a statement: "The president of Colombia could be courageous and greatly assist his country by throwing out Jorge Ochoa. Once Jorge Ochoa arrives in the US, he, like Carlos Lehder, will not be able to bribe, murder or intimidate his way out of police custody." The DEA brought an airplane to whisk away Ochoa.

Many Colombians thought Ochoa would be extradited as swiftly as Lehder, but Ochoa was only being held on bull-smuggling and the Supreme Court had ruled against extradition. The government's strategy was to keep Ochoa incarcerated, while arranging his extradition. The US government sent a legal team to Bogotá to find an extradition mechanism.

Unlike Lehder, whose status in the cartel had slipped, Ochoa was powerful and one of Pablo's closest friends. His extradition had to be stopped at all costs. El Patrón decided to target the owners of the newspapers encouraging Ochoa's extradition and Justice Minister Low Murtra, who was seeking a mechanism to legally hand Ochoa over to the Americans.

With Ochoa in a cell in a military complex, a dozen men prepared to kidnap Gómez Martínez, a mayoral candidate in Medellín and the owner of the city's biggest newspaper, *El Colombiano*. On November 22 at 7:30 AM, the kidnappers – including Popeye, Otto and Pinina – received word that Gómez Martínez was home, and headed out heavily armed in four vehicles. While Otto monitored the single policeman on guard, a girl working for the kidnappers approached the front door, intending to tell Gómez that she wanted to join his political campaign. After the girl had knocked, the politician's son opened the door slightly, without breaking the security protocol.

"Can I speak to Mr Juan Gómez Martínez?" she asked.

"My father is working long hours at the campaign headquarters." Pinina kicked the door and tried to force it open, but the politician's son managed to slam it shut, run inside and yell, "There are murderers outside! Father, grab the weapons!"

While more kicks were launched at the door, Gómez Martínez sprung up from watching TV, crouched behind a chair, grabbed a gun and started firing. Attempting to rupture a sheet-steel garage door, Pinina reversed a van into it multiple times, only bending it.

A man summoned the rest of the neighbours to arms. "They're trying to kill Gómez Martínez. Let's do something!"

Gunfire erupted. One of the kidnappers cradled his stomach to staunch the bleeding. His accomplices loaded him into a van. Finally, the garage door opened, but a radio warned that the police were nearby. Pinina sprayed the house with gunfire and ordered a retreat. The vehicles roared away. Dropped off at a hospital, the injured kidnapper learned that his colon had been shredded by gunfire.

Having failed to kidnap Gómez Martínez, Pablo issued a communiqué:

"Respected Sir,

We have found out that the government is trying by whatever means possible to extradite citizen Jorge Luis Ochoa to the United States. For us, this constitutes the vilest of outrages.

… in case citizen Jorge Luis Ochoa is extradited to the United States, we will declare absolute and total war against this country's political leaders. We will execute out of hand the principal chieftains …

The Extraditables"

A week after his arrest, Ochoa's six lawyers, including three former Supreme Court justices, started to demolish the case. They were aided by the departure of the US legal team in mid-December, 1987. By arguing that Ochoa had already served his time for bull-smuggling during his incarceration in Spain, Ochoa was released in time to celebrate New Year's Eve.

CHAPTER 14
WAR WITH CALI

In the beginning, the Medellín and Cali Cartels divided the US market and stayed out of each other's way. But over the years, the bosses eyed each other's expansion. Pablo's headline-making violence upset the sober-minded Cali godfathers. They blamed his assassination of Lara Bonilla for the reintroduction of extradition. Before the assassination, they sent him a message stating that they could not be counted on, and that the murder of such a high official would turn many traffickers against him. The Cali bosses were incensed by Pablo wanting to become the boss of bosses across Colombia. They had attended his super-cartel meeting, where he had pitched the economies of scale and the combined economic and political power they would wield. As its leader, he would be vested with the power to authorise every shipment, and would be paid 30 per cent of its wholesale value.

Sensing weakness in its rival, Cali started to move against Medellín in the late 1980s. Both groups had different organisational structures. Medellín was an alliance between independent operators, whereas Cali was run by a four-man executive board. Below the board were accountants, engineers and lawyers, and then the workforce. The executives, some of whom had law degrees, considered themselves more sophisticated than the rustic men from Medellín. They were known as the gentlemen of trafficking, whereas Medellín was regarded as thuggish. The Cali godfathers frowned on Pablo's motto of "silver or lead." They had their own saying: "Money opens any door." The head of the New

York DEA told journalists, "Cali gangs will kill you if they have to, but they prefer to use a lawyer."

An early warning sign had been Jorge Ochoa's arrest near Palmira, seventeen miles east of Cali. The police had found the girlfriend of one of the Cali Cartel's intermediaries with the Medellín Cartel in Ochoa's Porsche. Her jealous boyfriend had notified the police. With Gilberto in control of the authorities in and around Cali, Ochoa's arrest should never have happened. Even if a mistake had occurred, Gilberto would have been notified immediately and should have rectified the situation. Why did he abandon his partner in crime from Spain?

The cartels started telling the DEA about each other's shipments. In February 1987, the DEA's Miami branch received a letter postmarked from Cali claiming that a ship called Amazon Sky was on its way to Saint Petersburg, Florida, with cocaine valued at almost $2 billion. On April 20, agents arrived to inspect the ship's cargo. A broken cedar board roused their suspicion. A drill was extracted covered in white powder. Each board contained one kilo of cocaine. The DEA estimated that it must have taken up to 1,000 workers to load so much cocaine. Rather than bust the load, the agents used glue and sandpaper to restore the cedar boards. They put the ship under surveillance. It took four days for all of the boards to be moved to a warehouse complex in Saint Petersburg. The agents filmed the warehouse and listened to its telephone. After two weeks, three men were arrested.

The trigger for the war was a love-triangle incident among cartel workers including Blackie that led to Pablo demanding the assassination of the Cali godfather Pacho. After serving time in New York, Blackie, who had protected Pablo in prison in 1976, showed up in Colombia. During his visits to Pablo, Blackie was allowed to stay at the Monaco Building, where they smoked weed and chatted. Victoria moved Italian furniture into a third-storey apartment for Blackie. When Pablo changed hideouts, Blackie always visited.

"While I was in New York prison," Blackie told Pablo, "my

wife got together with Pineapple, who works for Pacho Herrera of Cali. This really upset me. I keep thinking about getting revenge on Pineapple because of the betrayal."

"Don't let this upset you," Pablo said. "I'll get the guys from Cali to give up Pineapple."

Pablo told Gilberto to sacrifice Pineapple or else suffer the consequences. Just like Blackie had protected Pablo in prison, Pineapple had protected Pacho, and they had bonded as cellmates. With Pacho supporting Pineapple, Pablo received a call from Gilberto refusing to hand over Pineapple. The two bosses argued. Pablo warned that anyone who was not with him was against him. After he found out that Pacho had agreed to protect Pineapple, Pablo extended the death penalty to Pacho.

While Pablo increased his security, the Cali godfathers protected Pacho. They tried to negotiate with Medellín, pointing out that a feud over such a triviality would damage them both disproportionately. Gilberto got on the phone with Pablo, who not only refused to change his mind, but ended the conversation with a declaration of war and threatened to kill all of the Cali godfathers.

After Pablo killed some of Pacho's men, the Cali godfather told his fellow bosses, "He cannot just go around killing anyone who comes to his mind." Believing that it was better to die in open warfare, he urged the bosses to go to war with Medellín.

Pacho decided to attack. While in a maximum-security prison in Madrid, Gilberto had befriended a bomb maker and electronics expert called José, whom he had promised to employ. With legal assistance provided by Gilberto, José had been freed and flown to Colombia. In Cali, Gilberto had hosted a party that lasted for several days to celebrate José's release. After the festivities had ended, José was transported to an exclusive estate by the Pance River, where he had trained some of Cali's most trusted hit men in how to make car bombs, letter bombs, and the art of blowing up houses, bridges, military installations …

In 1987, the new justice minister had issued extradition

warrants for the key members of the Medellín Cartel, so the traffickers were keeping low profiles and moving around a lot. Rotating through hideouts, Pablo watched TV for hours and formulated a new method of attack against the government. He dispatched his men to kidnap the son of a former president, who owned land and had directed a news programme.

With the war against Pablo heating up at the beginning of 1988, Pacho selected the Indian, a participant in the training provided by José, to bomb Pablo and his family in the Monaco Building, which he had under surveillance. As the Indian was on good terms with the Castaño brothers, he decided to involve them unwittingly by planning to stay the night at their Montecasino property in El Poblado, Medellín, before launching the attack. In a stolen green recreational vehicle packed with dynamite, the Indian arrived at Montecasino with a beautiful woman whom he introduced to Fidel Castaño and Don Berna as his wife.

After reminiscing about old times with Fidel, the Indian said, "Are we OK to spend the night, as we'd like to rest before continuing our journey to Cartagena in the morning?"

"You're welcome to stay at my property," Fidel said.

In the Monaco Building, Juan Pablo had just celebrated his first Communion. Victoria had spent a year planning the party, which was attended by Fidel Castaño and Kiko Moncada. On January 12, 1988, Pablo showed up at the Monaco Building to see a massive oil painting that Victoria had purchased by a Chilean artist. He greeted Juan Pablo. Manuela threw herself into his arms. While he hugged and kissed Victoria, the children demanded that he take them out for hamburgers, but he convinced them to eat at home.

Pacho sent a hit man to assist the Indian. After leaving Montecasino, the Indian transferred the vehicle loaded with 1,500 pounds of dynamite to his accomplice, who parked it at the Monaco Building.

After eating dinner in the Monaco Building, Pablo played with his children and listened enthusiastically to the small issues in their lives and their crazy questions and thoughts. After they went to bed, he made love to Victoria and they discussed domestic issues. As a precaution, he left just before dawn and hid at a farm ten miles away. Due to repairs in the master bedroom, Victoria and Juan Pablo were asleep in the guestroom. Under the supervision of a nanny, Manuel was asleep in another room.

Around 5:30 AM on January 13, the accomplice activated the vehicle's alarm system, which detonated the bomb. The explosion woke people up within a two-mile radius. The blast disintegrated two nightwatchmen, left a crater in the street thirteen feet deep, shattered windows through the neighbourhood, broke water mains and cracked the entire face of the building. Victoria saw a blue glow rise through the window. A slab of concrete from the roof fell, pinning her and Juan Pablo to the bed. Fortunately, a corner of the slab got caught on a Botero sculpture on the nightstand, otherwise they would have been crushed. Breathing awkwardly, Juan Pablo attempted to wriggle free, but was trapped to the bed.

At the farm, Pablo, his brother Roberto and their bodyguards felt the earth shake. Rushing to the windows, they saw a mushroom cloud in the vicinity of the Monaco Building.

Hearing Manuela crying, Victoria had a surge of strength, which enabled her to escape the rubble. "Wait a moment while I get Manuela." Rushing away, she found the nanny holding the baby.

Gasping for air, Juan Pablo managed to rotate his face towards a window. Somehow, Victoria managed to lift the slab, providing just enough room for her son to free himself. Standing on rubble, he tilted his head back, gazed at where the roof had been and admired the stars. He asked Victoria what would have happened if there had been an earthquake. She said she didn't know.

Victoria turned on the hallway lights. Attempting to find the stairs, the family and the nanny were blocked by rubble. Responding to their cries, bodyguards started moving debris, so that they could exit the building. A telephone rang. In shock, Victoria spoke to Pablo, who said someone was on the way to take them to safety. A maid gave Victoria shoes, but Juan Pablo couldn't find his, so he descended barefoot, his feet getting cut by broken glass, bricks, metal, splinters of wood and shrapnel. Outside, they rushed into an SUV, which sped to Pablo's hideout.

Pablo made a call. "Mom, you'll soon watch some news about a bomb in Monaco. But I just called you, so you'd know nothing happened to me." Pablo's brother Roberto and family showed up. They discussed the situation with Victoria's brother Mario.

The news broadcast live footage from the scene of rescue workers and panicked people milling around scorched earth in front of semi-destroyed buildings. A journalist asked the mayor about the nature of the explosion.

"There have been some phone calls," he said, "which haven't been checked yet, from the so-called Death to Drug Traffickers movement, but the authorities cannot say if this has any foundation because a careful investigation has to be carried out first. You all saw how difficult it was to identify the vehicle's plate. But of course, as usual, it must be a stolen car. Anyhow, further investigations are necessary to establish if there is any basis to this, particularly in the case of those who have made the phone calls."

"What information is there of the people who were at the building?"

"The building was empty with the exception of the penthouse. A very luxurious one …"

"Mr Mayor, what measures are going to be taken regarding these acts of terrorism?"

"It's very difficult to take measures. This must be done with the cooperation of the nation and the people. Notwithstanding the patrols and raids that have been going on these days, these acts have occurred at night, and in spite of all of the controls established by the Metropolitan Police, so it's not easy to make decisions and say that we're going to finish once and for all with these acts of vandalism. This is the product of the insanity of a society which is committing suicide."

Another news broadcast reported, "The building looked like a museum. It was full of works of art, sculptures, paintings. The eighth floor was the only one occupied, by Escobar's family apparently. And the second floor was occupied by his bodyguards and employees. There was a soccer field, a big warehouse full of sculptures and, in the basement, there was a collection of vintage vehicles. Eight floors completely destroyed." The news showed troops in green stood around classic cars, showcasing Pablo's wealth. They found latest-model cars, high-cylinder motorbikes and a six-door Mercedes-Benz limo – a birthday gift from Gacha.

On a twenty-five-page list, the police documented everything found. They photographed fine art, including works by Botero and Picasso and Colombian painters such as Grau and Obregón, as well as a sculpture by the Frenchman Auguste Rodin. They documented gold bathroom fittings, rare watches, diamond-studded jewellery, all of the classic cars and Pablo's jukebox, which offered a variety of songs by artists such as Madonna, Lionel Richie and Miami Sound Machine.

Pablo's phone rang. Gilberto said he had heard about the bomb and wanted to know if Pablo and his family were OK. Five minutes later, Pablo thanked Gilberto and hung up. Rumours were circulating that the bomb had been planted by DAS agents, but Pablo told his family that he suspected Gilberto, whom he believed had only called to find out if he had survived the attack.

After Fidel Castaño learned that the bomb had exploded in a green recreational vehicle with Cali license plates, he suspected the Indian and arranged an urgent meeting with his brother. At Montecasino, he told Carlos, "Before the bomb was detonated, the Indian arrived in a green recreational vehicle and spent the night. I noticed that he was a little uneasy. I never imagined that he would dare to attack El Patrón. I'm sure that the Indian was travelling in the vehicle with the bomb."

Contemplating the situation, Carlos stood up and lit a cigar. "Brother, the best thing to do is to tell Pablo everything that happened. The Indian used us shamelessly and if we remain silent and one day Pablo finds out, it'll be much worse."

"I agree. I'll make us an appointment with Pablo right away."

At the meeting, Pablo was angry. "The attack really scared my family, especially little Manuela, whose hearing is damaged. I'm completely sure that it was the Cali Cartel, but I don't have the full information yet." After taking a deep breath, Carlos detailed everything he knew about the Indian, while Pablo listened attentively. "You have nothing to worry about," Pablo said. "I have complete confidence in you. I need you to help me kill the Indian and I'll take care of the Rodríguez brothers [Cali godfathers]."

Corpses started to litter the highways, some perforated with drills, others burnt, some riddled with bullets. They all shared a sign in common: Members of the Cali Cartel for making attempts against the people of Medellín.

One of Pablo's men had spent time in American prison with Miguel, a bomb-maker. In ten days, Pablo located Miguel, asked him to train some of his workers and promised him excellent prices on cocaine to sell. After Miguel agreed, Pablo sent him $10,000. The bomb-maker arrived in Medellín and was escorted to a dining room at Hacienda Nápoles. Rubbing his hands, Pablo couldn't wait to see him. Their meeting lasted for three hours. He would be paid $300,000.

Pablo summoned Pinina. "Can you find someone intelligent enough to take courses and learn car bomb remote-control and slow-wick techniques?"

"I have the perfect guy," Pinina said. "My relative studies electronic engineering at the University of Antioquia."

"Perfect! I'm making you responsible for driving Miguel around and getting everything he needs, including dynamite. Set him up in one of my properties with all of the necessary comforts."

On the black market, Pinina obtained all of the supplies for Miguel, including dynamite from Ecuador. Electronics, slow wicks, pressure pots and milk containers were purchased in Puerto Boyacá.

Miguel operated with scientific precision, and avoided drugs, alcohol and partying with women. Pinina's relative, Cuco, arrived to join Miguel and specialised in exploding vehicles full of dynamite and making the force of the blast move in a targeted direction. He told Cuco to handle the dynamite carefully because it was like a jealous woman. Cuco quickly absorbed the techniques.

At a section of a Nápoles airstrip by a ravine, Miguel was ready for his first demonstration on a heavy old Buick. While Miguel and Cuco rigged the car, Pablo questioned Cuco about the technicalities. Cuco answered expertly. Miguel supervised Cuco as he adjusted a battery cable.

In a convoy of five jeeps, Gacha arrived and greeted everyone. For the benefit of Gacha, Pablo questioned Cuco, who said that 100 kilos of dynamite were going to be activated with a normal battery. For twenty minutes, Miguel chatted with Gacha and Pablo.

"I need everyone to stand at least fifty metres back," Miguel said.

The men scrambled for a ravine to avoid the blast and gazed at the Buick. While the ground shook, the car disappeared into a ball of fire. Pieces rained from the sky.

"Run for cover!" Pablo said. "We're still too close." After the smoke had cleared and all of the fragments had fallen, Pablo and Gacha emerged from behind a wall.

"Congratulations, Miguel!" Gacha said.

"Congratulations, Cuco!" Pablo said.

"I've got a supplier who can provide all of the dynamite you need," Pinina said.

"Buy 10,000 kilos," Pablo said, "and bury it throughout the hideouts in used plastic containers." Miguel quickly became one of Pablo's most trusted and valued men with access to secret hideouts.

A statue of Cano erected in his honour received a dynamite necklace. Pinina ignited its slow wick. The explosion launched the head flying into the middle of the park. After the statue was replaced, even more explosives were used the second time.

Gilberto called Pablo, protesting that he hadn't done the bombing. El Patrón told him to stop lying and get ready to be hit. Companies owned by the Cali godfathers, including pharmacies and radio stations, were dynamited. Cali focused on infiltrating Medellín, bribing police and army personnel and providing information to General Maza.

At night, Pablo used his telescope to watch the remains of the Monaco Building, while contemplating revenge. He offered $3 million for the whereabouts of the two men Pacho had hired to do the bombing. For several weeks, hit men stopped by to get intelligence on the suspects. Two pleasant young men showed up.

"You two need to be careful," Pablo said, doubtful of their ability to kill the Indian, who was living in Cali. "He's very dangerous."

The two men found out that the Indian was selling property that he had purchased with his payment for bombing the Monaco Building. Posing as a gay couple, they booked an appointment to see the house. After viewing it, they arranged to meet the Indian to discuss the price and killed him. The two men bringing photos of the Indian's corpse took Pablo by surprise. He was delighted by the assassination of an enemy who could have caused so much damage. Pinina captured the Indian's accomplice.

A car bomb exploded by Pablo's mother's house. Cut by glass, she was hospitalised. His pregnant sister had been asleep on the fourth floor. In hospital, she gave birth to a baby that had to live in an incubator for several weeks. Another sister on the fifth floor was treated for shrapnel wounds. Regarding Cali, Pablo told his mother, "If they broke my heart it was because they placed the first bomb."

He sent a team to Cali, including Cuco, Popeye and Pinina, with fake documents and a truck with 150 kilos of dynamite. They monitored Pacho's routine. Twice-weekly he visited a house behind the Dann Hotel, protected by bodyguards. After twenty exhausting days, they knew his routine. At 10 AM on Wednesday mornings, he crossed an avenue near 65th Street in a commercial zone. Although many innocent people would be killed, it was ideal for a car bomb. They planned the assault for on a Wednesday.

The bomb Cuco assembled consisted of dynamite mixed with steel shrapnel inside of two big milk jugs. One went into the trunk of a Renault 9, and the other was camouflaged between the back and front seats. They were connected to each other and to a remote control. The car was parked at the site. With a remote control, Pinina positioned himself on a street corner. After testing that the indicator bulb was lit, Pinina disconnected the mechanism and returned to his hideout.

On Wednesday morning at 9:45 AM, Pinina ordered the men to spread out within a 200-metre area. Nearby on the second floor of a gym, thirty women were doing aerobics. They would be consumed by the blast. A lady and a girl started to sell cigarettes at the street corner.

"Buy all of their cigarettes so that they go away," Pinina told Popeye, concerned about the woman and child because they were poor.

Popeye approached the woman. "How much for all of your cigarettes?" With the girl watching and smiling, he paid the woman. Back at his lookout point, he was thankful that they had left the area.

By 10:20 AM, Pacho had not arrived, and the area had become increasingly busy. The women were still doing aerobics, and the woman and child reappeared selling cigarettes.

"Do you want me to get rid of them again?" Popeye asked. Pinina shook his head.

At 10:35 AM, Popeye received a signal that Pacho was coming. Pinina put batteries in the remote control and moved away from the corner. Popeye imagined all of the women in the area covered in blood. They watched Pacho's truck draw near, followed by three cars. With the traffic light on red, Pacho was stopped next to the bomb. Pinina pressed a button. Nothing happened. Pressing the button repeatedly, Pinina kept crouching and standing up.

Nothing happened. The light changed to green, and Pacho proceeded. Pinina removed the batteries from the remote control and put them in his pocket.

"I have no idea what happened," Pinina said, "with this son of a bitch mechanism and remote control!"

"There's nothing we can do. Let's get in the car and go."

"Open the hood," Pinina said. "We need to deactivate the battery before we go to the hideout." Relieved that the civilians had survived, Popeye left.

The remote control had malfunctioned, so they bought a new one. The team returned to Cali to resume the mission, but were detected after leaving the airport. Although they managed to escape, two days later, the police raided the location of the car bomb. Pablo cancelled the mission, and the team returned to Medellín.

On February 21, 1988, Juan Pablo was about to participate in a motorbike race scheduled on streets in a housing project in northern Medellín. Ten trucks screeched onto the racecourse. Men with weapons emerged. In front of a startled audience, Pablo got out of a truck, approached his son and explained that he had learned of a kidnapping plot: the Cali Cartel had paid people to arrange a crash so that Juan Pablo could be abducted in the absence of his bodyguards. With all of his men there providing additional security, he urged his son to race, kissed his cheek, and patted him on the head. "Good luck. Drive well. Strap your helmet on tight."

Over four months, Pablo ordered the bombing of eighty-five drugstores that laundered Cali's money. The bombs in Drogas la Rebaja killed twenty-seven people, mostly customers and passers-by. Cali sent seven more killers after Pablo, who mailed boxes containing their body parts back to Cali.

Pablo targeted Gilberto's younger brother, Miguel, who oversaw the day-to-day operations of the Cali Cartel. Obsessed with managing minute details, Miguel used phones and fax machines to collect information and to issue orders. Employees viewed

Gilberto as a kindly uncle, whereas they were terrified of Miguel, who some had nicknamed Lemon Face due to his permanent sour expression. Miguel claimed to have a law degree, but a US government witness testified that he had purchased the degree by donating a library to a university and lavishing the dean with gifts. Despite their air of civility, the two brothers had raised money for their business ventures by kidnapping – just like Pablo – and had built dangerous reputations. They had been arrested for counterfeiting, but the judge had let the statute of limitations on their trial lapse because of the death threats she had received. Masters of avoiding detection, they operated under fake names, backed up by counterfeit passports and official documents.

A chief concern of the Cali godfathers was the safety of their family members. With almost twenty children and various wives and ex-wives, the brothers had such large families that during the war they had a permanent staff of 150 people protecting them. Miguel's children ranged in age from 3-year-old Andrea to William, a law student in his mid-20s. Gilberto's children were slightly older and were schooled overseas, including at Harvard and Stanford universities. After his eldest son was arrested for drugs and incarcerated in Cali, Gilberto stormed into the jail, extracted a belt and whipped him to teach him a lesson. In later years, Gilberto told *Time* magazine that his children had all grown up to be professionals and one was a student. After earning degrees at European and American universities, they had been employed by his legal businesses. The brothers also had to protect their mother, three sisters and a younger brother whom they called Good For Nothing.

While in their 30s, the brothers had founded the Cali Cartel in the 1970s with the third godfather, José Santacruz Londoño, a.k.a. Chepe. All three had been friends at high school. In the 1970s, Chepe had been arrested twice, including for a weapons violation in America. Money from kidnapping a university student and an industrialist had been invested into a fleet of taxis. Suspecting that his wife was going to move to Miami with his children, he had her killed because he thought he would never see his kids again. An informant told the DEA that Chepe's wife was always yelling and screaming and complaining, and he was not the type who would put up with that forever. A veteran Cuban-born US journalist who had criticised him was sitting at a bar in the Meson Asturias Restaurant in the Queens borough of New York when someone approached from behind and shot him twice in the head.

Following the rejection of his application for Club Colombia – exclusively for businessmen and industrialists – Chepe did not have the decision-makers killed. After he had calmed down, he decided to build his own club based on the design of Club Colombia on a hillside in a wealthy neighbourhood. He also commissioned a country club to be built with statues of heroes, three large white crosses and a bridge.

The earliest documented kidnappings were when the three godfathers were teenagers. A kidnapped fisherman earned Gilberto a day in jail. In the late 1960s, they joined a gang that kidnapped two Swiss citizens: a student and a diplomat. Aged 28 and running a gang of seven kidnappers, Gilberto negotiated a ransom of twelve million pesos, which was almost $1 million. The three godfathers invested it into cannabis and then into the far more profitable cocaine.

In the 1970s, Chepe started to build cocaine distribution throughout America. Gilberto and Miguel concentrated on processing the raw material in labs in Peru and Colombia. Individual parts of the business were set up as self-contained cells, so if raided, the workers genuinely couldn't provide any information about the bigger picture. Miguel took reports from the people in charge of the individual parts such as the regional bosses of South Florida and New York. Information concerning finances, security, drug shipments and the police was submitted to Miguel.

Pacho was the fourth godfather to join the executive board. Out of all of the Cali godfathers, he kept the lowest profile. He rarely allowed interviews. Due to his business performance, his homosexuality was accepted by the godfathers. Pacho had grown up in Palmira, a town less than an hour's drive east of Cali. In high school, he had studied technical maintenance. In America, he became a jeweller and a precious-metals broker until he began selling cocaine. In 1975 and 1978, he was arrested for cocaine distribution in New York.

After getting released from US prison in 1983, Pacho went to Cali to negotiate with the godfathers for supply and distribution rights in New York, where he started to build his empire. As law enforcement increasingly policed the Florida border, he used his contacts to shift the smuggling routes to Mexico, which was extremely lucrative. According to the DEA, Pacho ran one of the "most sophisticated and profitable money-laundering operations."

Pacho dealt harshly with his enemies. Those suspected of betrayal were invited to one of his ranches for a feast. After they had eaten, he would lead them to a room, put bags over their heads and torture them into confessing. Their corpses ended up in the Cauca River. He also flew traitors to Cali, killed them and sent lookalikes back on the return flights, so the authorities and the family members would believe that the victims had disappeared in their home cities.

Whereas Medellín members were sometimes at odds, the Cali godfathers never had a major disagreement. Pablo imposed his will upon others, but the men from Cali shared equal votes for key decisions. The war with Pablo had tightened their bond.

On a map of Central and South America, Cali's cocaine production started in the south with the growth of the leaves in Bolivia and Peru. To get the finished product north to America, the leaves were transported up to Colombia and processed into cocaine. Colombia was ideal for labs due to its size: more than four times bigger than the UK; almost twice the size of Texas or France. In the dense jungles and forests, illegal activity was easily disguised from the poorly funded authorities. With Colombia being at the top of South America, the cocaine continued north through Central America, stopping at transhipment points and finally crossing America's southern border.

Cali is the capital city of the Cauca Valley, on Colombia's western side by the Pacific Ocean, ideally placed to send cocaine out to sea. It's where tourists enjoy salsa music, panoramic mountain views, historic church buildings and constant tropical warmth as it's near to the Equator. This picturesque agricultural region is an industrial and commercial centre for coffee, cotton, sugarcane and soybeans, which are shipped through the city. Tyres, tobacco products, textiles, paper, chemicals and building materials are manufactured there. The town centre is noisy with traffic and bars playing Spanish songs. On the streets, poor people peddle their wares, including candy, clothes, shoes and little gold trinkets of Inca gods and frogs.

In the 1980s, Cali's population was over one million. The godfathers maintained control via the telephone company and taxi drivers. Through bribery, cartel technicians and engineers could listen to any calls. Clustered at the airport, taxi drivers reported the arrival of anyone who looked suspicious, especially Americans in case they were working for the DEA.

The godfathers split Cali into fiefdoms. Gilberto and Miguel controlled Cali's centre, an area around the Intercontinental Hotel in downtown Cali, and Ciudad Jardin in the southernmost part of Cali, home to the wealthiest residents. Chepe had the southern region of Cali. Pacho's cities included Palmira and Yumbo, north of Cali, and Jamundi, a city fifty miles south of Cali. Their luxury properties in each area had large protective walls, swimming pools, tennis courts, bowling alleys, cockfighting arenas, horse stables, dance clubs, private beaches and soccer pitches. To keep a low profile, they drove Mazdas, while loaning out their luxury cars to politicians and elites.

To control the population, the cartel bribed key people in politics, law enforcement and business. They threw parties for hundreds of officials. Gilberto's bank gave shareholdings to local leaders, some of whom ended up on the bank's board of directors, making them eligible for preferential loans and overdrafts.

The godfathers' grip on the police was so strong that when a love rival shot his competitor dead at a urinal during a salsa concert financed by the godfathers, the homicide detectives who arrived to investigate were instructed to wait outside so as not to upset the gentlemen from Cali or to disrupt the concert. After six hours, the detectives gained access. All of the witnesses were long gone and no one dared to provide any information. As the hit was unsanctioned, the godfathers summoned the murderer to appear before them. Miguel said that the godfathers didn't care why the man had been killed. They felt disrespected and they had a reputation to uphold in Cali. The man begged for his life, which was spared.

In the media, they credited their legitimate business interests for generating their wealth. If there were negative reports, Gilberto would often pick up the phone and chastise the journalists. During the war, they portrayed themselves as businessmen victims of a narco-terrorist.

Potential cartel employees had to fill out applications. They hired the most talented people, including accountants, economists and financial advisers. New employees were faxed the rules, which included living modestly and avoiding attracting attention. Stashhouse operators were instructed to keep the normal hours of a working person by leaving in the morning and returning at night. Out of the hundreds of traffickers in Colombia, the disciplined application of business techniques enabled Cali to forge ahead.

One of Miguel's houses had four bedrooms, seven living rooms, endless expensive furniture, a lion-skin rug, a stuffed lion, hundreds of porcelain figurines that cost up to $3,000 each, and a glass bead curtain hanging from a second-floor ceiling above an indoor reflecting pool. At each end of the house were spiral staircases: one led to a skylit gym; the other to a bar with an underwater view of an outdoor pool. Pablo's operation against Miguel was a disaster. A bomb exploded half a mile from Miguel's residence, destroying three houses and the assassins.

Working for Cali, a hit man called Flaco Osorio arrived in

Medellín. Pablo warned his men that Osorio was a professional killer and he told them a story: "Twenty years ago, Osorio robbed a bank with three other bandits. The police completely surrounded them in a small town. Osorio left in a blaze of blood and fire, and with the bank's money in his hands. Not only was he the only one out of four to survive, but he single-handedly took down six of the ten officers with his impeccable aim."

"He's much older now," Popeye said. "It's time for him to die. We'll attack him in the street. Eight against one."

Popeye watched Osorio leave his hideout at 7:30 AM every day, driving a white Renault 9. He organised the attack to be on a main avenue, with a two-mile approach. In stolen Renault 18s, the men waited with five guns, eight pistols and a machine gun. At 7:20 AM, Osorio walked to his car, scanning the area for threats. As he drove towards the main avenue, Pinina sped ahead. The other cars got next to Osorio, and the firing began. A bus on the avenue obstructed the assassination. The Renault 9 veered off the avenue, crashed into a house and flipped upside down. The men closed in and finished him off.

Both cartels hired the local police to interrogate anyone visiting from the opposing city. Law-abiding citizens would be released. Criminals would be handed over to the cartel's henchmen, tortured, killed and dumped on the roadside. Far more died in Medellín, where visitors from Cali were hung from posts after being drawn and quartered. The damage to each side shattered any prospect of peace and locked the cartels into a fight to the death.

General Maza protected Cali's infrastructure while pursuing Medellín with information provided by the Cali godfathers, including the whereabouts of Pablo's safe houses and hiding places. Special units of the Colombian police assigned to find Pablo were helping Cali expand its cocaine business.

With murder surging in Colombia, and Pablo taking the top spot on the FBI's Most Wanted list, he took time out to attend his son's 12th birthday party on February 24, 1989, at Nápoles. In a white shirt, dark sports shorts and with his face clean-shaven revealing a gain in weight, Pablo gave his daughter a white horse and danced with his wife. A photo taken at the party revealed the immensity of his troubles: next to his mother, he is sat at a table, gazing down forlornly as if trapped in his thoughts.

Everything was situated to make 1989 a terrible year for Colombia. Pablo put a hit on the justice who had indicted him for Cano's death. Two days after Pablo had been subpoenaed for the murder trial, the justice was packing his belongings, so he could flee from the country under government protection. Accompanied by two DAS bodyguards, he was assassinated in Bogotá. Thirteen days later, a lawyer investigating the case was murdered. Supported by the media and with his popularity surging, Galán was demanding that Pablo and the traffickers be arrested and extradited.

"What are we going to do about the traffickers?" asked President Barco, desperate to boost his image. Viewing him as a poor speaker, the media had described him as a "dishevelled, absent-minded and stuttering professor."

"We must be strong because nobody can be above the state," General Maza said. "We're going to fight a lot, but it'll be worth the pain. There's no alternative."

Pablo sent a lawyer to bribe Maza. "Pablo Escobar is interested in meeting you."

"I've nothing to say to him."

Maza received another visitor. "If you give the signal, we can make you the richest man in Colombia."

"Money is not the most important thing in life." From Maza's response, El Patrón realised that the head of the DAS had already been bought by Cali.

With information provided by Cali, Maza made numerous arrests. Many of the prisoners were tortured due to their association with Pablo and some were extradited. In Envigado, members of the DIJIN – the elite intelligence section of the secret police – located, tortured and killed two associates of Pablo because of information provided by Maza and the Cali Cartel. In Bogotá, the DAS killed one of the Prisco brothers, José Rodolfo Prisco, which incensed Pablo, who relied heavily on the Priscos' gang.

Pablo ordered Maza's death by car bomb. In Bogotá, Cuco assembled it, while others spied on the general to get his schedule and driving patterns. They noticed his official car had a protective shielding.

On Saturday, May 28, 1989, Maza attended a meeting where a general informed him of the arrest of an army captain who had been providing information to Gacha. To neutralise the threat, the generals planned to issue a press release on May 31. Maza left the meeting concerned about retaliation. By staying inside his home, he hoped to minimise his exposure.

On May 30, Maza went to his office and called his intelligence officer. He suggested that they use the compromised army captain as a double agent. As his armoured vehicle had broken down, Maza was transported by an old Ford. A remote-detonated car bomb with 350 kilos of dynamite exploded in northern Bogotá, lifting the Ford and enveloping the general in a deafening sound. Maza was shielded from the shock wave by a woman walking to her car. The blast killed her and seven of Maza's bodyguards. Although the undercarriage of his car was destroyed, the general opened the door and emerged through smoke and flames, holding an injured colleague. He saw rubble, broken glass, human remains, severed limbs, wounded men moaning and mangled cars. The media announced that the traffickers were using remote-controlled bombs, and that it was incredible that this monstrous practice had arrived in Colombia.

"All at once I felt as if I had been tossed into the air by the surf," the general said. Unfazed, he denounced his attackers: "In Puerto Boyacá, the base of this organisation, they have a large infrastructure: a clinic, a printing house, a drugstore, an armoury and a communications centre. They also possess thirty pilots and a fleet of planes and helicopters, 120 vehicles, mainly campers, bulldozers, motor graders and boats and slabs for river transport.

Henry Pérez, the Mexican [Gacha] (an emerald trader), Víctor Carranza and Escobar selected fifty men who, trained by English and Israeli mercenaries, became elite commanders."

"How was General Maza saved from that bomb?" Pablo asked his men. About the deaths of the bystanders, he said, "In every war innocent people die, but in the end the objective is achieved: to intimidate the government, to put people on their knees, to triumph. The gringos defeated Japan by killing thousands of innocents from Hiroshima." The boss wanted an even bigger bomb to annihilate the general in the multi-storey DAS building.

Years later, Maza said, "Pablo Escobar was a paranoiac who confused the real world with the surreal one, whereupon he went from being a good kind man to being a cruel and bloodthirsty man with great ease. He was a man who was born in the midst of financial limitations and dissatisfaction and, therefore, identified with the boys of the communes. There he created a sui generis personality full of resentment. Insofar as he was obtaining money and power, instead of creating a kind of antibody to those gaps, he instead fed them.

"He wanted to be more powerful than the industrialists Ardila Lülle and Santo Domingo. He lived for money. As a philosopher said, 'He was such a poor man that all he had was money.' I know that he respected me for two things: First, because he could not kill me and, second, because he never had an element that proved my dishonesty. He launched propaganda accusing me of being a friend of the Cali Cartel. He used all means to get proof to certify his position, and he instructed his political friends to look for millimetre-by-millimetre evidence against Miguel Maza. They paid to track my social and professional life and came to the conclusion that I had no shade. Escobar lived frustrated about Maza. He became obsessive with Maza. He said that he had to be destroyed in whichever way possible, but neither for him nor for the Mexican, who kneeled to proclaim his hatred against me, did things work out."

CHAPTER 15
EARLY ELITE KIDNAPPINGS

Pablo told his brother-in-law that kidnapping the big fish was the best way to negotiate. It would raise money for the war with Cali and put pressure on the government to halt extradition. He targeted Andrés Pastrana, the candidate for mayor of Bogotá, the son of a former Conservative president and a prominent journalist. Mayor first and then the presidency, Pastrana hoped. With the elections approaching, Pablo knew that Pastrana's father would do anything to get his son back, including influencing the political class to go against extradition. The ex-president was aware of Pablo's capacity for murder because, during his tenure, El Patrón had kidnapped Diego Echavarría Misas. With the public afraid, President Pastrana had ordered an air strike, door-to-door searches and rewards. Under pressure from the authorities, Pablo had executed Diego Echavarría Misas.

For ten days, Popeye spied on Pastrana's campaign headquarters near the Bogotá City Council. The area was so busy that the hit man was unnoticed standing around. Six bodyguards were stationed in the building. Pastrana left the headquarters numerous times, accompanied by four policemen on two motorbikes. At night, Popeye stayed at his grandmother's apartment. She thought he was searching for a good university to attend.

After gathering intelligence, Popeye returned to Medellín. With extradition gaining more support, Pablo wanted to strike fast. He devised a plan, and sent Popeye back to Bogotá. For twenty days, one of Pablo's helicopters flew back and forth from Bogotá to Medellín to prevent suspicion about its flight path on the day of the kidnapping. In a brown Renault 21, Popeye went about his business with a driver who knew the roads of Bogotá. An hour away from the city, Popeye scoped out farmland. By telephone, Pablo instructed one of the farmers to vacate his property. Pastrana would be held there.

"Will leaving your property be suspicious?" Popeye asked.

"I don't think so," the farmer said before getting paid.

Popeye instructed the driver to keep the Renault 21 on the roads near Pastrana's headquarters, especially near checkpoints, so that the troops would be familiar with it. The journeys needed to happen before 7 PM, the approximate time Pastrana would be in the car. He bought weapons, a green Mazda 626 and a white jeep. All of the kidnappers received elegant suits, shirts and ties. In the Mazda 626, Popeye and an immaculately dressed-up driver arrived at Pastrana's headquarters. The driver opened the door for Popeye, who paged the policemen at the headquarters' entrance, who allowed them to enter.

Inside, Popeye recognised the six bodyguards on the first floor whom he had watched. "I'm Dr Alexander Velez," he told the receptionist. "Can I get an appointment with the candidate?"

Writing his name down on a list, she said, "Can you please wait with those other men?"

After taking a seat, he studied the bodyguards, pleased that they didn't overreact to the arrival of any strangers. At 2:30 PM, he was authorised to see Pastrana's private secretary on the second floor. After ascending, he was asked to wait. The secretary scrutinised his clothes. After fifteen minutes, she authorised his entry into Pastrana's office.

On the phone, the politician motioned for him to sit. After concluding his call, Pastrana shook his hand, while examining his clothes. "What can I do for you, Dr Alexander?"

"My group has 1,500 votes to support you with," Popeye said. "I'm the spokesman. Our only request is that when you become the mayor, you help us set up headquarters in your city."

"Dr Alexander, I am very interested in your offer. We can discuss it with one of my advisers."

"Also, you should know that we are totally Conservative. We need assurance that whoever is in charge of the Department of Culture will support us, because we have many resources."

"That's no problem, doctor." Addressing his secretary, Pastrana made an appointment for January 16 with Dr Alexander.

On his way out, Popeye told the secretary, "With such a pretty secretary, the candidate's campaign is sure to be successful."

Descending the stairs, Popeye counted the steps and memorised every detail. After saying goodbye to the receptionist, he scanned the inattentive bodyguards. They had never searched anybody allowed up to see Pastrana. They seemed oblivious to their surroundings. He calculated that the kidnapping could be done on January 16.

On January 5, 1988, extradition was reintroduced. Galán, the media and the DEA celebrated, while continuing to blame Pablo for high-profile killings. Extradition warrants were issued for Pablo, Gacha and the Ochoa brothers. In response, Pablo wanted to accelerate the kidnapping of Pastrana, but Popeye and his men convinced him to slow down and stick to the plan. In the daytime, Pablo coordinated business out of Hacienda Nápoles, but in the evenings, he hid in the forest.

On January 15, Popeye returned to Bogotá to finalise the kidnapping. He told his accomplices that he would arrive at Pastrana's headquarters in the Mazda. More men would arrive in the white jeep, all smartly dressed. The jeep's doors would be adorned with Pastrana's campaign slogan "Talking the talk. Walking the walk," the sight of which would relax the police and the bodyguards. In the parking lot, the men would remain with the jeep, awaiting a signal from Popeye. The brown Renault 4 would be stationed around a corner with its keys in the ignition, waiting to receive Pastrana. The policeman at the door would be held at gunpoint and disarmed. More men would do the same to the bodyguards. With the building secured, Popeye would go upstairs, force Pastrana to the ground and inform him that they were a military unit of the M-19, that he was needed to convey a message to the government and that he would be freed within one hour. The phones would be disconnected to delay reporting the crime. Pastrana would be put in the Mazda and transferred to the trunk of the brown Renault. Popeye would be on the back seat with another accomplice, both dressed like business executives.

While they escaped, the men inside the building would close the door and warn the bodyguards that the door had been rigged with a hand grenade. They would escape in the jeep. Every five blocks, one would exit the jeep, leaving their weapons inside. The jeep would end up in a car park, with the campaign slogan removed. Travelling separately by bus, each accomplice would head to a different city. A helicopter would transport Pastrana. In case any of them were arrested and tortured, the accomplices did not know Pastrana's destination.

At night, Popeye rehearsed the plan in his mind. Pablo had ordered that Pastrana remain unharmed, but during a kidnapping anything could happen. If Popeye failed, the police would shoot him dead in the streets. He didn't want a repeat of the failed plan to kidnap Gómez Martínez, the candidate for mayor in Medellín. He hoped that the non-descript brown Renault would fool the authorities. Excited to be in charge of a plan that would shake up Colombia's political class, he looked forward to completing the mission, which would repay Pablo for everything the boss had done for him.

On January 16, he awoke with plenty of focus and prepared to die. Thoughts of Pablo contemplating his role in the mission excited him and made him feel proud. Over lunch, the accomplices joked about remaining calm.

At 4:20 PM, Popeye arrived at the headquarters. The driver opened his door. A policeman allowed him inside. "Good afternoon, miss," he said to the receptionist. "I have an appointment at 4:30 PM."

"I'm so sorry. The doctor is running late today. Please wait."

"No problem. I shall wait."

Sitting by one of the headquarters' guards, he contemplated

PABLO ESCOBAR'S STORY

possible reasons for Pastrana's delay. With the mission running late, he worried about getting stuck in heavy traffic.

"You can go up now," the receptionist said at 5:45 PM.

"Thank you," he said, smiling.

Upstairs, the secretary told him to take a seat as there was a visitor ahead of him. After watching Pastrana receive his guest, Popeye rose. "Excuse me, miss, but I left some papers in the car, which I need to get and I'll be right back."

"OK, but don't take too long."

At the foot of the building, he signalled to his accomplices outside. They entered with guns drawn on the receptionist, whom they locked in a bathroom. Popeye rushed upstairs and aimed his gun at Pastrana, who was on the phone. An accomplice grabbed the candidate.

"We are commandos of the M-19," he said, "come to take you to Commander Pizarro, so that you can send a message to the national government. In one hour, you'll be back in your office."

Studying Popeye, Pastrana was led out of the room without saying anything. They descended to the first floor. Outside, Pastrana was put in a car, which drove around a corner to the brown Renault. Within seconds, he was bundled into the trunk. Listening to the radio, Popeye and two accomplices drove away. Ten minutes later, a report was broadcast: "The mayoral candidate Andrés Pastrana has been kidnapped. Authorities are searching for a green Mazda 626 LS." Bracing for the riskiest part of the journey, Popeye tugged on the middle back-seat cushion to observe Pastrana.

"Commander, this is madness," Pastrana said. "We're going to get killed. If the police stop us, I'll handle the situation. Don't shoot. But why is Commander Pizarro doing this to me if we are friends?"

"Calm down," Popeye said. "In one hour, it'll all be over with. Don't speak. Just wait." While he readjusted the back seat, police cars and motorbikes with sirens blaring sped by.

The radio reported that Bogotá was in total chaos, with traffic unable to move. On main roads, the authorities were going car to car, ordering people to open their trunks. Several green Mazdas had been stopped. Despite the traffic, Popeye managed to escape in fifty-five minutes before any roadblocks had been established. In safe territory, he rejoiced over the gratitude that would be shown by Pablo and Gacha. The radio announced that Operation Lockdown was in effect, the entire city had been shut down and that Pastrana would be rescued within minutes because the kidnappers and the hostage were stuck in traffic.

At 7:10 PM, Popeye arrived at a safe house. "I'm so dizzy," Pastrana said, getting extracted from the car boot. After entering the building, he said, "Can I get a radio and a glass of water?"

After giving him what he'd asked for, Popeye came back outside and told his accomplices to return to the city, call the TV stations and ask that they have the police and the Army clear the streets so that they could move Pastrana and release him in Salitre Park. He ordered them to abandon their weapons and split up after the call. He hugged them goodbye.

Inside, he told Pastrana, "My men have the complex completely surrounded. It's only a matter of time before Commander Pizarro arrives."

"Good thing I'm not in the hands of drug traffickers," Pastrana said.

Listening to the news on the radio, Pastrana started to cry when he heard one of his friends praise him. The friend added, "It's ridiculous that from the very centre of a big city someone like Andrés Pastrana can be kidnapped and still not have been found by the authorities ... My sources in the palace have informed me that ex-president Pastrana has just arrived to participate in his son's rescue operation." Popeye assumed that the ex-president had got involved to prevent a rescue attempt because the authorities were notorious for shooting everybody and blaming the kidnappers if the victim was killed.

At 8:15 PM, a newsflash announced, "In minutes, Andrés

Pastrana will be released! The kidnappers have requested that the authorities loosen their control of the city."

Pastrana kept asking for Captain Pizarro, only to be told he was coming down the mountain. Wary of his escalating desperation, Popeye left the room to extract the bullets from his gun in case Pastrana attempted to wrestle it from him.

At 2 AM, the news announced that the authorities had located the green Mazda 626 LS used in the kidnapping. The news did not disclose that it had taken the authorities more than seven hours to find it only fifteen seconds from the crime scene, just around the corner from Pastrana's headquarters.

With adrenaline preventing sleep, Pastrana questioned Popeye throughout the night. Tired, but not wanting the candidate to complain of ill treatment, the hit man tried to answer politely, but realised he was giving away too much information.

At 6 AM, Popeye padlocked Pastrana's door and prepared a bonfire. After splashing cold water on his face to prevent sleep, he lit the bonfire at 6:50 AM and returned to Pastrana. At 6:55 AM, the whirring of a helicopter soothed Popeye but agitated Pastrana. The hit man left the building and admired the landscape. Holding his gun, he returned inside.

Pastrana stood and gazed at his captor. "I demand to know who you are!"

"Are you in any position to demand something from me?" Popeye said. "I am Jhon Jairo Velásquez Vásquez alias Popeye, head of the commandos of the Extraditables. You're going to Medellín."

After collapsing on the bed, the politician placed his hands over his face. He began to sob and repeatedly yell, "They're going to kill me!"

"No. If we were going to kill you, we would have already done it at your headquarters."

He was handcuffed and blindfolded with a pillowcase to prevent him from seeing the registration number of the helicopter provided by Kiko Moncada. Outside, his sobbing soaked the blindfold. He kept asking if he were going to be killed. "Why have I been kidnapped by the Extraditables? I have never said or done anything against them."

Having recently flown the route over and over, the helicopter pilot was confident that they would not look suspicious to the Air Force. Popeye assumed that the authorities would not believe that Pastrana would get moved from Bogotá by helicopter. In the air, they watched out for any threats. From an airport in Rionegro, the hostage was transported to another hideout.

At a separate safe house in the woods, Pablo congratulated Popeye for handling the job so well. After chatting, the hit man fell into a deep sleep. The next day, Santo called and Popeye answered. He wanted to meet urgently. Popeye met Santo at a church and brought him to the hideout. The politician was delighted that Pastrana had been kidnapped.

In Pablo's log cabin, Santo and Popeye sat in the living room. Pablo consulted Santo about what demands he should make from ex-president Pastrana. From his jacket pocket, Santo extracted the private phone numbers for Pastrana's father. "Who was the hero who made this great thing happen?" Santo asked.

"He's here at my side: Popeye."

Offering congratulations, Santo stood and hugged the hit man. "Pablo, you need to kill Pastrana."

Popeye and Pablo exchanged concerned glances. "Killing him would have been easy in Bogotá," El Patrón said, "but now it is impossible because his family will seek vengeance."

"Pablo, if they rescue him, he will surely become the mayor of Bogotá and the future president of this country. He is the son of the Conservative Party ... With Pastrana out of the way, a Liberal could rise to the presidency more easily. With a Liberal as president, extradition could be squashed."

After listening patiently to Santo list all of the reasons for killing Pastrana, Pablo said, "This is neither debatable nor negotiable."

On the drive back, Santo urged Popeye to convince his boss to kill Pastrana. "Pablo's making an error of judgement which needs to be corrected."

"I am only a simple worker. I am nobody to advise a man like Pablo Escobar. I only give him my opinion when he asks for it." Popeye detailed the kidnapping.

While the media reported that the investigation into Pastrana was advancing – the Toyota jeep used had been found – Pablo urgently wanted to transfer Pastrana to a hideout in the woods. But first, he needed to speak to Pastrana. With nobody suspecting that Pastrana was in Medellín, Pablo and his brother-in-law entered the hideout wearing hoods.

"Why are you doing this to me?" Pastrana asked, sat on a stool. "My campaign is in its final stages, and I'm going to lose the elections now."

"Pablo would not be—" Mario said, stopping mid-sentence, realising he had used the boss's name.

"Don't screw me again, Mario," Pablo barked, tearing off his hood. "Now you've given me away, these things have no purpose."

The blood drained from Pastrana's face. After attempting to regain his composure, he offered his hand and an effusive greeting, which Pablo responded to politely. "Please don't kill me, Pablo!"

"If we were going to kill you, we would have done it in Bogotá." After listening to Pastrana make political promises and beg for his life, Pablo cut him off. "You, the political class, are behind extradition. The war coming over extradition will be fierce. Remember, I'm the most moderate of the Extraditables. Serious changes are coming to this country. The first corpses are going to be from your class: the politicians."

"I don't have anything to do with extradition."

"You are very mistaken. You are the political hope of the Conservatives. Your father is the leader of your party. Your life depends on your stand on extradition."

"I am about to become the mayor. Whatever it takes, we'll resolve this issue soon."

"That depends on your father," Pablo said, assuming that the ex-president would do everything in his power to prevent a deadly rescue attempt.

After the meeting, one of Pablo's men called the ex-president. "Good morning. We are the Extraditables. We have your son. We need you to meet with President Barco and look for a way to make him change his mind about the extradition of Colombians to the US. We know he can do it. He can do it in the same way he continues to knock down the court's attempts to abolish extradition."

"How is my son? Can I speak to him?"

"In one hour we will call again and put your son on the line."

At the next meeting, Pastrana greeted Pablo with a handshake and a pat on the shoulders.

"I'm going to put you on the phone with your father. Speak only for five minutes, not one minute longer. Tell him that you're going to be taken from Bogotá to the forest."

"What? Why?"

"This is going to be a very long and slow, difficult process."

"And what about my election campaign?"

"This is one of your downfalls. You think only of maintaining power. Go out to the car phone and dial the number. Do not talk about anything I have not authorised."

Pastrana dialled. "Father, I'm fine. They're treating me very well. But I am worried that these gentlemen will take me from Bogotá into the forest. My election campaign will be jeopardised. Please find a way to stop the elections until this is resolved. We cannot lose that position. You must stop the elections."

"Stay calm. I shall work hard to ensure that everything is solved quickly."

Pablo ended the call, said goodbye to Pastrana and left the building. Outside, he told his man, "Call the ex-president again, and tell him that his son's life is at stake. He must do everything that he can to convince the president."

Speaking to his son had put the ex-president in a cooperative mood. He told Pablo's man, "Sir, I'm going to the president.

Please call me in the afternoon. My only request is that you don't take my son to the forest. You must understand that this is not easy. The state is in the hands of a Liberal president, and I am the opposition."

Pablo instructed his man to cover the phone's receiver, and whispered, "Tell him that it is not any easier for us to see the government take away our friends, men who have children just like he does." After the message was repeated, the conversation ended.

Rather than send Pastrana to the forest, he was kept nearby in case the ex-president needed to speak to him. Pablo ordered the disposal of the car with the phone. A new car with a phone would be stolen for the next round of negotiations.

The Pastrana family announced: "Andrés Pastrana is being held by a group of Extraditables, which is defined as a clandestine group, a kind of nationalist, ideological head of drug trafficking, which has become an armed force ready to do anything to prevent the extradition of Colombians to the United States."

Pablo issued a statement against imperialism and extradition. He said the traffickers were willing to be subjected to trials in Colombia and to accept high penalties without US interference.

In a meeting with Pablo, Carlos Mauro Hoyos, the attorney general, had promised to publicly oppose extradition. He had received $500,000 from the Extraditables to frustrate the extradition process. Having not followed through, and having ordered an investigation into Jorge Ochoa's release, he was targeted for kidnapping.

When a lawyer sent by Pablo showed up at his office, Hoyos refused to talk to him. "I do not speak with delinquents," he told his staff.

Having heard that Hoyos had struck a deal with the DEA which included an even bigger bribe than the $500,000, Pablo wanted to interrogate him on behalf of the Extraditables before making a decision about his life. Shadowing his movements, hit men learned that on the weekends he travelled from Bogotá to his hometown in Medellín to visit his mother. After double-crossing Pablo, Hoyos was going about his business with minimal security as if he didn't believe there would be any repercussions. Pablo gave Popeye a newspaper photo of Hoyos and sent him to the airport, where he was expected to arrive on an executive flight from Bogotá.

On January 23, 1988, Popeye and Pinina followed Hoyos, who left the airport in a Mercedes-Benz 230, accompanied by a driver and a bodyguard. They travelled to his family's farm by the city's main park. Observing from a safe distance, they were flabbergasted by his lack of protection.

At 11:30 AM, the Mercedes-Benz emerged, so Pinina drove after it. In the Villa Hermosa District, Hoyos met three other men in a house. Wanting to detect whether the Mercedes-Benz was armoured, Popeye walked over and touched its glass.

"It's not armoured," he told Pinina. "It has normal glass."

"OK, Popeye. Let's organise our operation, and we'll kidnap him on Monday."

Coordinating the operation, Pinina needed to determine which way Hoyos would travel to the airport. On the three most likely routes, he assigned a man with a radio. Each route converged on the public square, just 200 metres from the airport. At the public square, a Toyota would ram into the Mercedes-Benz and knock it into a ditch. If Pinina failed to intercept him on the way to the airport, the backup plan was to have Popeye capture him as soon as he exited his car at the airport. The driver and bodyguard would be killed. More men would provide cover from the police.

On January 25, by 5:35 AM, armed men with radios were positioned on each route. A report came in that Hoyos had set off without a police escort, accompanied by a bodyguard, and that he was travelling on the Santa Elena route. The Mercedes-Benz drove by a Toyota truck and a Renault with Pablo's men. They followed Hoyos to the public square, where the bodyguard quickly feared for his life as the truck knocked the Mercedes-Benz into a ditch. The first kidnapper to approach was mowed down by bullets from the bodyguard and bled to death. Five kidnappers blasted the bodyguard and the driver. By the time Popeye arrived, there were three corpses, and Hoyos was slumped as if dead.

"Remove the target," Pinina said, "and finish him off."

The command to execute Hoyos revived him. "No, no, no!" he said, rising up. "I'm alive. I'm only wounded." They seized him, but he couldn't walk properly due to a foot injury. They forced him into Pinina's car.

On the other side of the road, a taxi driver had watched the encounter. Gunfire had frightened him away. Twenty minutes later, the men, the corpse of their friend and the bodyguard's machine gun arrived at a hideout with a hidden chamber below its bath tiles.

"Can I get a doctor?" Hoyos asked.

Examining the wound, Pinina said, "We'll get you a doctor later in the afternoon." He gave Hoyos a homemade bandage.

Gazing at the corpse, Hoyos cried. With anguish, he watched his kidnappers open the trapdoor of the chamber.

"Help the man into the room," Pinina said. "Leave the door open and stay alert. If you see anything suspicious, you step in. Do not let Hoyos speak."

Pinina and Popeye left with the corpse, which they deposited by a road. The cars used in the kidnapping were disposed of in Medellín. In Pablo's cabin, the men detailed everything to the boss, who was eager for the radio to announce the kidnapping. Pinina agreed to return at noon with a doctor for Hoyos. Eventually, the news reported that Hoyos had been killed, which was based on the discovery of his blood-soaked shoe. The public braced for more violence.

During an extensive search, troops homed in on the locations of both hostages. One of Pastrana's kidnappers went to town to buy supplies. Drunk, he chatted excessively, rousing suspicion. The mayor of the town and six police set off for the hideout, expecting to find a cocaine lab.

When the authorities approached the ranch with Pastrana, a captor said, "We're surrounded by the police. Stay still. Don't move." After handcuffing him to the bed, he scanned the area, quickly realising that his accomplices had fled. He returned to Pastrana. "You are my life insurance, Dr Pastrana. If they want to take me, I'll take your life first. Leave slowly and shout that you are Andrés Pastrana." They emerged out into a garden, with police brandishing guns, posturing for a shootout.

More afraid of getting shot by the authorities than by the gun to his head, Pastrana repeatedly yelled, "I'm Andrés Pastrana!"

"Do not shoot Andrés Pastrana," the kidnapper said. "Stay calm. My life is not worth a peso, but Dr Pastrana's is worth millions. If you shoot me, I'll kill him."

"Surrender! You're surrounded!"

"No, no!" The kidnapper marched Pastrana into a garage, and unsuccessfully attempted to start a car. With his gun still at Pastrana's head, he demanded that the troops drop their weapons. After they complied, he emerged into the garden. "I will swap Dr Pastrana for a policeman." There was silence until a brave man stepped forward. The kidnapper demanded handcuffs. After the policeman was handcuffed, Pastrana was freed. Holding a gun to the policeman's head, the captor entered a pine forest at the back of the property, while threatening to kill the hostage if he were followed. In a remote area, he handcuffed the policeman to a tree and sprinted away. All of the accomplices escaped except for one, who jumped from a second floor down into a field, broke his foot and was arrested.

At 9:45 AM, a radio broadcast disturbed Pablo: "Extra, extra! The mayoral candidate to Bogotá, Andrés Pastrana Arango, has just been rescued in East Antioquia."

After contemplating the news, he said, "Popeye, did you escort Pastrana to the hideout?"

"No, sir."

The radio described a joint operation by the military and the police, who were going house-to-house in East Antioquia until Hoyos was found. Special forces from Bogotá would soon arrive. His rescue was imminent.

Pablo switched his slippers for sneakers. Holding his notebook to his mouth, he bit a small piece of paper and chewed it. "Popeye, there's only one way to stop the government from triumphing over us. If they rescue Pastrana and Hoyos on the same day, we, the Extraditables, will lose all credibility. You must go to the hideout and kill him. It's our only option. I need you to call the media and read the following note, which I'm going to dictate: 'We have just executed the Solicitor of the Republic of Colombia, Carlos Mauro Hoyos, for the crime of treason to the country.'"

In a jeep, Popeye travelled unarmed. He managed to get through an army roadblock and a police one.

"You're not allowed to pass," a captain said at another army roadblock. He silenced his engine and sat waiting. After ten minutes, the commander was reassigned to another roadblock.

"I'm going to get fired from my job if you don't let me go." He convinced a sergeant to allow him to proceed.

At the hideout, a kidnapper emerged, his face wrinkled with anxiety. "What's going on, Popeye? What's with all of the soldiers and policemen?"

"They rescued Pastrana."

"So now what?"

"The boss has ordered us to kill Hoyos."

"No, Popeye! A single shot and they'll fall on us like flies."

"There's no other way. We have to. It's a direct order from the chief."

With helicopters buzzing nearby, they extracted Hoyos from the chamber. "Boys, you are too young. Help me and I'll take you and your families to the US." Holding his foot, he cried in pain.

"This is more complicated than it seems," Popeye said. "You have been kidnapped by the Extraditables and you are to be executed in minutes for committing treason against the country."

"Who the hell did I betray?" he barked.

"You've betrayed your roots, your people, your country and yourself when you supported extradition and persecuted Pablo Escobar Gaviria."

"Call Pablo because I need to speak with him right away!"

"You rejected the lawyer he sent you, and I do not believe that he wants to speak with you now. You had your moment to speak with him."

Through the window, soldiers were visible crossing the mountain. Popeye's accomplice jabbed a forefinger in Hoyos' mouth to silence him. They escorted Hoyos to a gorge ten minutes away. The old man did not beg for his life. A bullet entering his skull collapsed him. The accomplice rotated his head for any signs of soldiers approaching, and shot Hoyos two more times in the head. With the noise echoing in the trees, they ran away.

The news broadcast Pastrana's ecstatic face. In Bogotá, he was reunited with his family. Having searched everywhere for him in Bogotá, the authorities were baffled as to how he had ended up in East Antioquia.

"Finally, we have confirmation of his release," the news reported, showing Pastrana on a balcony, dressed in the grey sports clothes his captors had provided. He said, "I always knew my captivity would be short and that I'd be OK. I'd like to thank the National Police. Above all, to [the captain] for his exceptional work in Antioquia. I hope they find the inspector general, too, and that they soon tell the country that he is safe and sound. Thank you."

Another broadcast announced: "The ordeal Pastrana went through in the municipality of El Retiro has been left behind. Thanks to God, the authorities and the courage of an officer who offered himself as a hostage, the story had a happy ending." Surrounded by officials in suits, Pastrana added, "A police officer, in a beautiful gesture, told my kidnapper to take him …" The report continued, "Eight days of captivity have become the symbol of what Colombia should be like: free and sovereign."

The footage showed Pastrana, holding his young daughter, with his father, and his wife holding their son. "Kidnapping is one of the most heinous crimes," Pastrana said. "Depriving someone of their freedom, using force over reason, taking someone away from their loved ones is a monstrosity. That's what the Extraditables did to me and to Inspector General Hoyos. The people have to demand that this group of criminals, who, in the end, just don't want to be extradited, release the inspector general and solve your problems before a judge, not with machine guns and kidnappings like they've done so far."

Popeye drove a jeep towards East Antioquia. He breezed through the first roadblock, but at another, he was instructed to pull over. After searching the vehicle, the police allowed him to continue. At a public phone, he called Caracol Radio and delivered Pablo's message. "Hoyos is in a gorge about a mile away from the magic store, close to a giant rock on the left side."

By the time Popeye met Pablo, Hoyos' body had been found. Pablo was listening to Popeye on Caracol Radio. When he heard Popeye add a sentence to the official statement of the Extraditables – "And the war continues" – he smiled. "Hey, Popeye, I didn't tell you to say that part. You are very creative." Pablo's appreciation of his work was a bigger reward than the money he was making.

Twenty minutes later, trucks arrived in the area with DAS agents. "Pablo, it's a raid!" yelled a lookout.

"Calm down," Pablo said. "There are only a few of them." After thirty minutes, the DAS agents left. Pablo ordered one of his men to call Pastrana's father. "Tell the ex-president that his son cannot identify our man who was arrested. He also cannot say that he spoke with me. Tell him that if he does, we'll assassinate him without a second thought."

Many wept for Hoyos at his well-attended funeral. The political elites feared that they would be next on Pablo's list. Two months later, the police arrested the drunken kidnapper who had led the authorities to the hideout with Pastrana. In prison, the kidnapper was murdered.

Galán held a press conference, surrounded by journalists: "The vile murder of Judge Hoyos is clearly a consequence of the decision made by Congress. I have no doubt Pablo Escobar and his men intend to scare this country because their plan to prohibit extradition using their political allies failed. I vehemently condemn the murder of this judge, and I ask the government to protect the lives of all members of the judicial power, paying special attention to the protection of the state's higher officers. Pablo Escobar wants to scare us again and we can't let him succeed."

"Dr Galán, do you think you could be a target of that retaliation?"

"Before worrying about myself, I worry about my co-workers, my colleagues; about you, the reporters that stand by us; about the police officers that chase drug traffickers; the judges that investigate them. We must protect all of them." Galán was gaining support by criticising Pablo, and the media was backing him to become the next president.

After getting attacked by a man with a machete, an inspector from the Department of Security and Control of Envigado was abandoned by his colleagues to die on a highway. The commander of the Army in Antioquia, General Barrera, responded to the situation and found the inspector begging to be saved. After he had recovered, the inspector repaid the general with information about how the traffickers had corrupted the authorities in Envigado, which had some of the highest living standards in the country and had earned the nickname the Monaco of America. In Envigado, the Mafia had co-opted the Department of Security and Control, which performed social cleansing, including murdering beggars and the homeless.

General Barrera, a stubborn man, decided to challenge Pablo by arresting some of his assassins in Envigado. He told his troops, "Escobar is a criminal and the state needs to subdue him. I will put an end to his immunity."

After learning about Pablo's strategic headquarters in the

mountains of Envigado, the general set up an operation to encircle the El Bizcocho estate. At 5 AM, Major Villegas contacted El Patrón: "I do not know where they are going but they are carrying out a special operation."

Accompanied by helicopters and tanks, troops ascended a mountain towards Pablo's hideout. A local couple and guards grabbed their radios and issued a warning. Escaping with almost ten hit men, Pablo was moving across the mountain when he was caught by surprise.

"Raise your hands and don't move!" a troop yelled, aiming his rifle at Pablo's chest.

Remaining calm, Pablo told the troop to relax because they were all going to turn themselves in. His men emerged from the vegetation towards the troop, who took his eyes off Pablo just long enough for the boss to disappear. Regaining his composure, the troop fired after Pablo. Bullets whizzed past him, causing debris to hit him in the face and for Pablo to sense his proximity to death.

Relieved he hadn't been shot, he hastened his pace. About fifteen minutes later, another troop tried to stop the group. Pointing his gun, Pablo said, "I'm from the F-2. I'm escorting prisoners down this road." He yelled for the man to move. After the troop had stepped aside, Pablo led the men down the mountain in front of a newspaper photographer who took their picture, which included Pablo without a moustache.

General Barrera next targeted Pablo's family. In eastern Envigado, Victoria and her sister Pastora were detained. During a raid, Hermilda was arrested. "Arrest me, too," said one of Pablo's sisters, concerned about her mother being incarcerated alone. They spent a day at a military headquarters and were released.

Pablo hired Major Villegas as a security chief, but learned that he was working for the Cali Cartel. Ordered to make an example out of him, Big Gun stripped him naked in a warehouse, drenched him with a hose and beat him to death with a board.

General Barrera offered a 100-million-pesos reward for Pablo, who printed leaflets offering a 102-million-pesos reward to whomever killed the general. By kidnapping the general's secretary, Pablo learned that he was friends with a famous bullfighter, who was promptly assassinated at a stoplight. The secretary was killed, and Pablo ordered that the general be assassinated only with dynamite. Shadowing his movements, the hit men learned where he ate, the roads he preferred, and even his secret places and lovers. Disguising themselves as guards at the general's destinations, they often opened his car door and greeted him. They decided to bomb him at an airport entrance, but after the button was pressed, the bomb failed to detonate, which lowered the morale of the superstitious hit men.

Hoping to restore their confidence, Pablo said, "He knows that we follow him day and night. He cannot sleep peacefully as we have tormented him."

The pressure on the general's family drove his wife to alcoholism, so he decided to abandon Medellín and the hunt for Pablo.

On March 3, 1988, Pablo activated a mission to demonstrate his power. At 11:40 PM, hit men dressed as Air Force officers entered Catam Military Base in Bogotá, where they had bribed some of the personnel. They managed to board a turbo commander plane that the government had confiscated from Gustavo. Upon taxiing, the plane came under fire. Emitting smoke from a damaged turbine, the plane took off with the hit men shooting back at the personnel and firefighters on the runway. After landing in the Middle Magdalena Valley, the hit team led by the Earring started to paint the plane and to convert it to carry cocaine, but an Air Force plane arrived and set off a flare.

"The operation has fallen, boss," the Earring reported to Pablo.

"Burn it so we can be tied 1-1."

While it burnt, the Air Force plane opened fire. Feeling a burning sensation in his chest, the Earring realised he had been shot and fled. After the Army raided Hacienda Nápoles and arrested thirty-five workers, Pablo released a statement:

"The military planes fired in a wild and bloodthirsty way at the facilities of Hacienda Nápoles, leaving several dead, including a pregnant woman, and approximately fifteen wounded. The people who were murdered in a dirty and cowardly way were cleaning staff and peasant workers of the region in the service of the Hacienda Nápoles. We will become a civil organisation immediately that will not rest until these miserable official assassins, murderers of innocent people, pay with all the rigour of justice for such an execrable crime."

CHAPTER 16
CALI'S FOREIGN MERCENARIES

Pablo's enemies were finding him difficult to capture or kill. The Cali godfathers turned to their head of security for ideas. Over six-feet tall, Jorge Salcedo towered over his peers. The softly spoken ex-army officer had short dark hair, thick eyebrows, a well-trimmed moustache and a firm gaze. He was a family man with degrees in mechanical engineering and industrial economics. Early in his career, he had designed forklifts and other machinery. His father was a retired Colombian army general and a diplomatic figure. Regarding himself as more of an engineer than a soldier, Jorge had become an expert in electronic surveillance, which had drawn him into counterterrorism assignments.

In a previous job for the military, financed by the Medellín Cartel's Gacha, Jorge had worked with mercenaries based in the UK. Enticed to Colombia on the pretext of fighting Communism, they had found themselves participating in a turf war with guerrillas over cocaine labs. Having been paid so well, their leader, David Tomkins, was enthused about doing more work in Colombia.

With coiffured grey hair, dark brows, narrow features and a tattooed arm, Tomkins was a demolitions expert and soldier of fortune who gravitated towards the hotspots of the world. His career had started in Africa. In Afghanistan, he had fought with the Mujahideen, in Croatia with warlords, and in Uganda he was involved in a plot to assassinate President Idi Amin. In Angola, a mine had exploded on him. After a medical operation, his wounds had deteriorated into near gangrene. Back in the UK, he had been hospitalised. Two days later, when the nurses came to dress his wounds, they found that he had returned to the battlefield.

As detailed in his book, *Dirty Combat*, Tomkins received a call from Jorge in February 1989. "Are you prepared to come back for another mission?"

"Yes, subject to terms and conditions."

On February 13, Jorge greeted Tomkins at the Bogotá airport. "Your prospective clients," Jorge said, "are a group of businessmen whom Pablo Escobar has sworn to kill. The Medellín Cartel has engaged in a bombing campaign against their business interests. They live in Cali, which is Colombia's third-largest city. More than thirty bombs have exploded in their Drogas La Rebaja chain of 350 stores."

"Why has Pablo Escobar targeted them?" He pressed Jorge into revealing that the clients were the Cali Cartel. The express purpose of the mission was to kill Escobar. Although the mission had no official government backing, the authorities had blessed it.

Back in England, Tomkins recruited some colleagues. On February 24, they flew to Colombia. In Cali, they were situated in a heavily guarded five-star apartment. They had their own bar, en suite bathrooms and money-counting machines. After they showered, land cruisers took them to a little town outside Cali called Jamundi, which Pacho controlled. The four godfathers arranged to meet them in a private sports facility with a swimming pool, gym, sauna and running track.

After getting into a complex surrounded by sheet-steel fencing and through security checkpoints, Tomkins and his three colleagues were escorted to the godfathers, who were sat around a table with drinks, wearing tailored shirts, designer trousers, Gucci shoes and modest watches made by Cartier or Rolex. In a Sergio Tacchini sports suit and with designer stubble, Pacho looked the youngest. Chepe wore overalls and no socks. A long-sleeved shirt hid a skin condition. As the godfathers spoke in Spanish and the mercenaries in English, Jorge translated. Discussing the operation, the godfathers were relaxed and congenial, as if it were just another day at the office.

Tomkins extracted a cigarette and scanned the room for ashtrays, but there were none. "Can I?" Miguel shook his head and his face puckered. The godfathers had zero tolerance for substances being used during work. Jorge explained that Miguel was allergic to smoke.

At lunchtime, the front gates let in a three-ton, open-back truck with over a dozen policemen. Their presence soothed the mercenaries' concerns about the authorities interrupting the meeting. They had come for lunch courtesy of the gentlemen of Cali.

Jorge got on a radio and equipment was brought for the mercenaries to examine: night-vision goggles, low-cost bugging equipment, Desert Eagle guns, crossbows and a sniper rifle. Tomkins rolled his eyes at the inadequacies. Addressing the godfathers, he started to ask questions from a list he had formulated. As the cartel didn't know Pablo's whereabouts, Tomkins said that he couldn't act without real-time info on Pablo's location.

"How long will it take for you to find Pablo?" Gilberto asked.

"With what you know: how long do you think it will take?"

"A couple of weeks."

Disturbed by their ignorance of the mission's complexities, Tomkins restrained himself from shaking his head. He needed much longer than two weeks. "I'll bring a team with all the military skills required to complete this mission. These people are presently highly paid in various parts of the world. I can't calculate how long it will take to complete this mission, but we need to be paid in accordance with the risk. To finance the initial twelve-man team, I need a three-month advance payment. No matter how long the mission takes, all payments are to be for a minimum of three months, with an operational bonus payment to be discussed when the mission plan is formulated." After holding the gaze of each godfather, Tomkins asked for $1 million.

Without hesitating, Gilberto said that amount was no

problem. If they killed Pablo, they would receive up to $3 million plus a bonus. Tomkins could barely contain his excitement. More weapons arrived in the night, including submachine guns and shotguns.

The next day, Tomkins was flown over Pablo's Hacienda Nápoles ranch. He took pictures of the huge building with terracotta roof tiles, an airstrip, two helipads, a lake, swimming pools, various other buildings for guests and bodyguards, a soccer field, a tennis court, aircraft hangars, a bullring and a massive satellite dish. The perimeter was protected by steel fencing and thatched-roof guard towers. Barriers to entry included trees, shrubs and lakes. Bodyguards lived in an L-shaped building, which contained a museum with the early 1930s Cadillac like Al Capone's. Surveying the location made Tomkins realise the magnitude of killing Pablo.

He left Colombia to recruit a team. He chose some ex-members of the Special Air Service (SAS) – a special forces unit of the British Army – and a couple of ex-South African Reconnaissance Commandos, some of whom he had worked with. The younger ones were lean, fit and muscular. They weight-trained constantly and ran long distances. The older ones were stocky, worldly wise, scarred from bullets and shrapnel and hardened by experience, their bodies ravaged by combat and booze. One had a scar from knee to ankle from an ill-fated parachute drop.

In the UK, Tomkins went on a shopping spree. Cartel cash paid for bugging kits, radio scanners, frequency counters, direction-finding equipment, portable searchlights with infrared lenses, infrared markers with strobe lights visible to night-vision equipment, and medical equipment, including tracheotomy sets and inflatable splints. A security guard at Heathrow airport allowed his bulky luggage onto the plane without any questions asked. Jorge did the same for his luggage in Colombia.

As a precaution, Tomkins told only one member of the team the nature of the mission: Peter McAleese, a former paratrooper, SAS Regiment soldier, South African sergeant-major and

Rhodesian SAS soldier. From Scotland, built like a tank, with hardly any neck and hair, McAleese was highly respected among the mercenaries; the majority of whom had signed up for the mission on his word. He was the team leader.

Settling into apartments in Cali, the mercenaries were warned to be vigilant as kidnapping was common. They were given arms, but advised not to take them outside. "We'll be moving to another place soon," McAleese said, "where we can start our training. While we're here, don't go around in more than twos or draw any attention to yourselves. You must behave in a touristy manner." At the morning meeting, McAleese chastised two men for getting drunk the previous night. "Our mission is to kill Pablo Escobar," he said. "It's called Operation Phoenix."

Tomkins showed pictures of Pablo and aerial photos of Hacienda Nápoles. Using maps, they planned various reconnaissance routes. Jorge said that any reconnaissance in the vicinity of Hacienda Nápoles would be reported to Pablo, whose guards would swoop down on the pale-faced strangers. Using radios, the group tuned into conversations between traffickers and producers. The Spanish was translated by a skinny Colombian from New York who worked for the godfather Chepe.

Exotic women and disco bars in busy Cali distracted some of the men. They were relocated to a heavily guarded hilltop retreat frequented by one of Miguel's wives. It included a leisure complex set on thirty acres of gardens with ornamental bridges and streams. Maintenance men tended the Japanese garden. The mercenaries swam in the pool, sweated in the sauna and had access to horse riding, tennis, indoor bowling and quad bikes. Their food was prepared by a female chef. Refraining from alcohol, they drank crates of Coca-Cola.

Worried about the luxuries softening their men, Tomkins and McAleese enforced a strict discipline. At 6 AM, a mandatory run around the track commenced, followed by breakfast. Then came weight-training, volleyball and other activities. To divide the men into sections, a secret ballot was held to nominate leaders. The mercenaries were instructed to write down the name of the man they would most want to be in a foxhole with during a crisis.

After a month, Tomkins was transported to the cartel's offices in a suburb of Cali called Garden City. In his typical low-key style, Gilberto ran the business from a complex of single-storey terracotta buildings. His weapons of choice were phones, fax machines, telex machines, typists and secretaries. Tomkins was escorted to a workshop which received incoming goods. Refrigerators were unpacked and their back panels removed to reveal weapons manufactured in America that had travelled via Mexico. They were hidden in the false floor of a van, which was activated by tilting the vehicle to one side.

The mercenaries were delighted with the weapons' shipment: an assortment of guns, anti-tank rocket launchers, C4 demolition charges, ammunition and night-vision equipment. With the new arms, they performed a week of drills until everything was second nature. They practised repelling attacks by helicopters and night-time raids by Pablo's men. At a remote hilltop farm, they did drills with live ammunition, machine-gunning down imaginary enemies.

On their way back with their weapons, they went to a village bar. A policeman on a motorbike noticed them and stopped. Approaching them, he observed their black combat boots. After he spoke in Spanish, one of the mercenaries' escorts from the cartel intervened. Toting a mini-machine gun in a shoulder bag, Mario was ex-army, so he displayed his military ID. The unimpressed policeman yelled in Spanish, and both men argued. Some of the mercenaries started to move towards the truck to get weapons. Jorge told them to stay put and to not do anything drastic. Mario produced a radio and made a call. A man showed up on a motorbike with a bag of cartel cash. Mario gave the bag to the policeman, who departed.

In the second month, one of the South Africans quit as he believed an attempt to kill Pablo was a suicide mission. Tomkins flew to England for a replacement.

The Cali godfathers hosted lunches for Tomkins, McAleese and their two chaperones: Jorge and Mario. Gilberto assured them that Pablo had been seen in many places, but Tomkins viewed the information as stale and of no tactical value.

The mercenaries stayed focused on Hacienda Nápoles. Jorge and Mario provided detailed information about the property, and military and police reports on attempts to capture Pablo. After processing the info, Tomkins realised that some of his earlier assumptions were wrong. Originally, they had intended to land on the soccer field, but as they examined the photos under a microscope, they spotted anti-helicopter wires on the field. The helipads were wired. The only option was to land on a tennis court.

A jungle cabin fifty miles west of Cali was transformed into a base camp. Built on wooden piles, it had a big room with tables and benches, a kitchen and bathroom. Animal skulls adorned the back wall. An electric generator pumped water from the Manguido River. The cabin was equipped with a cook, a barbecue, mosquito nets, mattresses, cooking appliances, and food and drinks for the mercenaries, who arrived via helicopter. To avoid getting kidnapped by guerrillas, the men took turns on lookout duty.

A Huey helicopter arrived for the assault, which they painted emerald and white to appear to belong to the Colombian police, complete with a Colombian flag under its tail rotor and Policia Nacional on both sides of the fuselage. The jungle drills included firing rockets and detonating grenades. On the beach, they shot at the river and killed imaginary enemies. They rehearsed landing at Hacienda Nápoles and bringing in additional helicopters by using coloured smoke. Yellow meant safe to land, whereas red indicated landing in hostile fire. Using maps, they chose emergency rendezvous points in case they had to evacuate the mission on foot because the helicopters had been damaged. If that happened, they would broadcast emergency radio transmissions to aircraft circling above.

They sprayed a Hughes 500 helicopter olive to match military colours and altered the doorway to accommodate a mounted machine gun. Previous raids from the air on Hacienda Nápoles had met with no resistance. Pablo's staff had even offered refreshments to the authorities. The plan was to deceive the staff with the helicopters, and to mow them down with machine guns before the mercenaries were spotted. Explosives would be dropped along the front of the main house. Upon entering the property, any locked doors would be blown open with C4 explosives. The men received black ski masks and combat vests with special pockets to hold equipment such as grenades and radios. Backpacks were stocked with emergency supplies such as civilian clothes and medical emergency shock packs with syringes and morphine.

By the fourth month, Pablo's location was still unknown. Torrential rain trapped the men in the cabin, where they sweated blanketed by the humidity. Tomkins and McAleese were summoned to give a progress report to the godfathers at a ranch belonging to Chepe surrounded by cattle fields. Chepe's recently constructed mansion still had protective sheeting over its windows. The men arrived at a massive front door with Doric columns. About sixty armed bodyguards were on duty. Others were playing soccer.

Gilberto revealed that although there had been no sighting of Pablo, he knew that he was going to hold a family party at Hacienda Nápoles. It would be large and he would definitely be there. Although pleased that the cartel finally had info about Pablo being at a specific location at a certain time, Tomkins declined the opportunity because there would be women and children attending and they would get killed by machine-gun fire.

In ski masks and camouflage gear, the mercenaries resumed drills by the cabin. They practised launching assaults with rockets and grenades. From helicopters, they fired machine guns at the jungle. Practising so much gave them a permanent stink of guns and gunpowder. Equipment was adjusted after weaknesses were exposed and flimsy combat vests were replaced.

Months of rehearsing as if their lives depended upon it exhausted the mercenaries. Jorge flew all of them except for

Tomkins and McAleese to Panama City for a break. They partied in clubs and bars and took a scuba-diving course.

With the team absent, Tomkins and McAleese requested a meeting with the godfathers. They were transported to a luxury home, where they constructed a model of Hacienda Nápoles. They dangled aircraft from threads attached to the ceiling. They positioned helicopters on poles, so that they could replicate flights by hand. After they rehearsed the mission, they requested the godfathers.

The godfathers and four senior cartel members entered and sat down. Explaining what was about to happen, Tomkins and McAleese spoke in English, which a translator converted. They demonstrated the assault and ended with Pablo getting killed and the mercenaries leaving safely.

Gilberto stood and clapped, immediately joined by the rest, which delighted Tomkins and McAleese. Speaking in limited English, Chepe told Tomkins that he would pay an additional million dollars if he fetched Pablo's head. For that price, Tomkins agreed to make room for a piece of Pablo on the helicopter.

On June 3, 1989, the mercenaries awoke as usual to the cawing of jungle birds. The men swore at each other in a comradely way. Some shared sexual fantasies. Armed with guns, they went to the river for toilet purposes.

Hours later, their radio came alive in coded Spanish: Pablo Escobar was at his swimming pool at Hacienda Nápoles. Gilberto gave the go-ahead for the operation, which required two Huey helicopters. As one of the Hueys was getting repaired in Brazil, Gilberto proposed that a smaller Hughes helicopter be used. As the lone Huey would have to be overloaded to compensate for the missing helicopter, McAleese and the pilots objected on safety grounds. Having waited so long to get Pablo, Gilberto overrode the objections. He told the pilots to figure out how to handle the extra load. A pilot agreed that it could be done by redistributing the passengers and cargo. Gilberto ordered them to go as it might be their only chance and he announced another change. As soon as the mercenaries had landed and launched the attack, a plane was going to land on the opposite side of Pablo's ranch with over a dozen hit men sent by Pacho, who had a score to settle with Pablo.

The excitement was palpable as McAleese told the team to get ready. The men cheered and grabbed battle gear. Steel clunked and rattled as each of them checked their equipment, which was double-checked by another man. They tested their radios. An hour later, McAleese addressed the men with a final briefing. "I have colour-coded the areas of Pablo's mansion, which I've divided into three sections. The back of the house is black. The right of the house is red. The front is white. Once inside, the house team will advise me in the gunship which section they're in and they'll call out their position as they move. The support group will target the area one section ahead of the position of the house team. The gunship will act as an aerial stop group that can eliminate runners into or out of the building. I have 300,000 pesos emergency money for every man in case you have to make your way to an emergency rendezvous point."

Helicopter blades swooshed. The Hughes 500 buzzed like an angry bee. "Let's do it!" McAleese said. Packed into the helicopters, the men sat cramped amid weapons, explosives, ammunition and fuel tanks. Before noon, the helicopters set off on a two-hour journey to a refuel site, ten minutes from Hacienda Nápoles. The men were quiet and focused.

Eighty miles away from the refuel site, rain lashed the helicopters. Wind rocked the men from side to side. The helicopters attempted to climb above the low clouds. Approaching a ridge called Silent Knife, the two helicopters separated to find the safest ways to ascend. One minute they were in a cloud, the next they could see a section of a green mountain.

Within a cloud as thick as cotton, the Hughes 500 struggled to ascend. At 8,200 feet, wind and rain tossed the helicopter around. The pilot tried to navigate between the mountain peaks, which were suddenly visible, but a cloud filled the space and he was flying blind. The dense cloud muffled the sound of the helicopter as if someone had turned down the volume of its propellers.

Crunch! The helicopter crashed. Tomkins was thrown upside down and his head throbbed with pain. The other two men in the cabin were gone, and so was the helicopter door. Tree branches reached inside through the door space.

Bracing for an explosion, Tomkins grabbed onto the branches and crawled out on his hands and knees. He ended up in a forest with no sign of anyone who had been in the helicopter. In shock and confused, he went downhill to a clearing, where he took some deep breaths to regain his thoughts. Gazing up, he saw the helicopter on its side, sizzling and emitting steam. Perplexed, he wondered whether he would be killed if the satchel charges exploded.

Further up the slope, McAleese limped and staggered out of the vegetation. Tomkins climbed up to help him. He found the satchel charges, cut the fuse trains and removed the detonators. Two crew members limped out of the vegetation, one's face covered in blood. With broken ribs and barely able to walk, McAleese had been injured the most. Bleeding from the skull, Tomkins was afraid to touch himself in case he could feel his own brains. He suspected his rifle had penetrated his head.

Noticing the pilot was absent, they scanned the area. Forging his way through vegetation, Tomkins managed to crawl back to the helicopter, which was on its side. Entering the cockpit, Tomkins found the pilot in a contorted position, his face deathly pale. Upon hearing Tomkins greet him, the pilot opened his eyes, but didn't move. In Spanish, he mumbled about his leg. Tomkins felt the pilot's leg for broken bones. It seemed OK. A wound at the back of the pilot's hips shocked Tomkins. His liver was hanging out of his torso. By moving his hand across his throat and shaking his head, Tomkins signalled to the others at the helicopter's doorway that the pilot was dying.

"You're going to be OK," Tomkins said.

In the vegetation, they searched for medical supplies among

the debris, but most of it was damaged. Holding a morphine injection, Tomkins checked for a vein on the pilot's arm, but they had all collapsed from shock. His left arm had been sliced from his shoulder to his hand. Bone was jutting out. He started mumbling prayers. Several times, Tomkins stuck a needle in the side of the pilot's neck and injected morphine. Minutes later, the pilot died. Tomkins removed his dog tags, which ended up at the pilot's military funeral, where he was honoured for dying on an official anti-drugs operation.

Tomkins searched for a vein on McAleese's arms, but they had collapsed. He cut open a saline drip bag, and McAleese drank from it. They moved him to cover and tried to minimise his discomfort. They found a radio and told Jorge that they had crashed and the pilot was dead. Tomkins gave a compass bearing and draped a red towel over a shrub, so the location could be identified.

A Huey helicopter arrived and swayed in the wind, unable to land. The pilot radioed that he would land at the bottom of a stream that started west of the crash. Using C4, Tomkins lit a fire for McAleese, who was trembling with pain. They insulated his bulletproof jacket with shell dressings from the shock packs. Hoping to find a stream, Tomkins took off through the jungle canopy, mindful of stepping on rotten trees, which acted like trapdoors. He headed towards the rays of daylight penetrating the vegetation, and found himself on a cliff. Eventually, he located the stream and followed its curves down the mountain, obstructed by dense foliage. As the stream widened, he crawled down through the cold water, rather than battling the vegetation.

Another cliff stopped his journey. He trekked along the ridge, searching for a way down. It had been an hour since he had left the crash site and daylight was fading. Hearing branches breaking and voices, he froze. This was Pablo's territory, and if the locals found him, they would surely take him to El Patrón. The voices belonged to the other two crew members. Although relieved they were comrades, Tomkins was upset that McAleese had been left alone with no radio. They said McAleese had told them to go.

Fifteen minutes later, they reached another cliff. Due to zero visibility, they stopped near the edge. Soaked and cold, they couldn't sleep. Wetness prevented them from lighting a fire. Dawn brought light and the sound of a helicopter. Assuming that their rescuers were ascending the mountain, the three men entered the vegetation again, and attempted to make their way down. After four hours, they heard branches breaking below them. Armed with a submachine gun, they listened to the Spanish voices approaching. The absence of English made Tomkins fear the worst: they were Pablo's men. He hid.

Two unarmed peasants appeared. Mario yelled at them. They identified themselves as friends sent to rescue them. The three men emerged from the vegetation and claimed to be a military operation in need of assistance to get McAleese down. Nimble like animals, the rescuers guided the men down a steep rock face covered with moss. To steady themselves, they clutched onto trees. Six hours later, they arrived at a dilapidated shack enclosed by a tree-branch fence. Hot chocolate in tin cups warmed them.

A farmer announced that the military had arrived. Soldiers were scouring the mountainside. Tomkins assumed that the aircraft activity in the area had been spotted, and Pablo had ordered the search. Mario picked up the submachine gun and ordered everybody to leave. They abandoned the shack for the cover of the jungle and ascended the mountain at its edge, so that they could see what was happening below.

By late afternoon, the farmers had taken them to a small valley dappled with cowpats, and into another shack. Mario and the farmers left for food and so that Mario could contact the godfathers. In case Pablo's men approached, Tomkins and the other crew member found a hiding place. As the sun set, Tomkins noticed that his knee had swollen and he was caked in blood. His head was still throbbing.

After darkness, Mario and the farmers returned with food and drink. They all got in the shack and lit a fire outside the doorway.

The cold kept Tomkins awake. He worried about McAleese freezing to death on the wet mountain.

Dawn brought rain and fog. By late afternoon, the mist had cleared and a helicopter arrived. Unable to land on the rough terrain, it hovered low enough for a rescue team to jump out, armed with machetes and ropes. The three crew members scrambled on board the helicopter, which flew to a ranch airstrip. A small plane brought them to Cali, where vehicles took them to an apartment. They were greeted by Gilberto and a doctor, who gave them first aid. They showered and changed into regular clothes.

With broken ribs, McAleese spent three nights on the mountain shivering, delirious and caked in the pilot's blood. He wrapped himself in jackets, but stayed cold. On the second night, he had an out-of-body experience: he floated away from his painful existence. Dawn snapped him out of it. He lit plastic explosives to keep warm. On the third night, he dreamt that he was in a grave. The next day, he searched the helicopter for supplies. The cold had suspended the decomposition of the pilot's corpse, which was free of flies and a grey-blue colour. He found a drip and some sweets.

Back on a mountain ledge, he heard Colombian voices. He grabbed a submachine gun, rolled onto his stomach and prayed that enemies were not approaching. As the dark hair of the first man appeared, he aimed his gun and told the son of a bitch to stop right there or else.

The man yelled amigo, and gave Jorge's name as a code-word. McAleese lowered his gun and smiled. One of the five men poured a Pepsi down his throat. Another cut off his boots and trousers to see his injuries. They dressed him in fresh clothes. The journey down through thick jungle vegetation and waterfalls was agonising. It took over a day for a helicopter rescue. He was transferred to an airplane, which Jorge piloted.

Even though the mission to kill Pablo had failed, the team was awarded an operational bonus for risking their lives. The godfathers wanted to resume the mission as their sources had revealed that Pablo was unaware of the aborted attempt. Tomkins agreed with one condition: he would hire his own helicopter pilots. The godfathers accepted. To prevent any overloading of helicopters, they ordered two more, so that three would be available.

In June 1989, Tomkins flew back to England, followed by two female Colombians who had smuggled money to pay for the mission. He recruited two pilots and returned to Cali, where McAleese was still recovering. While the team leaders stayed in Cali, the rest of the men were moved to Panama to await the signal for the next mission.

CHAPTER 17
GALÁN ASSASSINATION

At his 46th birthday, the popular presidential candidate, Luis Carlos Galán, came across as preoccupied and uncommunicative. Questioned by his brothers about who wanted to kill him, he responded the traffickers, some politicians, the military and the guerrillas. While reading his palm, his sister saw something terrible. His family said that they could do without having any more martyrs and that only alive could he best serve the country. Encouraged by his family, he moved to England, but after six months, he felt as if he were failing the people, so he returned to Colombia. From the airport, he travelled in an open-topped car as if challenging death. His family's suffering resumed.

An astrologer warned that he would be betrayed and that he needed to be alert for danger in August. Living in the same building as his parents in Bogotá, he learned that it would be bombed, so he moved to get them out of danger. Before his family even knew his new number, the first call was a death threat.

The "some politicians" Galán had referred to included Santo, who travelled to East Antioquia to meet El Patrón. "I warned you, Pablo, that if you did not kill Pastrana, he would become the Mayor of Bogotá, and eventually the President of Colombia. But your worst enemy now is Galán. He is rising in the political polls because he is openly speaking out against you, the Mafia and drug trafficking." Hiding in the forest surrounding Hacienda Nápoles, Pablo contemplated Santo's advice.

Their next meeting was in a small house six miles from the main house on the estate. "Pablo, I bring you grave news. Galán will be the next president of Colombia. He is receiving support from the US Embassy. There's nothing we can do. After he becomes president, he'll extradite you. Using all of the power of the state, he'll get you. I am telling you, Pablo, you must kill him." Santo was the voice of Galán's enemies in the political establishment, powerful people receiving drug money who were afraid that Galán's crusade against corruption would expose them.

Pablo and Santo analysed the possible consequences in light of the aftermath of Lara Bonilla's assassination.

"Galán is going to seriously investigate Lara Bonilla's death," Santo said. "They were inseparable friends. You need to kill him now while he is vulnerable, Pablo. When he's president, you won't be able to get to him."

"What's the word in political circles?" Pablo said, sitting in an armchair. "Are they certain he'll win against Gómez?"

"Gómez will never be the president of Colombia. Of that you can be certain. The future president of Colombia is Galán."

"Who's going to be the next president of Colombia?"

"Look, Pablo, it's going to be Galán, but it actually doesn't matter who it will be. Galán is your enemy. He threw you to the DEA. He humiliated you."

Pablo contemplated in silence. His bodyguard, Popeye, wondered what would happen to them all if the boss agreed to the assassination.

Santo broke the silence. "Kill him, Pablo," he said in a slow, coaxing voice. "Kill him. Kill him."

For five minutes, Pablo remained silent. Gazing at Santo, he stood up. "Go to Medellín," he said to Popeye, "and find Ricardo Prisco."

In north-eastern Medellín, Ricardo Prisco ran a gang in Aranjuez. Tall and athletic, Ricardo was popular among the masses due to an altruistic streak running through his crimes. He sold stolen clothes to the locals for a pittance. Indigent students and impoverished families received his financial support. He built three sanctuaries devoted to the Blessed Virgin Mary Helper of Christians, a.k.a. the Virgin of the Assassins.

Out of four brothers, Ricardo was the oldest. He posed for mugshots with an unnerving gaze. Below short, thick, wavy hair, his face lacked emotion. If Pablo wanted somebody killed, Ricardo had a network in the Medellín slums with endless assassins. Adept at high-profile hits, he had coordinated the murders of two judges: Hernando Baquero, who had drafted extradition laws, and Bogotá Superior Court Judge Tulio Manuel Castro Gil. The reputation of the Prisco gang had caused some judges with contracts on them to flee from Medellín. In his letters to Pablo, he offered his services and unconditional support, and signed them, "With you until death."

While Popeye travelled to Prisco, Pablo researched Galán's schedule. On his campaign tour, he was due to lecture at the University of Medellín. Pablo instructed Prisco to form a team armed with rockets and guns. They would blast Galán with the rocket on his way from the university, and finish him off with the machine guns. He ordered Popeye to buy a Mazda station wagon in the full legal name of the Cali Cartel leader Pacho Herrera, which would be used for the assassination. With two ex-soldiers experienced in handling rockets, Prisco left for Medellín to organise the assault.

At a meeting with the Extraditables, Pablo announced his decision to kill Galán. The majority objected on the grounds that the backlash would be terrible. They urged him to discuss it with the whole cartel to avoid repeating the Lara Bonilla situation. "I am not consulting you! I am informing you so that you can start looking for good hideouts. Either we finish Galán or he finishes us!"

The hit team was in place long before the arrival of Galán, whose late lunch had delayed his schedule. From a third-floor window, a woman spotted a man hiding in the grass and called the police. When the authorities arrived, the ex-soldier hid his rocket, dropped his trousers and pretended to pee. While the police under Colonel Quintero's command questioned the ex-soldier, his twelve associates escaped. More police arrived and found the rocket and weapons.

Quintero called Galán. "They are offering 200 million pesos for your head. We have just neutralised an attack." He urged Galán to cancel the event.

"Dr Galán," a journalist asked, "there is concern about money being offered for an attempt on you. Is that true?"

"I am really offended," the politician said, "because everything goes up in value except the price of my head, which has been costing the same for a decade … That's the elementary version of the person who moves within the criminal world and enters into a chain of psychopathic and criminal acts, thinking that because I am a protagonist of Colombian politics, who expresses my worries about the problem and invites the national and international society to move before it. So they think they can build their criminal empire by eliminating me, but they are totally wrong because men can be eliminated, but not the ideas. On the contrary, when sometimes men are eliminated, ideas grow stronger. Therefore, even from the strategic point of view, it is the most absurd method." To a packed audience at the University of Medellín, Galán lambasted Pablo.

The news reported, "After the failed attempt on his life in Medellín and despite multiple threats, [Galán] and his head of debate [Trujillo] continue their tireless tour throughout the country to win the Liberal Party candidacy in the upcoming elections. Over the month of August, he has visited over 100 municipalities, taking the project of renovation he has defended for over several years. Galán continues to score first in all surveys and is beginning to look like the next candidate for the presidency." The broadcast showed Galán in his signature red shirt, surrounded by cheering supporters. "With clear, diverse and complementary answers that contribute to the development of rural Colombia to rescue it and transform its life conditions. However, talking only about peasants isn't enough. Because among them, the ones who suffer the most and have fewer opportunities and face the highest risks for the dignity of their existence, are the peasant women and the elderly peasants."

The failed plan prompted Pablo to arrange some meetings at Hacienda Nápoles. He posted lookouts by the Oro River on the road to Medellín and on the Magdalena River on the way to Bogotá. His contacts at a military air base were on alert to report any suspicious aircraft. Paramilitaries working for Gacha and Henry Pérez bolstered security. After having a bath, Pablo dressed in jeans and a blue, short-sleeved shirt. He instructed his lawyers and gave them files.

Popeye interrupted the meeting. "A caravan of military trucks is coming down the highway."

"Stay cool. They are heading to Bogotá," Pablo said.

Popeye hurried away, but returned more agitated. "Boss, the trucks are entering Nápoles."

"Stay cool. They want to see the zoo and then they'll move on." The military trucks parked at the zoo. "Take them sandwiches." Finished with his lawyers, Pablo went outside to greet the traffickers, including Gacha, Henry Pérez, Kiko Moncada and Negro Galeano. While rolling a piece of paper in his fingers, he proposed the assassination of Jorge Enrique Pulido, who produced TV programmes.

"He's working with the DEA."

"And he's a magistrate of the Supreme Court of General Maza."

They agreed he had to go and also Colonel Quintero.

"We have to kill Quintero now," Gacha said. "The bastard arrested and harassed my son at Medellín airport."

Pablo picked the paper ball from his mouth. "We'll take care of that one. I have information obtained by Santo: Galán will be elected president. If we allow that to happen, we are all screwed. The time has come. I tried unsuccessfully to kill him in Medellín. Because of the failure of the operation, nobody can get near him now. The new attack will have to be carried out in Bogotá." Responding to objections raised by Gacha and Kiko Moncada, he said, "If you don't support me, I'll do it alone. What happens, happens. If Galán comes to office, extradition will be impossible to abolish. We need to scare the politicians, and Galán's death will send a clear message to the others. The persecution that will follow won't affect us too much. We all know how to move under pressure."

For two hours, more objections were raised. Turning to Gacha, Pablo said, "Friend, it is Galán or us." Towards the end of the meeting, Pablo had steered them into agreement. The presidential tour would take Galán to Soacha and Villeta, both in Gacha's territory. If they couldn't assassinate him in Soacha, they would blow him up in Villeta. One of the Extraditables, Henry Pérez, put forward his best man to lead the operation: Jaime Rueda. Pérez was a paramilitary leader who protected Gacha's cocaine facilities from guerrilla attacks. In return, Gacha provided arms to Pérez.

With the meeting over, food was served. Around 1 AM, a group of virgins whom Pablo had flown in sashayed naked around the pool. Traffickers who took the women back to rooms were recorded. The sex broadcasts were part of a collective voyeuristic enjoyment.

Three days later, Rueda arrived with five men. "I'm offering you 200 million pesos for this work," Pablo said.

"I'll need more than that," Rueda said.

"The money is no problem. You can have it from the Extraditables fund. I'll even throw in some merchandise to make things fair," Gacha said, referring to a cocaine bonus.

"In that case, let's call it even," Rueda said, smiling.

"What do you need?" Gacha said.

"A travel allowance. A mini submachine gun."

"Popeye, buy him a mini submachine gun," Pablo said.

"Rueda is my best man," Pérez said. "Galán's death is certain."

Two days later, in a bar called the Black Dog, Popeye paid 200 million pesos for a mini submachine gun, which he took to Pablo at Hacienda Nápoles, who said, "Now we just have to wait. Our lives are in Gacha's hands."

On the morning of August 18, 1989, Colonel Quintero was travelling discreetly with a driver and a bodyguard. Shots from long-range weapons stationed in two cars ended his career of thirty-four years and seriously wounded the bodyguard.

On the afternoon of the same day, Galán was scheduled to speak in Soacha, south of Bogotá. He told the media: "The recent events, the death of Colonel Franklin Quintero and Judge Valencia, are saying that anyone who fights to eradicate our conditions of injustice and social backwardness is at serious risk. This will be a difficult campaign. The enemies of democracy are becoming more sophisticated. But we'll keep going. We knew it would not be easy."

The intelligence services had warned about an assassination plot in Bogotá. His staff had tried to divert him to Valledupar instead, which was near Barranquilla, where Galán was going to attend a 1990 FIFA World Cup qualification soccer game, which included the Colombian team. Instead, he made a last-minute decision to go to Soacha, after receiving assurances from his head of security, Torregrosa, who had been assigned by General Maza after Galán had met the general to demand security improvements. The other bodyguards were suspicious of Torregrosa, whose appointment had divided the group. They frowned on his personal use of cars and for sending them out prematurely and unnecessarily to locations. They heard him in Galán's office, speaking English on the phone. Unsettled, they had asked Galán to remove Torregrosa, but Maza had responded that he had complete confidence in him.

"The security of the square is guaranteed," Torregrosa said. "The people at the front holding placards will be from the DAS. There'll be 200 policemen taking care of everything."

In a prophetic announcement, Galán said: "Today I received another invitation to abandon the public activity, but I assumed politics as a service action that demands sacrifice and implies vicissitudes you should handle. I couldn't disappoint the thousands of Colombians I meet every day at the public square. I would never forgive myself for that, and I would prefer to die in the attempt."

At the massive event, two hit teams arrived, carrying secret police ID cards. One four-man team waited up the road with a rocket launcher to finish Galán off if he attempted to escape. Members of the second team dispersed among the excited and drunken spectators, wearing beige hats to identify each other. In the event that the hit teams in Soacha failed, dynamite had been planted in the town of Villeta and at the stadium in the city of Barranquilla.

At 8:30 PM, Galán arrived in a blue car, lifting the spirits of the boisterous crowd of 10,000. People cheered and waved red flags and banners. With security lax, one of the accomplices easily passed the machine gun to Rueda, who hid under the speakers' platform, disguised by banners. His widow later described security that night as practically nothing. The majority of his bodyguards had been sent to the location of his event the following day. Due to the density of the crowd, Galán's vehicle was unable to get him to the platform. Wearing a bulletproof vest, he assured his staff that they would not stay long due to security concerns. As he cruised along on an open-back truck flanked by bodyguards in suits, the crowd repeated, "Galán! My friend! The people support you!"

Exposed on the truck, he was advised to walk the remaining distance to the platform. His bodyguards and DAS agents forged a way through the placard-waving crowd, but Torregrosa avoided going onto the stage, which was his duty. Carried by aides and besieged by animated supporters who were attempting to touch him and shake his hand, Galán moved briskly past a cluster of pink balloons and arrived at the podium. On a wooden stage supported by a steel frame, his bodyguards scanned the area for threats and signalled the all-clear. Back on his feet, he ascended the stairs.

On the platform, he was greeted by a councilman, standing next to men in light-coloured suits. Galán raised his arms, waving at the supporters, who cheered riotously. With his target's

PABLO ESCOBAR'S STORY

midsection exposed, Rueda emerged from under the platform and fired dumdum bullets – which expand on impact – upwards into Galán's stomach. Blasted in the abdomen, side and groin, Galán collapsed with severe internal bleeding. While gunfire sprayed multiple times and supporters screamed, several people fell, some hit by bullets – including the local Liberal Party leader – others just scrambling out of the way. Hoping to shield themselves from gunshots, some pressed themselves to the side of the podium and clutched onto the wooden frame. As shots continued from the accomplices, most of the people in the area remained crouched. Bodyguards in suits drew their weapons, but Rueda had acted too fast for them to retaliate. Guards in beige suits, one holding a machine gun, dragged a body to a car. Rueda rushed to a transit office, put on a grey sports jacket and escaped through the crowd.

The whole scene was caught on camera and is available on YouTube under, "The Luis Carlos Galán Assassination." While everyone fell to the ground, the brave cameraman kept recording with his trembling hands.

"They got him!"

"Oh my God!"

"Come on! Move aside! Help us here!"

A radio station announced: "When there's news, Caracol lets you know about it. Extra! This is a last-minute news broadcast on Caracol. There has been heavy gunfire at the main square in Soacha. The candidate for nomination for the Liberal Party was about to deliver a speech at the square. Early reports claimed that some people were injured. Yes, we have received a report from the police that [Galán] was injured in the shooting which occurred in Soacha."

While members of the terror-struck crowd scattered, Galán lost a massive amount of blood. Eventually, bodyguards carried him to a car. Instead of taking him to the nearby hospital in Soacha, they took him further away to a health centre in Bosa that lacked resources.

At home, Galán's wife and children heard about an incident

at Soacha. Like many times before, they assumed that the news was false and that Galán would call at any moment to tell them to remain calm because everything was fine.

"News flash! [Galán] was the victim of a terrorist attack tonight. This happened at a political rally in Soacha, near Bogotá. He was taken to a [hospital], according to the first reports. We don't know how badly he was injured. He was wounded in the head and the stomach. He has two wounds in his stomach."

Glued to developments, Pablo, Santo and Gacha were disappointed by the news, which devastated Galán's wife and children, who questioned the police assigned to protecting their house and raced to the hospital, hoping his bulletproof vest had saved him.

The news announced: "The Boso Police Department just informed us that [Galán] was wounded in the shooting that took place at Soacha. He was taken to the Bosa Hospital according to early reports. We still don't know the severity of Galán's injuries."

In an operating theatre, a doctor gave Galán a blood transfusion, but didn't have the necessary equipment to perform surgery. He was transferred to another hospital. Galán's frantic wife and sons arrived, only to be told he wasn't there.

"We regret to inform you that [Galán] is currently being treated at the National Welfare Clinic … The cameraman closest to Galán confirmed that he was not shot in the head. He saw him being shot in the stomach, and told us that Galán was conscious through it all. So, let us pray and send our good wishes that nothing bad happens to Galán."

Galán's private secretary, Juan Lozano, saw Torregrosa talking suspiciously on a phone. Lozano grabbed the receiver and heard a voice: "Is he dead yet? Did he die?" The other bodyguards, some wounded, implicated Torregrosa, who disappeared under the protection of General Maza, rumoured to have been sent to Venezuela.

In a TV interview, Santo said, "Me and Senator Galán don't agree on many subjects, but I must say that he is a valuable asset to the Liberal Party and the country. I'm so sorry about what happened. I hope his condition is not serious and my prayers are with him."

Pablo told Popeye, "We must remain alert because if he survives, we'll never be able to get near him again."

Galán's family arrived at a hospital surrounded by hundreds. The crowd let them through, and they were shown to a waiting room. At 10:15 PM, he died on the operating table. A surgeon told his family that they had done everything possible to revive him but he had lost too much blood from getting shot in the groin. They all wept, including his father, who sobbed in front of his children for the first time.

His death was headline news:

"We regret to inform the people of Colombia that Galán has passed away. Senator Galán suffered several gunshot wounds when he was about to deliver his speech at Soacha's main square."

"Galán died tonight. This is a dark day for Colombia. They killed him. The chief of the Antioquian police was killed this morning, and in the evening they also got Senator and candidate for president Galán."

"He has died. We're sorry to inform the Colombian people that Galán, the candidate for president, according to medical sources who have spoken with our reporter, has died at the Kennedy Hospital."

Judicial officials wanted to take the corpse for an examination by a forensics team, but the family objected, and an autopsy was performed at the hospital. Out of nine impacts to the body, only one had been fatal. Examining his bulletproof vest, his sister noticed a small dent in the lower part. She imagined him waving his arms and how the bullet would not have entered if his hands had been down. Believing that his spirit needed gentle love and attention to counteract the violence, she caressed his hands, arms and legs, while whispering for his spirit to have a happy trip. Next was his mother's turn. She addressed the corpse as if it were a baby. His wife was surprised by the warmth in his hands. They dressed him in a dark tie, striped with the colours of the

Colombian flag. After pondering what to put on his feet, some of the family removed their socks and offered them to him.

After turning off his radio, Pablo – in the mountains west of Medellín – warned his guards to be alert. In a kiosk facing the river, he sat alone, lost in thought. Bracing for a strong response by the government, he reassured himself with the knowledge that many powerful people were involved.

Two hours later, Gacha arrived in a victorious mood. "This is a great day for the Mafia and the Extraditables. Now that the easy part is over, the hard part will come."

"I'm pleased with the death of Colonel Quintero since he touched my family," Pablo said. For hours, they discussed the possible consequences in a sombre tone with alcohol absent. Prepared for war, Pablo pledged that he would not go on the run like in the aftermath of Lara Bonilla. Around 2 AM, he took three drags from a joint of weed and slept at dawn.

At 4 AM, the family left the hospital with the coffin and travelled through a city full of flags outside of homes and on cars, while appreciating the peaceful resolve of his supporters.

"If he had been violent," his wife said, "or an inciter like Gaitán, the Liberal leader of the first half of the twentieth century, who preached against the oligarchies, there would have been another destruction of Bogotá. In this century, the three most important leaders of Liberalism – Uribe, Gaitán and Galán – died violently without becoming presidents of Colombia."

The Spectator published the headline "Galán Killed." With Galán gone, the staff worried that the Medellín Cartel would target them next. They prayed for Pablo to die before he could murder them. With Galán gone, Pablo was formulating a plan to attack the offices of *The Spectator*.

The newspapers headlined with:

"The Mafia killed Galán" – *The Time*
"Assassination of Hope" – *La Presna*
"The Country Crumbles. Galán KILLED" – *El Siglo*
"Colombia Loses Hope" – *Cromos*
"Grief and Scandal Over Galán's Murder" – *La Republica*

In the aftermath of Galán's death, the president declared a state of siege. "The assassination that took place in our country is definite proof that a small group of terrorists, drug dealers and murderers has declared war on Colombia. The government must wage this war. We must strike down with the full power of the law. We must enforce martial law. We deeply regret Galán's death, and we promise his family and this country that his murderers, the masterminds and perpetrators will be punished severely.

"The death of two important, bright, intelligent Colombians, who were important to our country, makes us profoundly sad, but it must also make us hate their murderers. I want to share my condolences with the families. What was started by Colonel Quintero and Senator Galán will be carried on by this administration. We will find and punish their murderers. That is the promise this government is determined to keep."

The president issued executive orders to establish an elite task force, consisting of top members of the Army and police, to hunt down Pablo and the Medellín Cartel. Colonel Martínez was put in charge. He intended to use wiretaps, rewards, rural patrolling, checkpoints and intelligence. With thousands of hit men at his disposal, Pablo intended to counterattack the task force.

President George HW Bush made a statement: "In such difficult times, democratic nations faced with such common threats to their national security must stand together. Today we stand together with Colombia. The narco-traffickers who again have robbed Colombia of a courageous leader must be defeated. Colombians must know that we stand by its efforts to move aggressively against these criminals who seek to destroy both our societies." When it came to battling traffickers, never had such strong words of support been issued by a US president to the rulers of Colombia. Bush was itching to send troops.

Before Galán had even been buried, Santo proposed – to the other three nominees for the leadership of the Liberal Party, including César Gaviria – that the polls should be called off and that the four of them should choose the next candidate.

At Galán's funeral, people chanted, "Galán, our friend. We will be with you until the end." Adorned with white and red flowers and a Colombian flag, his coffin was carried down a street crowded with people waving white handkerchiefs and holding flowers and banners.

"What a flawless, transparent life," one son said, fighting back tears. "What an honourable man! Colombians stand up and demand justice. I pray to God that this sacrifice will serve to make our society react in support of the government and the institutions. While calling for a more efficient administration without giving into those who murder and commit other violent actions. I also wish to ask Mr César Gaviria, on behalf of the people of Colombia, to pick up my father's banners. You can count on our support to become the president that Colombia wants and needs. The legitimate heir of the flag of my father is César Gaviria and he must be the president of Colombia." After the speech, he hugged Gaviria, who now was sure to win the election with Galán's support behind him.

Enraged by Galán's son's proposal, Santo decided that the future president was not going to be decided by a teenager. Despite Santo's insistence that the four nominees should make the decision, Gaviria objected: he wanted to submit his name for the popular consultation. He believed that Galán's son had significantly changed his prospects. Santo argued that cancelling the popular consultation would unite the Liberal Party and that the candidate should be chosen from the previous shortlist of nominees, which excluded Gaviria. Believing that Galán would have wanted the candidate to be chosen through a popular consultation, Gaviria pointed out that he had received Galán's banners and that the people would support him despite Santo's plan. Pablo assured Santo that Gaviria would soon join Galán.

Under General Maza's leadership, the DAS claimed that the Medellín Cartel had put a $500,000 contract out on Galán. Pablo and Gacha were blamed.

With the news reporting Pablo as a murder suspect and the government offering a reward for his capture, Pablo's mother visited him, hoping to get an explanation. "Did you see the news?"

"Yes, Mom," Pablo said, "but don't believe that I did everything they say. I'm not that bad, and the first person I would tell what I do is you. I'm not a saint, but if they forced me to be bad, what can I do?"

Behind the scenes, Galán's family suspected Maza of being a co-conspirator in the assassination. As well as issuing the order to move the bodyguards to the next location, which left Galán exposed, Maza had removed the leader of the bodyguards whom Galán trusted the most and put Torregrosa in charge. The family was convinced that those decisions were part of a bigger plot.

With pressure on them to produce results in the wake of Galán's murder, dozens were arrested, five of whom were paraded on TV. General Maza and the National Police director Colonel Oscar Peláez announced that Alberto Júbiz Hasbún was the main suspect. To support their claim, they put up reward posters in Soacha showing pictures of Júbiz Hasbún and his alleged co-conspirators. Enticed by reward money, a dozen people claimed to have seen Hasbún and his accomplices at the crime scene. Even though their testimonies contradicted each other, General Maza endorsed the evidence and published a chart of the criminal organisation. By solving the case so quickly, Maza and the National Police director became national heroes. It took years for Hasbún and his accomplices to be acquitted. Shortly after his release, Hasbún died from a heart attack.

Pablo joked that he couldn't possibly have killed Galán because the assassins had been arrested. With the case solved, Rueda's accomplices easily left Medellín and eluded capture.

Some journalists claimed that Galán had been shot again on his way to the hospital.

While the authorities retaliated, Pablo and the Extraditables hid and moved around. The police raided 920 properties, confiscated 744 weapons, 1,128 vehicles, 106 aircraft and nineteen helicopters. Pablo sent Popeye to Medellín to pay Rueda 200 million pesos. Popeye changed his appearance and travelled with fake documents to fool the checkpoints. Demonised by the media, Pablo planned to bomb the headquarters of *The Spectator* in Bogotá and *Vanguardia Liberal* in Bucaramanga.

The first clue about the real assassins came from a former partner of Gacha in the emerald business. Dissension among the emerald traders had caused a rebellion against Gacha, who had ordered the assassination of his first boss, Gilberto Molina. After arriving at a party at Molina's house, two-dozen hit men had assassinated Molina and sixteen guests. A former partner of Gacha's in the emerald business, Pablo Elías Delgadillo, was studying the cover of *Cromos* magazine, which featured a photo of the crime scene at Soacha, including the stampeding attendees. With his eyes drawn to a lone man in a white hat stood by the platform seemingly unfazed by the chaos, Delgadillo recognised the man holding a banner as an emerald miner. Suspecting that the miner had been involved in the assassination, he informed the military and helped to capture him. In captivity, the miner gave up Rueda Rocha.

Suspected of cooperating with the police, Rueda and three of his men, including his half-brother, were killed. Before his death, his half-brother wrote a letter to his mother to explain what had happened: it was a conspiracy between corrupt politicians and the Mafia to eradicate their common enemy. Galán's widow even noticed a triumphant look on the faces of some of Galán's political enemies.

Eventually, Juan Manuel Galán, the candidate's son, wrote a book about his father. He blamed Maza and General Peláez of the DIJIN for framing Hasbún and his associates to derail a legitimate investigation and to hide that the perpetrators were paramilitaries trained by mercenaries in the Magdalena Medio region. He claimed that Maza was a willing accomplice even though he was Pablo's enemy because the general was working for the Cali Cartel. Although the cartels were at war, they were in agreement about eliminating Galán. With Maza's oversight, the DAS had dismantled the bodyguards before the attack, and during the attack the DAS had pretended that security was in place. After the attack, the DAS had led the investigations on false paths and fabricated evidence. He cited the co-conspirators as paramilitaries and Liberal Party politicians who worked for the traffickers, voted for their laws and had attempted to overthrow extradition multiple times. With the polls showing his father with a 70 per cent probability of winning the election, some corrupt politicians had joined the conspiracy to safeguard their dark interests. The only one a judge recommended to investigate was Santo, but in the immediate aftermath, the prosecution found that the recommendation had no merit.

Galán's family wanted Pablo captured alive in the hope of learning the truth. In one of his final letters before his death, he wrote: "If I paid to kill Cano, I will acknowledge it. If I gave money for Galán, the same. But, if those who are against me had to do with those [crimes], they will also pay. It will be the total clarification."

On May 13, 2005, the former justice minister and congressman of the Colombian Liberal Party, Santo, was arrested and accused of being the intellectual author of Galán's murder. According to the confession of Escobar's former hit man, Popeye, Santo had suggested Galán's murder at a secret meeting in order to eliminate his competition should Galán ever win the election. During the original murder investigation, Santo had been mentioned and his involvement was rumoured, but no direct evidence existed. From prison, Popeye told the media that he had earlier denied Santo's participation due to the congressman's political power at the time. On October 11, 2007, Santo was sentenced to twenty-four years for the murder. He was released on appeal, but in August 2011 the Supreme Court reinstated the conviction, and he surrendered himself.

In 2009, General Maza was questioned about Galán's death. The authorities wanted to know why he had suddenly replaced Galán's head of security with Torregrosa, when his duty had been to protect the candidate, who had received numerous death threats and one attempted murder. Investigators knew that the hit men had been working with the official security on the night of the assassination. In numerous interviews, Virginia Vallejo confirmed that Torregrosa had been working for the traffickers, including Escobar, and that the hit teams and Torregrosa had all been murdered in the years following the assassination. In 2016, General Maza was sentenced to thirty years for conspiring to murder Galán and for committing homicide with terrorist ends by reducing the candidate's security in the days preceding the assassination.

On August 21, 1989, the authorities arrested over 10,000 people. Seizures included 1,000 buildings and ranches, 350 planes, seventy-three boats and five tons of cocaine. Riveted to the TV, Colombians watched the security forces raid Hacienda Nápoles. Another of Pablo's properties, a two-storey hilltop cabin, was seized. Inside, they found thirty-eight Italian shirts and a mirrored ceiling over Pablo's brass bed. The raids on Gacha's property were just as impressive. Outside a mansion was a stone bridge over a man-made pond. Inside were porcelain cats, crystal coffee tables, Chinese vases, a pool table, a white marble bathroom with gold plumbing fixtures and Italian toilet paper with prints of naked women on each sheet.

Worst of all for the traffickers: extradition was reinstated with a new set of rules. Traffickers could be extradited to America by executive decree, without being processed through the courts or the government having to utilise the antiquated treaty that had been suspended in 1987. On August 21, 1989, the police arrested a cartel treasurer and started extradition proceedings.

Pablo entered a stage of war uninhibited by limits or consequences. A communiqué announced "now the fight is in blood … We declare total and absolute war against the government, the industrial and political oligarchy, the journalists who have attacked and insulted us, the judges who have sold themselves to the government, the magistrates who want to extradite us, the union leaders and all those who have pursued and attacked us. We shall not respect the families of those who have not respected our families. We shall burn and destroy the industries, properties and mansions of the oligarchy. From the Extraditables and the Expropriated to the people of Colombia."

On August 24, the Medellín headquarters of the Liberal and Social Conservative parties received bombs in the post. Some politicians' houses burned down.

George HW Bush sent $65 million to Colombia in emergency aid, including twenty Huey helicopters, eight A-37 reconnaissance and attack jets, five C-130 transport planes, anti-tank weapons, assault boats, machine guns, grenade launchers … Dozens of US military advisers arrived with equipment. "We will provide only material support and training," Bush said. "The United States has complete confidence in the capability of the Colombian police and military to deal with this situation."

Based on information from ninety-three US attorneys, the Americans released a Top 12 Most Wanted list. The top five were Pablo Escobar, Jorge Ochoa, Fabio Ochoa, Juan David Ochoa and Gustavo Gaviria. Gacha was only ninth. According to the US Attorney General, the purpose of the report was to compile "the business structure of drug trafficking … find out once and for all how the deadly game is being played. Demystify it. Drag it out from under the rock where it lives and breeds, so that we can fully educate the American public as to the size and breadth of these illegal and insidious business operations."

According to the report, the Medellín and Cali Cartels "control approximately 70 per cent of the cocaine processed in Colombia and supply 80 per cent of the cocaine distributed in the United

States. These cartels act as true cartels in the classic sense that they attempt, through collusion, to set prices and to eliminate any effective competition … Among the cartels, the Medellín Cartel is the most sophisticated organization." It controls "most of the modern office buildings in the city of Medellín and many of the retail establishments. Overseas communications are done by fax. In the US, cartel managers serve on a rotating basis … Of the three other major Colombian organisations, the Cali Cartel, founded in the late 1970s or early 1980s, comes closest to rivalling the Medellín Cartel in wealth and influence … A tacit agreement of ten years' standing, giving the bulk of the New York City cocaine trafficking distribution to the Cali Cartel, was breached, and tons of cocaine were shipped directly into that market by the Medellín organisation."

On August 25, the Medellín Cartel announced that ten judges would die for every Colombian extradited. Over a hundred judges resigned. Seventeen bombs exploded within a few days, all blamed on Pablo. The Ochoas and Gacha tried to make peace with the government, but the president said that he would not rest until the traffickers were destroyed. Over a two-week period, the price of cocaine in Miami rose from $13,000 a kilo to $19,000, indicating that the crackdown was disrupting the short-term supply.

On August 29, old Fabio Ochoa Sr wrote an open letter to the president, identifying himself as the father "of so-called Extraditables, poor fellows, may God protect them," who "prefer a tomb in Colombia to a life term in a cell in the United States – in other words, a living death …" But they "are also human. They have mothers, fathers, children, brothers, relatives and friends. They also have a heart. We are all brothers." He asked the president to "let there be dialogue, let there be peace, let there be forgiveness, let us try wiping the slate clean and starting a new account. Let us forgive as Jesus Christ taught us." The president ignored him.

CHAPTER 18
ELITE POLICE

In response to Galán's death, President Barco created and dispatched the Search Bloc to Medellín. It worked alongside an intelligence group from the Judicial Police. It was similar to the Elite Force based in Bogotá, established in 1986 to fight the paramilitaries. Aiming to capture or kill Pablo and the traffickers, it was a special unit of the National Police trained by the Army. Directed from Bogotá and under specially appointed police officials called in from outside Medellín, its members had been carefully selected in the belief that they were incorruptible by drug money. One of its leaders would become Pablo's new nemesis.

Six-feet tall and lean, Colonel Martínez was a quick thinker with a calm demeanour. In the 80s, he had seen Pablo on the news, building soccer pitches and homes for the poor. As chief of police intelligence in Cali, he had watched the godfathers walking the streets and wondered why nobody had arrested them. Researching, he discovered that the government files on the godfathers were missing, having being sold to the Mafia. Frustrated, he asked the courts whether there were any arrest warrants, and the judges replied that there were none for the leaders of the Cali and Medellín Cartels. He was flabbergasted by the traffickers having corrupted the police, the Army, judges and politicians.

After Cali, Martínez headed the Police School in Barranquilla, and by the middle of 1988, he was commanding the Police Department of Caldas. He learned that an overweight helicopter that had crashed had been on a mission for the Cali Cartel, who had paid the pilot, a police lieutenant, to attack Hacienda Nápoles.

In Spain, Martínez studied criminology. He demonstrated an outstanding ability to complete tasks, and his results enabled him to graduate at the top of his law-school class. After Spain and in his 40s, he became the director of the National Police School in Bogotá, where he analysed intelligence sourced from across the nation. His oldest child, Hugo Martínez Jr, respected his father's profession so much that he had joined the police.

The assassination of Colonel Franklin – who had detained El Patrón's family and refused to give Manuela a bottle – was devastating to the National Police. Martínez had to tell Franklin's son, a police cadet, "Your father was just killed in Medellín." The son's anguish and devastation increased the colonel's resolve to get the traffickers.

In Bogotá, a hit team contracted for 150 million pesos shadowed Judge Carlos Valencia. During the long hours of surveillance, they befriended local transvestites. Seeing this, the judge's bodyguards thought that the hit men were gay civilians. As the judge was about to sign a draft resolution against Gacha, the Mexican offered the hit team an additional fifty million pesos to finish the job before anything was signed. The judge alternated four routes, so the team timed how long it took to get to each traffic light and they selected two places. Disguised as street vendors, they waited for the day of his arrival.

"He is heading there," the first group warned the second at 7 PM.

At a traffic light, two hit men opened fire, one at the judge and the other at the bodyguards. The judge compressed himself down, so a hit man approached the vehicle, aimed his machine gun at an angle through the window and killed the judge. Unknown to the hit team, just before leaving his office, the judge had signed the papers against Gacha. Due to his death, his colleagues approved the indictment the next day without reading it.

Following the assassinations of Gálan, Franklin, Judge Valencia and the governor of Antioquia, a letter was penned from the Extraditables dated August 23, 1989, and sent to a radio station with twenty kilos of dynamite: "[We seek] absolute and total war on the government and the industrial and political oligarchy, to the journalists who have attacked and insulted us, to the judges who have sold themselves to the government, to the extraditing magistrates, to the guild presidents and to all those who have persecuted and attacked us."

President Barco responded: "Colombia, listen well, it is a war. This is not a simple rhetorical expression. The country is at war with traffickers and terrorists. Neither the government nor the country will rest until we have won this war." Aware that the traffickers had corrupted every branch of law enforcement, Barco decided to launch an offensive in Medellín by sending the Search Bloc.

The local police in Medellín were purged of anyone suspected of working for Pablo. DAS agents from Bogotá were kept separate from their colleagues in Medellín, who were suspected of corruption. Information provided to General Maza from the Cali Cartel was forwarded to the Search Bloc.

On September 2, 1989, Pablo lured Search Bloc members to a false threat, while a car bomb arrived at the offices of *The Spectator*. Fortunately, the building was mostly empty when an explosion rocked the area, injuring seventy-five people. Windows were shattered and the newspaper's photo lab was destroyed. The damage totalled $2.5 million.

The news reported: "Attention! Right here on 68th Avenue, in front of *The Spectator*, between 100 and 150 kilos of dynamite were placed in a vehicle which was completely destroyed. The anti-explosive technicians at the National Police have indicated that the bomb's blast towards the base caused a depth of four feet six and a ten-foot-long crater. This bomb contained numerous elements, especially pellets, screws and nuts and pieces of road. The bomb's blast reached a range of about 600 feet, causing serious damage here in the Interior Custom's building of Bogotá, to Corpoacero and to other buildings nearby. The fire department of Bogotá is here on the west side, one block away. A building is completely roofless because of the powerful impact. Ten cars suffered damage."

In the following days, the newspaper's staff, assisted by emergency workers, the police and the military, worked around the clock to clean the debris. The news broadcast images of people in hazard suits removing rubble and of staff cleaning up glass from work desks and sweeping the floors. Some desks, cabinets, telephones and typewriters had been mangled together by the blast. Other newspapers offered the use of their rotary presses.

The news reported: "At this time, *The Spectator* continues to work in order to give the Colombian people their edition on Sunday. Most of the people are working and making significant efforts to release their morning newspaper all over the national territory. Serious damage was done to the newspaper facilities. At this time, they are being reassessed by the directors. They have informed us that there are no press releases right now, but on Sunday there will be a special editorial." The Sunday edition's cover photo showed the rubble-strewn office. The public bought half a million copies to support the newspaper.

One of Cano's sons gave a radio interview: "First of all I would like to say that I'm here giving this interview contrary to the teachings of my father, Guillermo Cano, who always told us that our opinions should only be seen reflected in the newspaper's editorials. Our correspondent in the Amazon, and later my father Don Guillermo Cano, were the first victims of this atrocious war that Pablo Escobar began against *The Spectator*. From the very beginning, we knew there would be others, as was confirmed yesterday with the bomb they placed at the newspaper building. And also the statement of the so-called Extraditables group on behalf of the Medellín Cartel, which was published this morning, where they make both a frontal attack against the country's political establishment and the judiciary branch, and also against the freedom of press. But as today's headline of *The Spectator* reads, we shall continue to move on, and we shall also wait for the newly formed Elite Group of the Army to give us results."

PABLO ESCOBAR'S STORY

In September 1989, in the Carlos Holguín Police School in Medellín, Colonel Martínez strategised with his most trusted officers. On a piece of paper, he attempted to sketch a rudimentary structure of the Medellín Cartel. He listed four main families involved in exportation – the Ochoas, the Galeanos, the Moncadas and the Tomates – all of whom paid taxes to Pablo. Gacha was described as an independent military power operating a satellite group of the Medellín Cartel in Bogotá and the emerald area of Boyacá. He listed Gustavo Gaviria as a chief coordinator of exports. As a military leader, Pinina controlled the offices – groups of killers with abundant criminal history – that operated in different parts of the city. Ricardo Prisco's area was Aranjuez. Big Gun's was La Estrella.

La Kika controlled a gang in Castilla in north-west Medellín. He was known for marking his corpses with KK. From the Muñoz Mosquera family of fifteen brothers, he prayed to Saint Jude with faith inherited from his father, a policeman who had converted to evangelicalism. Although La Kika and his brother Tyson had asked God to protect them during the commission of crimes, they had both been arrested and received long sentences. Astonished when Tyson received twenty-five years, the family had prayed for a miracle.

Pablo had sent a helicopter painted with police colours, which had landed on a terrace at the Bellavista prison. While men aboard had fired at the guards, La Kika and Tyson had climbed into the helicopter. In a cove called La Pesebrera, the brothers had received thirty million pesos each from Pablo, to whom they now worshipped more fervently than Saint Jude.

Despite identifying the principal players, the colonel was daunted by the size of the area that Pablo controlled. It included the Aburrá Valley, a region of three million people. Pablo's safe houses were spread across an area he had known since childhood. The thick forest and jungle in which he moved was impenetrable to the police, which, combined with the false information they were receiving, had created lots of wild goose chases for the authorities.

Sketched by Martínez, the organigram of the Medellín Cartel was on two pieces of A4 paper, divided into two sections: smugglers and bandits. As intelligence came in, real names replaced nicknames, and those captured or killed were removed. In response, Pablo drew an organigram of the Search Bloc, with Martínez at the top.

Listening to cartel calls, Martínez heard a familiar female voice, insisting that she was in the correct place but she couldn't see what the man had asked her to find. Despite the man's repeated demands, she was unsuccessful. It dawned that the voice belonged to a woman who cleaned the colonel's office. The trafficker on the call had wanted her to remove his picture from the organigram. Investigating the woman, the colonel learned that she had cooperated with the cartel because they had threatened to kill her and her family. He transferred her away from his office, but shortly after, she was executed in her home.

On September 5, President Bush delivered a speech: "In Colombia alone, cocaine killers have gunned down a leading statesman, murdered almost 200 judges and seven members of their supreme court. The besieged governments of the drug-producing countries are fighting back, fighting to break the international drug rings. But you and I agree with the courageous President of Colombia, Virgilio Barco, who said that if Americans use cocaine, then Americans are paying for murder. American cocaine users need to understand that our nation has zero tolerance for casual drug use. We have a responsibility not to leave our brave friends in Colombia to fight alone.

"The $65-million emergency assistance announced two weeks ago was just our first step in assisting the Andean nations in their fight against the cocaine cartels. Colombia has already arrested suppliers, seized tons of cocaine and confiscated palatial homes of drug lords. But Colombia faces a long uphill battle, so we must be ready to do more. Our strategy allocates more than a quarter of a billion dollars for next year in military and law-enforcement assistance for the three Andean nations of Colombia, Bolivia and

Peru. This will be the first part of a five-year, $2-billion programme to counter the producers, the traffickers and the smugglers.

"I spoke with President Barco just last week, and we hope to meet with the leaders of affected countries in an unprecedented drug summit, all to coordinate an inter-American strategy against the cartels. We will work with our allies and friends, especially our economic summit partners, to do more in the fight against drugs. I'm also asking the Senate to ratify the United Nations antidrug convention concluded last December.

"To stop those drugs on the way to America, I propose that we spend more than a billion and a half dollars on interdiction. Greater interagency cooperation, combined with sophisticated intelligence-gathering and Defense Department technology, can help stop drugs at our borders.

"And our message to the drug cartels is this: the rules have changed. We will help any government that wants our help. When requested, we will for the first time make available the appropriate resources of America's Armed Forces. We will intensify our efforts against drug smugglers on the high seas, in international airspace and at our borders. We will stop the flow of chemicals from the United States used to process drugs. We will pursue and enforce international agreements to track drug money to the front men and financiers. And then we will handcuff these money launderers and jail them, just like any street dealer. And for the drug kingpins: the death penalty."

On September 17, Pablo responded to Bush. Near the US Embassy – which was on a high state of alert – a man was taking a stroll in a park. After scoping out his surroundings for witnesses, he pulled out a rocket-propelled grenade launcher, took aim and fired. The rocket hit the embassy building, but failed to explode. It only damaged the cement facade. Diplomats sent their families home.

CHAPTER 19
DEATH OF MARIO HENAO

Pablo went on the run with less bodyguards because he believed that the reward money could tempt anyone. He stayed at a farm forty miles away from Medellín, with his brother and a couple who lived there. Visitors such as politicians or lawyers were brought to him blindfolded. He stationed lookouts in the neighbouring farms, which he owned. He passed the time swimming in a pool by apple and orange trees, playing dominoes outside with a barbecue cooking or with a dog, Hussein, which had bitten him when he had bought the farm.

The police arrived one morning, so Pablo moved into a secret compartment built into the house. Pretending to be an artist, Roberto answered, wearing a cap and an artist's glasses. In the living room was an unfinished painting of a farm and a small cow. The police said they were searching the neighbourhood because they had found a head on one side of the road and a body on the other. Roberto said he had been painting and was oblivious to the goings-on outside. The police came in, drank some coffee and left. To let Pablo know that the police had gone, Roberto knocked in a special way that only they could decode.

An intercepted call raised the hopes of Colonel Martínez. Pablo asked his brother-in-law about someone named Maria. Mario Henao then contacted a volleyball coach who procured young athletes for the traffickers. "El Patrón wants me to bring Maria to him," Mario said. From the volleyball league, Martínez obtained a list of players and wiretapped the phones of every

Maria. Eventually, the coach contacted Maria with the news that she was going to travel to see the man.

At a safe house on a farm called The Parrot by a river so clear that all of the fish were visible, Pablo hugged his mother and wife. He greeted Juan Pablo, and Manuela pounced on him. "Please pretend to be a horse," she said. On all fours, he carried her until he grew tired.

Juan Pablo enjoyed hanging out with the bodyguards. Pablo was raising him with survival skills. From an early age, he had been taught to ride motorbikes and cars. Encouraged by his father, his interest in weapons had been criticised by Big Gun, who said, "We have to take our children away from all this and make them study."

Earring defended the boss. "Pablo knew that the boy was going to be involved in the war and he taught him how to defend himself and to handle the way things were played. What other heritage could Pablo have left him? He could not hide the truth from him."

At night, Hermilda consulted her son about problems and he gave her instructions. Years later, she said that little Pablo had always obeyed her, but the tables had turned. Everything required his consent, but he never lost his exaggerated attachment to her, a.k.a. mama-itis by the countrymen. He constantly arranged meetings, and she happily took multiple cars, crossed rivers, risked snakes and dangerous animals and slept on a mat to see him.

During the night, Pablo lit a candle and Hermilda woke up afraid of a tarantula. "Oh my God! Will it eat us?"

"No, Mom. These are my friends. Sleep calmly." His confident tone reassured her as it did when other dangers arose. The next day, with his business partners and the young volleyball player scheduled to arrive, he told his family that they needed to leave due to security concerns.

On the journey from Medellín, eight undercover elite policemen followed Maria in various vehicles. Eventually, they exited the highway and travelled down an unpaved road. Maria stopped at a small port and boarded a boat. Afraid of being detected, the undercovers left the area for where the boat was heading.

In Puerto Triunfo, a farmer eager to earn a reward offered information. "Man, I know where Pablo Escobar is because I've seen that there is a party and lots of movement."

"Could you take us there?" a policeman asked.

"I can't because they'll kill me, but I can point out the site from a helicopter."

With six helicopters at his disposal for the operation, Martínez pondered the situation. With the Air Force nearby, he would need authorisation to enter the airspace, but Pablo had spies in the Air Force who would immediately inform him from the control tower. He decided to launch the helicopters from the port of Barrancabermeja on the Magdalena River, so that they could fly upstream at a low altitude to avoid radar detection.

While Martínez made preparations, Gacha left the party in the afternoon. Mario Henao, Jorge Ochoa and his wife decided to stay overnight. Pablo's brother Roberto had a bad feeling, so he made sure the boats had plenty of fuel. After eating in the evening, Roberto went to bed early as in the morning he wanted to mark cattle in a neighbouring farm with Jorge. While Roberto was sleeping, Pablo placed a plastic tarantula on him, so that he would get a fright when he woke up. After 7 AM, Roberto and Jorge were about to leave when a warning came about six helicopters travelling up the river.

Roberto rushed to his sleeping brother. "Pablo, get up! There are six helicopters in a caravan."

"They are not heading here. They are going to Bogotá."

Roberto radioed the bodyguards. "Be ready, brothers, for what may happen."

Another warning came about the helicopters plus twenty-five trucks full of police.

"Pablo, be alert," Roberto said.

"What time is it?"

"7:30."

"I still have a little more time to sleep. At 8 I can get up." Eventually, he rose and entered the bathroom, where he sang the Corrido de Lucio Vasquez:

Uaa!
The peacocks flew
towards the Sierra Mojada, they
killed Lucio Vazquez
for a young woman he loved.

At 11 o'clock at night
Lucio was having dinner.
Some friends came
to invite him to a fandango.

AAAAAu aayayyaa!
Corrido de Lucio Vazquez a man, yes gentlemen.

His mother told him,
my heart warns
not fences Lucio to that dance take
care of a betrayal.

They mounted their horses
to the wet sierra
where was the young woman
who wore so much adored.

AAAAY ahahaha, Lucio Vazquez a man

When they arrived at the dance
Lucio did not want to take
one gives him a drink
and another sticks in a dagger.

After emerging from the shower, he sat at the kitchen table. "Where's breakfast?"

"Pablo, the helicopters are coming here," a bodyguard said. "They already warned from Nápoles' radio that they are coming to this side. Let's get out of here."

Pablo called the helicopters mosquitoes and gestured slapping them away as if they meant nothing. "Ah, let's wait and see." No sooner had he replied than the helicopters were heard. He grabbed a rifle and everyone fled outside for the mules and boats.

Aboard a helicopter, the farmer was struggling to pinpoint the location due to the aerial view of dense green vegetation. Knowing that they were in the correct zone, the helicopters circled. "There's the site!" the farmer pointed.

El Patrón and his men shot at the helicopters. Amid noises like popcorn crackling, a pilot said, "We're being hit."

"Open fire to prevent them from firing on us," Martínez said, watching people scramble around below.

Pablo, Jorge and his wife, and two other men headed towards long grass, which had been planted to enable escapes. Emerging from the house, Mario intended to board a boat until he suddenly fell from the force of bullets. A helicopter aimed its gun at Roberto and unleashed an onslaught but a massive tree shielded him from death. They were so surrounded that Jorge Ochoa took his gun out as if contemplating the suicide pact agreed by the Extraditables, but Pablo told him that the time wasn't right.

When the helicopter left for refuelling, the escapees attempted to hide, while other helicopters kept shooting, their bullets cutting through and scorching the vegetation. With more helicopters leaving to refuel, Pablo and his group ran through the long grass. Eventually, they submerged themselves into water up to their necks, and then walked uphill with bullets raining down.

Separated from Pablo, Roberto and some men dashed for a mountain slope. "I see the police there, but remain calm," Roberto said. Panicked, one of them launched into a meadow, breaking some ropes. The snapping sound drew gunfire. Roberto jumped from a boulder and slid. By the time he had finished falling, his jeans had been torn from his legs and his buttocks were bleeding.

Helicopters attempted to land, but were prevented by ropes tied onto guadua trees similar to bamboo poles. From the air, they found a landing site 3 km from the safe house, which gave Pablo a thirty-minute advantage. By the time they arrived, sixty people were on the ground ready to surrender, alongside twenty rifles and radio equipment. The detainees refused to provide information, so the police searched the safe house and found phone numbers, codes and lists of people on Pablo's payroll.

After walking for hours, Pablo and his group stopped to rest. "There's the police," said Jorge Ochoa's wife. Lying flat on a carpet of leaves, they watched the police and some DEA agents about thirty metres away. After the authorities left, they continued to walk. On a radio, Pablo attempted to contact Mario, but got no response.

At night, with his knowledge of the area, Pablo guided the group alongside a road. Intercepting their radio transmissions, Martínez listened, but could not act in the darkness in unfamiliar terrain. Avoiding police checkpoints, Pablo led his group across a river and into the Nápoles estate. On horses, they fled to safety.

Overnight, a peasant provided sanctuary in his house and fresh clothes for Roberto and his men. They ate, showered and dressed their wounds. Breakfast was eggs with rice, pastries, cheese and chocolate. To clear the Medellín-Bogotá highway of police checkpoints, Roberto got on a radiophone and said they were heading to Puerto Berrio, and the police left hoping to intercept them. On TV, Roberto laughed as he watched the police announce that they had them completely surrounded in Puerto Berrio. Roberto ended up delirious and with a dangerously high temperature from dengue fever, which almost killed him.

The next day, Martínez overheard Pablo on a radio reprimanding the air base for failing to alert him to the helicopters.

"We did not realise they went through. The radar did not detect them."

For five days, El Patrón cried for Mario. His men had never seen him mourn for so long. He spent the nights recording his family messages, stating how special they were and how much he loved them. They received them in the mail.

Having not slept for two days, Martínez washed his underwear in the safe house, left them drying in the bathroom and fell asleep in Pablo's bed. He awoke to a helicopter full of journalists demanding a tour of the house. In a hurry, he hid his underwear under Pablo's pillow and got dressed. The journalists were thrilled to find the underwear, which they assumed was Pablo's. The newspapers printed cartoons of Pablo escaping half-naked into a forest.

The president announced Mario's death: "The death of Mario Henao is the first blow to the Medellín Cartel. He was Pablo Escobar's brother-in-law. This shows that the government is producing concrete results. I'd like to congratulate the Elite Force, which was recently established. And also to remind you that we will be continuing the persecution."

After wanted posters were dropped by helicopter and plastered on walls, Pablo told his men, "History shows that he whose boss has a price on his head is a dead man." He told them to brace for an escalation of the war and advised them to move around using disguises and fake documents.

In Medellín, Elite Group checkpoints stopped every expensive car and compared the passengers to wanted photos. They were so rude and brutal to passengers that the public began to hate them. They told passengers, "Tell those motherfuckers, Escobar, Otto, Popeye and Mugre to stop hiding like cowards and show themselves."

Getting plastic surgery on his nose and chin altered Popeye's appearance from the picture on the wanted poster, which was from his passport application. Stopped at a checkpoint, he was handed a wanted poster of himself and told to keep an eye out for assassins.

With all of these forces pitted against him, Pablo learned that the order had gone out to kill him using any means necessary – sanctioned by President Bush, the Colombian president and his military commanders. With so many people from the neighbourhoods he had supported getting killed by the police, Pablo decided to retaliate hard.

At a meeting with his top men and associates, Pablo announced, "We cannot continue to allow the police to kill the youngsters on the streets, so we are going to challenge them. Death to the city police and the Elite Group!" He offered rewards for dead police: $1,000 for a regular policeman, $2,000 for a sergeant major, $5,000 for a lieutenant, $10,000 for a captain, $20,000 for a major and $30,000 for a colonel. People reported crimes to entice police to locations where they were surrounded and massacred. Collecting a reward required the shooter to obtain a newspaper report and bring it to one of Pablo's offices. His stashes of weapons were distributed throughout Medellín: pistols, machine guns, revolvers, hand grenades … Cuco prepared more bombs. Unwitting suicide bombers were given dynamite packed to appear like cocaine. Sent nearby to police stations and checkpoints, they were enticed by the prospect of making fast cash. The bombs were activated by remote controls used to fly model airplanes. Rival criminal gangs united against the police, turning Medellín into a battlefield. The criminals knew that if they were caught, they would be tortured to death at the police academy.

Pablo announced that he would destroy the Search Bloc within eight days. On the first day, nine police were shot dead by killers who lived in their neighbourhood.

At a press conference, a general announced: "As you know, the public order situation in Medellín is delicate. The National Police Institution is fighting a dirty, merciless war that has already taken the lives of ten of our men."

"And what is going to be the response, General?" a reporter asked.

"The usual one. Go against those criminals all the way till the end. Finish them."

"When you talk about criminals, do you refer to Pablo Escobar?"

"Everything seems to imply that character is behind this entire situation. The Medellín police has taken some steps to counteract this dirty attack by the criminals. They include the prohibition of motorcycle rear-seat passengers, the helmet use by drivers, and all vehicles running at night must keep their lights on."

Targeting the Elite Group, Big Gun managed to get a car bomb on a truck carrying police. The blast launched the truck to the other side of the road, killing fifteen police and wounding ten. Civilians and other cars were blown to bits. Policemen on fire ran around screaming. From September to December 1989, over 100 bombs exploded across Colombia. By July 1990, hundreds of police had been murdered in Medellín.

Amid the war, Pablo documented his thoughts:

"Why in the highest spheres of the government do they all look towards Antioquia and point the finger at us every time a bomb explodes, a massacre takes place, violence is rampant? Isn't there much gratuity in that hatred? Why does General Maza Márquez have that special hatred for us and point at us with an accusing finger for everything that is wrong that takes place or will take place? Every day, the media records the murders of policemen in Medellín! This news is so painful that it must fill everyone with anguish. What they do not register is that at the same time in the neighbourhoods, scores of boys are killed in massacres that never become known. The most general explanation is that it was a fight between gangs, a settling of accounts, etc. There is another explanation that is much more cruel and more certain: an institution is annihilating them.

"There is an organisation that goes out at night and fumigates unmercifully all the boys that you see in the corners, in the streets, in the cafes, in the cantinas, etc. That organisation acts apparently in good faith, supposedly to clean the city because it was taught that the drug traffickers were hit men of the worst kind and that all the boys from the poor neighbourhoods were part of that ilk that had to be extinguished. As long as things continue as they are, the abyss that separates the poor classes and police officers will continue to dig deep and instead of one dead agent per day, the number will continue to grow. Currently, there are 4,000 police officers in Medellín, however there are 200 schools of assassins who have half a dozen members each. The [police figures] are not true, and this deception will harm us all. There are 1,200 people who oppose the actions of extermination by the police. We are all united and must be united. The [police methods] are not the way.

"If in a family there is a black sheep in a neighbourhood, a hit man … we do not have to exterminate the whole family or the entire neighbourhood! We must put an end to the massacre of the boys and the police agents who also belong to those same neighbourhoods. For this we must stop, now, this preaching of hatred that is being inculcated from above. It is necessary that the high spheres of the government change all the violent and oppressive rhetoric they are throwing against Antioquia, against the people of marginalised sectors, against all of us who have to suffer the excesses of the encounters between these two polarised sectors of our society that are so linked they should be having the same roots."

Years later, Colonel Naranjo commented on the war:

"When Galán died, and the establishment, President Barco, launched The Offensive, the police acted as an emotional, reactive harlot, which created a strategy not rational enough to channel all the necessary institutional power as the strategy was put into place.

"It was operated in a hostile environment. Pablo Escobar, who wanted to assimilate the figure of Robin Hood, not only had obtained some legitimacy, but had been turned into an invincible, almighty and non-debatable myth. Those hostile to Escobar acted upon two lines: one, penetration via intelligence processes to get to know the functioning of the cartel and another, a permanent pressure and harassment not only on the cartel but also on its support nuclei, which meant that the people in Medellín, the good people; would also pay a high cost because the police could not discriminate who was or was not Pablo Escobar's sympathisers, and so the task of pressure was inflicted upon the [innocent] population.

"The arrival of people like Colonel Martínez, with other instances of the government, allowed the police to outline a more articulated strategy. And as the strategy of the police was rationalised, Pablo Escobar's strategy became insane. Two contradictory, antagonistic processes finally ended up producing costly results for the country in terms of human lives, in terms of the climate of coexistence, and in terms of the very values that kept the regime functioning.

"The police acted without meaning, without planning, and resorted to the use of force as a basic element; ending up with a strategy that attacked the middle and lower levels of the Medellín Cartel, where the last one to be annihilated would be the boss. Unlike the case of the struggle against the Cali Cartel, developed a few years later, where we did not face low and medium levels, but rather the [organisation's] dome. At first, people believed Pablo more than the authorities but people believed [him] only on a certain basis: the police behaved in an aggressive way with the citizens, but that aggressiveness was not predisposed unto the normal people, but it was a task of pressure designed to close in on the social spaces of Pablo in Medellín. Many people who greeted Pablo, who received him in the clubs, under pressure [by the authorities], broke up. Thus, we were closing the spaces of mobility, of sociability and of economic alliance with sectors that in the past did not feel threatened by the authorities – and that, let's say, is what gave results.

"The point of equilibrium was broken when Pablo resorted to terrorism. It is clear that society, after a terrorist campaign, ends up transferring responsibility to the government that does not protect them. That was Escobar's ability at that time. And in that, it must be said clearly, he overcame all the institutional capacity of the police and the state using terrorism."

CHAPTER 20
AVIANCA AIRLINES FLIGHT 203

Refusing to meet anyone, Pablo ran his operation by phone. Denying individual responsibility for Galán's death, he credited the Extraditables, a group of which he was only a part. Santo requested to meet, but Pablo declined. Over the phone, they discussed what would happen if Gaviria became the president.

Pablo decided to assassinate Gaviria with a car bomb in the main square of Pereira, a city in the mountains of western Colombia. The bomb would have to be detonated from afar due to the high level of security. It would require a huge amount of dynamite, and cause untold casualties.

The car bomb plan was abandoned after Pablo learned that on November 27, 1989, Gaviria was scheduled to board Avianca Airlines Flight 203 from Bogotá to Cali. At a meeting with Pablo present, it was decided to eliminate Gaviria by using a briefcase bomb manufactured by Cuco – consisting of five kilos of dynamite. Airport security was bribed to allow the briefcase onto the plane.

A young man was offered a large amount of money by Earring to agree to carry the briefcase. Having been told that it contained a recording device, he was instructed to open the briefcase when the plane reached its cruising altitude. "We need you to record the conversation of two passengers from Cali in the row in front of you." His ticket had been booked under the name Pedro Santo Domingo. The plane belonged to the Santo Domingo Group, one of the largest Colombian conglomerates, owned by one of the wealthiest families in Latin America.

With the bomb aboard the plane, Pablo's men at the airport watched for Gaviria and his bodyguards. By 7 AM, the politician hadn't arrived. Unknown to them, Gaviria's head of security had advised him not to get on the flight. Even when they finally realised that Gaviria had changed his mind about flying, Pablo's men had no way to deactivate the bomb.

At 7:13 AM, the plane took off. It was in the air for five minutes and flying at a speed of 794 kph when the briefcase was opened. At an altitude of 13,000 feet, the bomb blasted a hole in the floor and the side of the plane and ripped the airliner apart. The nose section separated from the tail section, which tumbled down in flames. All 107 people on board were killed, as well as three on the ground from the falling debris.

The radio announced: "Breaking news. We've received many calls from listeners saying that a plane has allegedly crashed over the city of Bogotá."

"I saw a trail of smoke coming from it," said a female caller to the station. "Then the plane caught on fire and fell near the Cazucá area."

"Yes, but what type of plane was it? What exactly did you see?"

"I saw a smoke trail. OK? Then flames, and then the plane falling towards Cazucá. That's all. I was quite far away."

"Did the plane fall?"

"Yes, it fell."

"A big plane?"

"I don't know. I didn't see it pass."

"Thank you for your help, ma'am. We have another caller. Who is it?"

"Well, I live in the Marco Fidel Suárez neighbourhood. I was on the terrace at home, following the plane with binoculars that someone lent me."

"This is unbelievable."

"I didn't see a small plane. It was a big Avianca plane."

"Let's not be too quick to say it was a commercial aircraft, please."

The radio presenter contacted an official, who said, "According to the investigation, the plane departed from Bogotá to Cali and hasn't made contact with any city."

"That means you tried … to contact the aircraft."

"Yes, sir, destination Cali."

"At what time, sir?"

"At 7:13."

"7:13?"

"Exactly."

"It has just been confirmed that the HK-1803 flight that was covering the Bogotá-Cali route is the plane that crashed. They don't exactly know what happened, but multiple callers said it exploded in the air and fell to the ground."

"I work here at the Muña Three power plant. While having breakfast, we heard a loud sound. The plane exploded. I went to the crash site and, unfortunately, there were no survivors."

"Emergency relief personnel are on their way to Soacha, where the aircraft remains have been sighted."

The country watched in horror as the TV broadcast the crash site, including views from a helicopter and from the ground. Soldiers dressed in green guarded the remnants of the plane, some of which was still on fire, surrounded by debris strewn across green slopes.

"The first impression of the explosion site is very painful," a presenter said. "I'm at the Canoas Ranch. There is an enormous pipe filled with gasoline here, and we've seen the mangled bodies spread over an area of approximately three kilometres. This place is five kilometres away from Indumil, south-east of the Colombian capital on a hill called Canoas in a huge old ranch called Fiques. The Bogotá River is at the bottom. The sky is too dark, too grey. When we arrived, we could smell the acrid carbon monoxide. I am at the peak of the edge, and at the bottom I can see scattered bodies, life vests, pieces of what used to be an airplane. It is really shocking and no survivors."

After it became known that Gaviria should have been on the

plane, people started to suspect that the crash wasn't an accident.

"Gaviria, how are you?" a radio host asked.

"Fortunately, I'm all right, but what happened was terrible."

"Sir, we have been informed that you were in that plane."

"No. A few days ago I stopped using commercial planes. I was travelling, but in a light aircraft."

"Why did you change your travel plans? Were you threatened? Did you know?"

"No. The truth is that whenever I get in a plane, people get out. That's why I decided to stop travelling in commercial planes. We managed to find a light aircraft, but what happened is very serious."

A later news broadcast zoomed in on the debris: a bent bicycle tyre, a woman's white boot, a photo of a baby, a greeting card with hearts, flowers and butterflies titled "Especially For You, Mom, WITH LOVE," a picture of the holy infant next to a young person's ID card. It showed a field with a crowd gathered around rows of corpses wrapped in large black plastic bags, and an official ordering men dressed in orange to search the hills for bodies.

Family members of victims were arriving on the scene, and an official said, "We need them to expedite the operation and identify the bodies." Devastated parents collapsed and sobbed. After identification, each plastic bag containing a corpse was put on a stretcher and carried to a van. Out of 107 victims, 106 were identified by family members, leaving the bomber unidentified, which provided the police an investigative lead. The bomber's fingerprints could produce his real name, but the police were unable to obtain prints from his body parts.

The Spectator reported: "Today, Colombians feel threatened and frightened because of the power of the Medellín Cartel. The killing of one minister, two colonels, several judges and magistrates, the director of this newspaper, the attorney general, the future President of the Republic, not to mention the bomb placed in this newspaper office, wasn't enough, but now they are also the possible perpetrators of the explosion of a plane in mid-air that killed 107 innocent Colombians. How long will President Barco keep us in this hell? Do we have to wait for an even worse tragedy to see results?"

The assassinations included Judge Espinosa, whose car Pablo had continued to burn or steal over the years since she had presided over his 1976 cocaine case. His thirteen-year vendetta had included publishing photos of her in the newspapers with the caption: "Judge Espinosa, who suffers from mental disorders, disappeared from her home a week ago. We appreciate anyone who can provide information about her whereabouts." In November 1989, the Priscos' gang gunned her down as she arrived home.

A Bogotá radio station received a call from a member of the Extraditables, claiming responsibility because the passengers had included five informants. Fidel and Carlos Castaño were suspects, but the absence of evidence prevented any charges. Four years later, the bomb maker confessed to the DAS that he had been paid a million pesos by a senior Medellín Cartel member. Also, years later, while in custody after surrendering, Earring said that the bomb had been a gelatinous explosive activated with a detonator and battery, and confirmed that a young man had been duped into carrying it.

The death of two Americans on board Avianca Airlines Flight 203 prompted the Bush administration to classify Pablo as a clear and present danger and to begin Intelligence Support Activity on him. George HW Bush dispatched the CIA, a secret surveillance unit called Centra Spike and Delta Force, the top counterterrorism unit. Mostly language experts and technicians, Centra Spike specialised in eavesdropping on electronic communications to find people. By tracking Pablo's phone calls, they mapped out the members of the Medellín Cartel. They forwarded the information to the elite police and provided eavesdropping technology.

Despite Gaviria dodging the disaster, the traffickers intended to use the terror to force the government into negotiations. A few days after the Avianca bombing, the traffickers contacted Diego Londoño White, the manager of the Medellín Metro, who had directed Betancur's presidential campaign. He was transported to a safe house north of Medellín to discuss the possibility of a negotiated solution. He was received by Pablo, the Ochoa brothers, Kiko Moncada and Negro Galeano. "How are we going to talk about dialogue after you exploded that airplane?" he said.

The traffickers were denying responsibility until Pablo said, "May they suffer on their own the violence that we have suffered with our families."

"I see it will be difficult to make contacts. I think you should look for other ways."

As well as scaring people from getting on planes, the cartel intended to frighten them from being on the streets of Bogotá by bombing targets, starting with the building housing the DAS. The principal target was General Maza. A bus full of explosives would be detonated when Maza arrived to work, so that the building would collapse upon him.

CHAPTER 21
BOMBING BOGOTÁ

On December 1, 1989, Pablo turned 40, frustrated that he couldn't celebrate with his family due to the war. With bodyguards, he arrived at a farm in Sabaneta owned by Chuchilla, the bisexual son of a barber who played soccer in the lower divisions. Chuchilla was known for driving at high speeds, holding the steering wheel with one hand, while rolling a joint with the other. At night, Pablo drank mineral water, smoked cannabis and chatted to his men. The arrival of the president of the Patriotic Union (UP) interrupted the conversation. Pablo's lawyer Guido Parra had arranged the meeting. Bernardo Jaramillo was a tall man with a moustache and a happy spirit. With Fidel Castaño and Gacha at war with the guerrillas, Jaramillo sought a peace agreement.

"I'm a guy with left leanings," Pablo said, impressing Jaramillo with his slow speech and commanding aura. "But in some moments, I've leaned towards the right. For example, the National Liberation Army placed two kilos of dynamite in one of my houses. They put me into a fight over stupidities. I've never wanted to fight against the left, among other things, because I'm not a landowner and I do not grow or process cocaine. My business is transportation. I do not get involved with anything else." Over the years, his business had transformed into providing routes and taxing traffickers. Jaramillo gazed at Pablo as if trying to ascertain his sincerity. "We were all blamed for Galán's death, and since we are a family, we all go to war. I am going to place a hundred bombs in Bogotá, so that the oligarchy will know the meaning of war! At this point, a war has already been declared and this war is going to last, at least until the end of the government of Mr Barco."

"Well, I don't think that bombs are the solution. That's terrible," Jaramillo said.

"No, no, no! If the oligarchs have me running around, I'll make them run around. Either all in bed or all on the floor. The war is going to get serious and hard. It's not just a war in Antioquia and Puerto Triunfo. Next month, I'm going to put bombs in Bogotá, so be careful where you walk."

In silence, Jaramillo contemplated Pablo's wicked and arrogant side. He decided that Pablo had so much money, he had lost touch with reality. He had created a world in which he had power over so many lives and other things, but he had no way to switch it off.

"The only possibility of a negotiated solution is with the next president," Pablo said. "With Gaviria, there is nothing to do, he will continue Galán's stubbornness. Santo is my friend, but he's not going to win the election. Then the only possibility is with Samper. I don't like him, but we have to support him anyway. I spoke with Santo, and he said he would support him. Suddenly, you support him, and I get some votes and put money into that and we look for a way out of the situation. And I would be willing, if you give me the guarantees, to go talk to the FARC and then talk to Gacha to fix all the problems." Jaramillo paid more attention now that Pablo was addressing his problem: Gacha's war against the Patriotic Union. "The Mexican was preparing an attack, but I stopped him. I recommend that you leave the bodyguards of the government because they will sell you for five million pesos. Do as I do. See these guys: they've known me since childhood. They've been my lifelong friends. They'd get killed for me."

"That's impossible for me," Jaramillo said.

"The other problem is Fidel Castaño. You guerrillas committed the stupid mistake of kidnapping his father, asking him for a big sum of money and killing him. Fidel asked me what he was supposed to have done, and I told him, 'For the family, you have to do whatever it takes. Pay if you have money.' Fidel showed me a threatening response letter, in which he said that if they did something to his father, he would declare war on them to the death. I told him, 'If I were from the FARC and I received this letter, I'd kill the old man immediately.' And sure enough, they killed him. Hence, it became an obsession of his life to kill Communists. But if we reach an agreement, I'll see to it that Fidel respects the agreement and if he doesn't agree, I'll see that the agreement gets respected."

Jaramillo believed that Pablo wanted peace between the guerrillas and the traffickers to help Samper become the president. Then Samper would allow a negotiated settlement with the traffickers. "I'll get you a response promptly," Jaramillo said. While eating beans, they watched TV and engaged in small talk until Jaramillo left for his hotel at 10 PM.

Previously, Pablo had viewed the DAS as too corrupt to be harmful, but with General Maza challenging him at every media event, something had to be done. After watching Maza on the news, Pablo said to his men, "What does Maza do in the DAS? What is the purpose of this institution? Where are the detainees and the results of their investigations?"

Sat at his work desk, Maza received a package, which he started to open with scissors. Observing plastic sealing the package, he grew suspicious and took it to the Explosives Group. In a courtyard, two agents handled the package carelessly. It detonated, killing both.

On December 6, 1989, Pablo upped the stakes on Maza. A bus brought a gigantic bomb to the DAS building. Inside the lobby, Earring waited for the arrival of Maza and his bodyguards, ready to give a signal. A man who had been duped into the mission was supposed to drive the bus into the lobby, but Maza had rose early, walked through a street market in front of the building and took a different entrance, frustrating the original plan. Exasperated waiting for Maza – who was in his office – Earring gave up and exited the building. Spotting him, the driver clumsily drove the bus towards the building, running over street vendors and finally crashing into a money-transportation van. Instructed to turn on the sound system, he unwittingly activated the bomb. Just past 7:30 AM, tons of dynamite exploded, almost killing Earring, who was picked up and carried by the blast wave. A mushroom cloud rose over the city as if a nuclear bomb had exploded.

A male presenter on Caracol Radio reported: "At first, the ground felt like, I don't know, like a buzzing, then there was a huge explosion. Our journalists are already arriving at the site. I repeat, it was a powerful blast. We don't know what caused it. The police authorities have been informed immediately and we indeed don't know the origin of this disaster. It's 7:33 in the morning. We are located on 19th and 8th, and now we are on the fourth floor. The blast was violent and the structure was shaken. At this time, we're trying to find out what exactly happened. The authorities are arriving at the explosion site."

A female radio presenter said: "What we can inform Caracol listeners is that, as Juan Dario said, we are on the fourth floor. The first thing we felt was the floor moving, and then two very strong successive shakes that made us think it was an earthquake. But after we heard an explosion, we understood that something very big had happened here in downtown Bogotá."

A male radio presenter said: "Breaking news! A huge explosion has just taken place in the neighbourhood of the Security Department in west Bogotá, apparently caused by a car bomb. It's estimated that the blast has affected at least three surrounding blocks and authorities estimate that there are at least 100 injured people."

It was one of the biggest-ever explosions in Colombia. If the bus had entered the lobby, it would have annihilated the DAS building. The blast opened a crater ten-feet deep and demolished a complex of two-storey commercial buildings next to the avenue where the bus had been parked. The entire facade of the eleven-storey DAS building was gone and its interior destroyed.

The fronts of the elevators had been ripped off, exposing the dead inside. Numerous buildings were damaged and windows shattered in a twenty-six-block area. Out of the almost 1,000 injured, those who could stand wandered through an area strewn with rubble, pieces of cars, corpses, blood-splatter and body parts. So many needed blood transfusions there was a medical crisis.

A radio presenter said: "Yes, Juan Dario, I am close to the scene of the tragedy. Many floors of that building suffered extreme damage. On the east side of 27th Avenue there is a large crater. Several employees were injured and they are still being evacuated by the police, the Red Cross and the Social Security Institute ambulances."

A TV presenter said: "The wave of terrorism spreading over Colombia in 1989 continues. Employees' relatives are advised not to come to the area. All injured people have been moved to different hospitals. We plead with you not to come close. We are dealing with a critical situation. I repeat, at least 100 wounded employees have already been taken to different hospitals in the capital of the republic."

The TV broadcast the remnants of buildings, piles of rubble, fire engines with their sirens blaring, firefighters on ladders scaling the skeleton of the DAS building, medical workers dashing around with stretchers, a person's limbs dangling from a mangled car: "The police have brought out shovels as they have started to remove debris from the building, trying to find wounded people who might be trapped."

"Well, according to information provided so far by the security agencies," said the mayor of Bogotá, "it seems it was a bomb with high explosive yield. Apparently, it was a truck that was parked by the east side of the building, and it's been confirmed that it is the largest bomb ever set off in the city. It seems there are many victims. An evacuation of the injured is under way ... and many blocks around the area have been affected by the explosive wave.

"The general and director of the DAS have come out of this unhurt. I repeat, General Maza came out of the attack alive."

Prior to the explosion, Maza had arrived and greeted his secretary, who gave him coffee. Usually he would chat with her, but instead, he took the coffee and a newspaper to his office, where his bulletproof window imploded and fell on his desk. If it had fallen on him, it would have crushed him to death. A wall collapsed onto his secretary and a bodyguard. Less than ten feet away, his secretary died. Blinded by dust, the survivors attempted to escape by feeling their way along walls encrusted with shards of glass, which shredded their hands, painting the walls with blood. Descending the stairs, Maza was shocked by the corpses and the wounded. As the dust settled, arms, legs, hands, fingers and toes appeared. Outside, the area had been flattened. Despite the devastation and over 100 deaths, Maza emerged without a scratch, having been shielded by his office walls.

"It was like a mini-atom bomb," he told reporters. "The ceiling fell down on top of me." He said that the bomb was positioned to aim shock waves at the upper floors of the building. "Without a doubt, it was aimed at me." He credited his survival to the grace of God and the steel protecting his office. "It wasn't just an attack on the State Security Department, it was an attack against democracy, against all Colombians. The terrorists want to destabilise this country with their savagery by killing innocent people."

"Do you think you were the main target of this attempt?"

"I'll ask you a question: do you think that to kill one person the terrorists had to use a bomb that could kill hundreds?"

"I don't know. That's why I'm asking."

"I repeat, this wasn't an attack against just me. It was an attack against all Colombians."

"Could it be that the Medellín Cartel now has the government cornered?"

"No way. Nobody here has the ability to subvert the state order! Two police operations are under way to capture the Mexican and Pablo Escobar."

"Does that mean they've claimed responsibility for the attack?"

"No more questions."

Worldwide news reported the terrorism. Watching on TV, Pablo smiled and issued a $1.3-million contract on Maza. Although disappointed by Maza's miraculous escape, he viewed the bombing as a success because it had increased the public's paranoia. If the government couldn't protect its citizens, it would be forced to negotiate an end to the war. With the Colombians losing faith in their leaders, a sense of hopelessness spread across the country. After the attack, he wrote: "Our military actions have been the only means of defence against abuses and barbarities committed against the extradited and their families."

An investigation traced the bus to a storage warehouse. General Maza invited the media along for the raid. The police went in and cameras flashed, but the smell of dynamite caused a quick evacuation.

The Spectator asked: "Now what follows after the bombing of *The Spectator*, Avianca's airplane and the Security Department? After these three devastating terrorist attacks, all of which took place in a three-month period, most Colombians anxiously await the end of this tragic year 1989, and to start a better year. The terrifying acts of the Medellín Cartel have the people of the capital living in fear and paranoia. At this time, Bogotá is a city where nobody knows what can happen. Its citizens pray each day so as not to become victims, while the police chase and try to capture the criminals who seem to be winning, one by one, the battles of a war, which seems to be never-ending."

CHAPTER 22
DEATH OF GACHA

Reluctant to negotiate with the Medellín Cartel, the president wanted to restore the people's faith in the government by capturing or killing one of the bosses. Such a success would demonstrate who was in command. An operation was launched: The Beginning of the End. Special agents arrested many of Gacha's men, dismantled some of his infrastructure and reduced the area he controlled. Information from those arrested, from Gacha's enemies in the emerald trade and from the Cali Cartel, enabled the authorities to have Gacha on the run in his zone.

In December 1989, on a deserted runway near Hacienda Nápoles, Pablo met Gacha. During a two-hour conversation, El Patrón proposed purchasing the mountain of Aquitania, which bordered a 30,000-acre forest, a national reserve they could hide in. Despite Pablo's insistence, Gacha refused.

"Pablo, I'm on my way to Cartagena to coordinate a new route with the Navigator," Gacha said. "I want to take my son Freddy, so he can get an education. I won't be long." In November 1989, Freddy had been released from jail. Two months earlier, he had been arrested by Colonel Franklin Quintero during a raid on a ranch north of Bogotá, and charged with possessing illegal arms. Hoping that he would lead them to Gacha, the police had watched him.

"Don't go to the coast. You'll be exposed there."

Ignoring Pablo's advice, Gacha left to see the Navigator, who coordinated cocaine shipments on the Caribbean coast. The Navigator had informed Cali about the meeting, and the Cali godfathers had told General Maza, who was attending a ceremony at the Military School of Cadets.

At a small ranch, Gacha reunited with Freddy. The government sent more than 1,000 police and Marines to the area. Informed about the arrival of special commandos, Gacha left Cartagena for a resort town in northern Colombia called Coveñas, accompanied by bodyguards and Freddy. General Maza dispatched two helicopters.

At night, Gacha attempted to escape on a yacht, but got lost at sea. After abandoning the boat, he headed for an island to pick up reinforcements. Guided by the Navigator, helicopters located the yacht and interrogated its skipper.

"I left him at the El Tesoro estate in the Coveñas resort. He went to a nearby island to collect a group of paramilitaries to strengthen his security."

On December 15, 1989, the elite police sent two helicopters. The Navy was stationed to prevent him from escaping over the water. At mid-morning, the two helicopters flew over El Tesoro with loudspeakers asking him to surrender. There was no response, but a red Chevrolet truck was seen. The helicopters split: one towards Tolú and the other towards Coveñas. The helicopter heading for Tolú spotted the red truck and followed it along the road to the city of Sincelejo until it stopped. Four bodyguards and Freddy jumped from the truck to confuse the police, and shot at the helicopter, which fired back. While the helicopter killed two bodyguards, Gacha sped away. After descending, the helicopter put elite troops on the ground, who opened fire and killed Freddy and his men.

Up the road, Gacha spotted a Marine checkpoint. The troops were vigilant because the shots had led them to believe that a guerrilla attack was in progress. Assuming that the checkpoint was for him, Gacha and a bodyguard leapt from the truck and fled into a banana plantation in a farm called La Lucha. With two helicopters in pursuit, the hunted men fired back, but the bodyguard fell. Spotting Gacha behind a banana tree, a helicopter gunner aimed at the tree and blew off a chunk of Gacha's skull.

Initially, the extent of the head damage and the noise of the grenades led some witnesses to believe that the Mexican had committed suicide by holding a grenade to his head, upholding the Extraditables motto that it was better to die in Colombia than to rot away in an American jail. But as his hands were undamaged, the grenade theory was debunked. The official report stated that a bullet to the face from a helicopter-mounted machine gun killed him, but Popeye later claimed that Gacha was killed by a shot from a Marine before the helicopter arrived.

The news reported: "A National Police source has just informed us that a few minutes ago, the Elite Group commanded by Colonel Martínez eliminated José Gonzalo Rodríguez Gacha, a.k.a. the Mexican! After the death of Mario Henao, Pablo Escobar's brother-in-law, this would be the largest blow the government has struck to drug traffickers because the Mexican was one of the main heads of the self-called Extraditables group. Although our information is totally confirmed, the police will perform fingerprint tests on the corpses in order to rule out any type of doubts. Together with the Mexican, his son Freddy Rodríguez and a group of men belonging to his personal security were eliminated. The Elite Group is now centred on Pablo Escobar and Jorge Ochoa, who continue to be in control of the Medellín Cartel's group of delinquents and drug traffickers."

Photos of the corpses showed Gacha, Freddy and their bodyguards on the ground, filthy and blood-stained. The Mexican was so disfigured that fingerprint tests were needed to establish his identity.

The president announced: "We have important news for you. This government has eliminated one of the worst criminals ever."

Death had come to Gacha so fast that the marble-plated chapel he had commissioned for his corpse was incomplete. Dedicated to the Holy Child, it was under construction in his hometown of Pacho. On December 17, 1989, his unrecognisable corpse ended up in a coffin in a common grave, shattering his aura of invincibility to some of the attendees. The media reported that up to 15,000 mourners had arrived. Many viewed him as generous due to his building projects and assistance to the poor. His death restored some faith in the government, and exposed the vulnerability of the Medellín Cartel's bosses.

Cali celebrated its first big result from providing information. The Navigator entered the United States Federal Witness Protection Program and wrote a book about his role in Gacha's downfall.

Having warned Gacha, Pablo was unsurprised. His death ended Pablo's relationship with the paramilitary groups of the Magdalena Medio associated with Gacha. Their leaders such as Henry Pérez now schemed against Pablo. Realising that he had overestimated the government's willingness to negotiate, El Patrón decided to respond with more bombs and terrorism. To spoil the government's victory, he would escalate the war.

The spearhead of the Search Bloc was a branch of the police called the DIJIN, nicknamed the Reds because of their thirst for blood . They dressed as civilians and had names similar to Pablo's hit men, such as Pencil, Motor and Tube.

A car bomb near a soccer stadium killed six policemen and wounded twenty. Seeking rewards from Pablo, killers shot five policemen on the same day. The Reds waited until dark to round up and kill more young people in the poorest neighbourhoods of Medellín.

Using 2,000 kilos of dynamite stored in toilet-paper rolls, Cuco organised a truck bomb in Bogotá. The driver of the truck headed for an exclusive neighbourhood, where General Maza and senior politicians lived. At dawn, the slow wick was lit and the driver fled. A military bodyguard grew suspicious, found the bomb and extinguished the wick. A statement from the Extraditables promised more attacks in Bogotá in response to the victims of the Search Bloc and Colombian citizens who had been extradited.

Hiding in a farm, Pablo orchestrated bombings against the government and the Cali Cartel, including dynamite attacks on police barracks and remote-control car bombs. A bomb manufactured out of an experimental type of dynamite accidentally detonated in a home, converting the area to rubble.

Hoping to reduce the violence, the occupants of embattled neighbourhoods demanded that the police leave. On the streets, the police braced for car bombs to go off at any moment and for assassins seeking rewards to shoot them. The risk was so high and pressure so unbearable, that the police retreated back to their academies and the Antioquia police headquarters. Across the country, police were trained in anti-terrorist techniques and put on standby to replace the dead police in Medellín.

In Cali, Cartagena, Bogotá, Medellín and Pereira, eighteen car bombs exploded, killing ninety-three, injuring 450 and creating damage in excess of three billion pesos. Years later, Colonel Martínez admitted that, at first, he felt small in the face of Pablo's hellish death machine and that Pablo, at the beginning, looked at the men of the elite with detachment, without perceiving them as a threat but merely as operatives continually on his heels, while valuing them as enemies. Martínez said:

"Five million dollars or something like that he ordered them to offer to me, but since he could not get the agreement, he set car bombs on us. He had a hit man infiltrate our commandos, sent attacks on my family, and paid lower-ranking people from the Elite to obtain information and affect the operations. However, above all, he proposed to take us out using bombs. He killed about thirty-five of our men in three attacks in a week. The police commanders in Bogotá thought of withdrawing the Elite Corps from Medellín, but we asked that they let us continue working, so to give the signal that the fight was not with an officer or with a group, but with the state.

"We went from 100 to 300. Escobar focused his interest on the people on top. He found out our backgrounds, got our resumes and, to make us look like criminals, he accused us of kidnapping and torture. It was his job, he was defending himself, avoiding capture.

"I observed Escobar for several years, not as a personal enemy, but as an enemy of the State, and I considered him a criminal with a lot of power, but a criminal, a kidnapper, a drug trafficker. He was seeing us the same time we were seeing him, so it was like a race – who would arrive first? If we acted with professionalism, with serious and responsible work, we would win. It was considered that we could all die, and he would win. The officers had to go out and knew that at any moment a bomb could explode, but they had to set an example. As we progressed, we lost the initial fear."

Hundreds of reinforcements were based at the Carlos Holguin Police Academy. Before long, the new troops were employing torture and execution in Medellín. In the academy, prisoners endured extreme heat in what became known as "the Sauna Room." Some of the survivors of the torture returned from the academy missing nails and eyes, their bodies covered in cuts. Some were permanently disabled from drills piercing their backbones.

Acting as a death squad, the Reds would arrive at a spot in the city, round up a group of young people and shoot them on the assumption that they worked for Pablo. Due to the nightly killings, seventy young people were executed within twenty days, mostly innocent as Pablo's men were in hideouts, alert to the ways of the police.

Pablo assassinated the Medellín police captain and lieutenant, who were assisting the Reds. The killer was abducted by the police and tortured to death. To earn rewards, policemen with Mafia associations killed their own colleagues and sold weapons provided by the government to the Medellín Cartel.

CHAPTER 23
CHRISTMAS KIDNAPPINGS

El Patrón believed that targeting the most elite and powerful families would bring the government to the negotiation table. Abducting them quickly would spread shock over Christmas. Rather than killing people, kidnapping them would instil even more terror in their family members, who would live in perpetual fear of their loved ones getting tortured and disposed of. He drew up a list of almost twenty names and sent his men.

In December 1989, he kidnapped Diego Montoya, son of Germán Montoya, President Barco's personal secretary. Also taken were Patricia Echavarría, from the wealthy textile family, and Roberto Zuluaga, the son of the owner of the largest retail chain in Colombia.

"I'm certain that the Extraditables kidnapped your son," General Maza told Germán Montoya. "You need to look for people in Medellín who could help you."

Santiago and Diego Londoño went to find out if the Extraditables had Montoya's son.

"Yes, we have him," Gustavo said, "and this time we have him to negotiate. You'll see if you get into this, we'll not let them take us for a fool." He reminded them of the previous negotiation with Germán Montoya that had failed in 1988. Back then, the Antioquian writer and businessman Joaquín Vallejo had published a newspaper article calling for dialogue to end the war with the traffickers. The lawyer Guido Parra had arranged for him to meet Gacha, Pablo and the Ochoas.

"We want to lead quiet lives with our families," Jorge Ochoa had said, and complained about their treatment by the authorities.

"If we reach an agreement," Gacha had said, "I'll give the government something bigger than the Colombian Petroleum Company."

Joaquín Vallejo had met Germán Montoya, who asked, "But do you believe in these gentlemen?"

"They, for the sake of peace, are willing to sacrifice many things, and are willing to hand over weapons, laboratories, airports and 5,000 men that can be put at the service of the state to end the guerrillas. Maybe we should close our eyes a bit, cover our noses a bit. The means would not matter because if they created a solution, the drug trafficking would end."

Montoya had hinted at making progress and, during a speech, President Barco had proposed using dialogue to solve the violence. Through Joaquín Vallejo, the traffickers had resurrected the proposals made in 1983 to Betancur, and added the possibility of a patrimonial amnesty. Montoya had told the traffickers to lobby the highest levels of the US government, but they hired a second-class firm which made no progress.

Under pressure from George HW Bush, Barco had U-turned. "No more dialogue," he had announced. "The only option is for those men to surrender."

Montoya had fallen into line with the president, and denied negotiating with the cartel. Government action against the traffickers had resumed.

With the December 1989 kidnappings of people from wealthy families, Pablo believed that the outcome would be different, as Montoya's son's life was at risk. "Let's see how Montoya behaves now that we have his son tied up," he said.

The Extraditables announced: "We ordered the leaders of poor barrios to take hostage members of the traditional oligarchy, especially those that have never undertaken social works to benefit the community of those without protection." The ransom, "will be used 50 per cent to finance the war declared against the political oligarchy and the other 50 per cent for the construction of housing for those without shelter. These measures are being taken in response to the official persecution of our families and organisations."

The radio reported: "Shortly after the national government surprised the country with the elimination of the drug trafficker José Gonzalo Rodríguez Gacha, bad news returned again. In the midst of the Christmas season, and during unprecedented action, seventeen people were kidnapped in Medellín. The inhabitants of the capital of Antioquia are living with fear and uncertainty caused by the so-called Extraditables group. They are the ones who claimed responsibility for kidnapping citizens as retaliation for the death of the Mexican. It seems that a relative of an important member of the government is one of the hostages."

Against the wishes of his family, Santiago Londoño agreed to mediate again. He hoped to demonstrate that, "a negotiated solution to the traffickers would be more convenient for the country than an intense and endless war." For the negotiations, Germán Montoya also suggested including the Antioquian businessman J. Mario Aristizábal.

They both met Pablo, who said, "I want a negotiated exit, but I must clarify to them that my offensive capacity is not diminished."

After listening attentively, J. Mario said, "The narcos not only have to dismantle the business, but surrender to justice. In the end, they don't have to ask permission from anybody to do so. To set the mood for the dialogue, why not announce a unilateral truce?"

With the political class plunged into a crisis, powerful people including three former presidents tried to resolve the situation. A group of elite family members joined forces to mediate between the government and the traffickers.

The Notables held a press conference: "Colombians can't allow their country to become a war scenario, or that their brothers end up being victims of a battle that doesn't concern them. Colombian people claim their right to live in peace. That's why we, the Commission of Notables, ask all extraditable individuals in the spirit of the Christmas season to give Colombia the best present they can: freedom for all hostages! Free the hostages and leave behind the dynamite, and please surrender. That's the only way you can expect justice, a fair treatment."

After accepting the idea, Pablo freed a hostage and surrendered a bus full of dynamite, a helicopter and a lab in the Chocó jungle, but he ran into difficulty attempting to stop a hit on Low Murtra. He told Guido Parra, "I sent people to kill Low Murtra because he signed some extraditions. We entrusted the task to the people of the ETA, and since these people are clandestine, we have not been able to locate them. Tell the former Minister Low Murtra to seek protection until I manage to stop the order." As a protective measure, Murtra had been assigned as an ambassador in Switzerland. Germán Montoya told him, "Look for protection because there is an attack in progress against you." The Swiss government gave him a bodyguard.

The Extraditables announced: "We want to let the public and national government know that we agree with the most excellent Commission of Notables in order to live in a peaceful Colombia. We already released one of the hostages held by us. The other sixteen will be released in the next few days. We will also return properties, cash and infrastructure. And we will face Colombian justice. The Extraditable Group, full of love for the country, accept the elusive call for peace and announce our total and absolute surrender."

Letters arrived to the government urging diplomacy with the traffickers, including from the ex-presidents Pastrana and López Michelsen, and the archbishop primate, Monsignor Revollo.

At a Security Council meeting, President Barco sought a consensus for a negotiated solution but General Maza objected: "It's morally reprehensible to hear these spokespeople. I am very sorry but Escobar has tried to kill me and done plenty of damage to the country. I do not consider that this dialogue is good for Colombia."

A deal was made to ensure Montoya's release, timed to coincide with the arrival of George HW Bush for a War on Drugs meeting in Colombia. A week later, Montoya was freed. After money was exchanged, the remaining hostages were returned to their families.

On a radio interview, a Notable said: "I can't help feeling pleased because the Extraditables accepted our call for peace. They not only sent their declaration of surrender but also showed with facts their real intention for peace. They not only released the hostages, which is the most important thing, but they also delivered a great amount of explosive material, and I know that in Antioquia they delivered a helicopter, several thousand dollars and a cocaine processing laboratory. Those, in my view, are coherent actions that guarantee the Colombian people their real intentions for peace."

Pressure on Barco came from President George HW Bush, who classified the traffickers as a threat to national security and pushed for war. Not wanting to risk the aid coming from America, Barco dropped the dialogue with the traffickers and resumed a hard approach. The media leaked information about the negotiations. After denying that they had taken place, Germán Montoya stated that contact had been made on a humanitarian basis to obtain his son's freedom.

The radio announced: "Your attention, please! The newspaper *The Spectator* revealed in today's edition that what has so far been known as the surrendering process of the so-called Extraditables Group is nothing more than a negotiation of the National Government with the Medellín Cartel."

Pablo exploded: "What I do worry about is seeing prude people who hide behind false morals and pretend to cover the sun with their hands, like our president Mr Barco, who declares with a loud voice that he is fighting against drug traffickers, while under the table he does not hesitate in making arrangements with them. And then [he] gets upset, screaming at everyone that he will never negotiate with them. Impudent!"

In late 1989, President George HW Bush ordered the invasion of Panama and the capture of General Noriega, whom Bush had helped to put in power. On January 3, 1990, Noriega surrendered. Pablo documented his thoughts in a memoir found by the police years later in a jungle shelter:

"Noriega forgot a social and political principle that has a special validity. There's nobody more dangerous than an ex-friend. Bush, when he was the boss of the CIA, was his godfather, benefactor, friend, confidante and accomplice. When Noriega could not continue to lend him the 'valuable and cheap' collaboration, [Bush] began the pressure, the accusations, generally false and tendentious, to discredit and make the general fall, among them, obviously, the simplest: drug trafficking. When the gringos did it through the same channels as always but with monetary benefits for the Contras in Nicaragua … nobody said that anything bad was happening, but now it was very serious!

"After what has just happened in Panama, and given the US imperialist antecedents, a fatal shadow falls on our future and that of the entire world. At any time and according to the whim of the reigning satrap [provincial governor], [they] will do whatever pleases them under pain of the Marines disembarking, giving us death, destroying what we have and leaving.

"When being left without a job, unemployed, useless, dissolved, all the American armies deployed in Europe, Asia, etc., when there is no longer Communism, or the Soviet Union, potentially dangerous enemies, those war machines, those planes, aircraft carriers, tanks, frigates, cannons, rifles and all those guys who run them will be unemployed, and to justify their positions, the Pentagon's top brass will rush to look for some marginal occupation, and there is talk of sending the Sixth Mediterranean Fleet to patrol the waters of the Caribbean, in front of Colombia, under the excuse that they are in international waters, and also to send squads of the Air Force or military satellites to patrol our skies, with the declared purpose of ending drug trafficking. Those boys will be given some weekends off and we'll see them soon in Santa Marta, Cartagena, Tolú, and soon after we'll see how AIDS spreads in an exponential way in our country."

CHAPTER 24
DEATH OF PININA

Pablo assigned Popeye to kidnap Senator Federico Estrada Vélez. The senator had once refused to help Popeye get a job at the municipal transit. Having grown up where Vélez lived, Popeye entered the Éxito District in disguise. He watched the senator's driver go from Hugo's Store and collect Vélez at 7:30 AM. The driver knew who Popeye was, so it was essential that the driver didn't see him. Travelling in the back of an unarmoured vehicle with no bodyguards, Vélez seemed an easy target. Every day, he kept regular hours and took two routes to work.

Pinina arrived with four policemen who worked for the cartel, and discussed the plan with Popeye. He would stand by Hugo's Store, while Popeye walked around. Stationed at a car park outside a department store, the four policemen would abduct Vélez on the avenue and transfer him into a car. After a second car transfer, Popeye would take him to Pablo to discuss extradition.

By 7 AM, everyone was in position. At 7:10 AM, Vélez got in his vehicle. By radio, Popeye reported the target's movements. On the avenue, the four policemen kidnapped the senator and threw him into Pinina's car's trunk. Two blocks away, while getting transferred to the second car, the senator recognised Popeye, but pretended not to.

With the driver having reported the first car, Popeye believed the police would be looking for the wrong vehicle. Twenty minutes after the kidnapping, the authorities had blocked all of the roads leaving Bogotá. According to the radio, a witness had observed the transfer to the second car. Tuned in to their radios, the occupants of other cars were scanning the roads for the second car. With the Army and the police on the streets, Popeye drove to one of Pablo's warehouses. With radio broadcasts continuing to alert people about the kidnapping, Pinina ordered everyone to stay in the warehouse, where the senator was allowed to get out of the car.

"Can I have some water?" Vélez asked. Popeye brought him some. "Why have I been kidnapped?" After Popeye didn't answer, the senator looked terrified. While Pinina went to find a new drop-off spot, Vélez tried to get Popeye talking, but he remained quiet. While contemplating how much power he had over the senator who had once refused to make a call to help him get a job, Popeye felt strong.

Exasperated by the senator's small talk, Popeye snapped. "You know me. I work for Pablo Escobar, and as soon as everything calms down, I'm going to take you to him." The senator didn't speak.

With Pinina gone for too long, Popeye feared they had been seen entering the warehouse. He tied up and gagged the senator. With his hostage in the trunk of another car, Popeye headed for one of Pinina's apartments in El Poblado. Despite police being everywhere, Popeye travelled unnoticed. At a red light, two policemen on motorbikes stopped next to him. Grabbing his gun, he watched the police until the light changed and they proceeded.

Finally, Popeye parked in a covered area at the apartment. Again, Vélez, still in the trunk, asked for water, only to be told he would have to wait. "I'll leave the gag off, but if you make even the smallest noise, I'll have to shoot you."

"Yes, sir."

After closing the trunk, Popeye sat in the car for two hours until Pinina arrived with more men and three cars. With the senator in the trunk of the middle car, the three cars headed out and took back roads. With no problems encountered, the senator was transferred to another safe house.

Hiding elsewhere, Popeye received a call warning him not to

go back to the senator's district because people had reported that he had kidnapped the senator and suspicious cars were getting stopped. He responded that anybody who reported him would be killed.

Two days later, the senator was brought to Pablo. In armchairs, they chatted for hours.

"I'll try and convince my colleague to fight for the abolition of extradition," Vélez said.

"Don't mention me to the authorities," Popeye said, and the senator agreed.

After shaking hands with Pablo, the senator was transferred to a safe house, to await his release with a note from the Extraditables. Just after Pablo's men left, the Elite Group arrived. Vélez walked out to the police. The government announced that the senator had been rescued by the Elite Group.

While publicly condemning extradition, Vélez secretly supported it. After Pablo found out, he ordered his assassination. The authorities were expecting Popeye to return to the senator's district because Vélez had described him to them. Aware of the senator's routine, Popeye sent two men, who killed the senator and his driver.

Colonel Martínez was in Medellín coordinating operations against Pablo when an explosion outside of his home in Bogotá shattered the glass in his TV and his windows imploded. After hearing news of the bomb, he called his terrified wife. With her children, she abandoned the apartment for a safe house, leaving it littered with their belongings and glass. For their safety, the children had to stop attending school.

The colonel assumed that the bomb had been a warning, as Pablo could have easily killed his family. Resolved to maintain pressure on Pablo, he returned to the apartment a week later. Nobody knew he was there. With a guard downstairs protecting the building and allowing no one access without prior permission, the colonel felt that he had enough time to pack his belongings.

A harsh knock on the door sent a shiver up his spine. When he had been ordered to lead the Search Bloc, his colleagues had assumed that he would be dead within months – and perhaps now the moment had come. As the guard had issued no alert and the colonel had not preapproved any visitors, he assumed that Pablo's men had infiltrated the building, which mostly housed senior police.

The next loud knock prompted the colonel to yell, "Who is there?" The voice on the other side of the door was unintelligible, so the colonel yelled, "Who is it?"

The knocker said a name, which the colonel recognised from four years previous, a policeman he had worked with. Due to irregularities in a case, the colonel had asked him to resign. Opening the door revealed his colleague in a suit and tie, his sweaty face pinched, his gaze low.

"I've come to you with a message, my colonel. I've come to you obligated." The man raised his eyes. "The message is from Pablo Escobar. If I didn't come, they were going to kill me or my family. That's the threat I'm under."

"Look, I understand your position," the colonel said, perplexed as to how the visitor had arrived by bypassing the guard, plus nobody was supposed to have known that he was in Bogotá. Suddenly, he felt unsafe, as if he could be killed at any moment. "If you want a response, first tell me how you got here. Who told you that I was here? If you don't tell me, then I have not received your message."

"Escobar sent me to offer you $6 million." The man studied the colonel's impassive face. "The only thing he asks is that you keep on working, that you continue your job, that you keep carrying out operations against him. But if you're sending an operation to capture him, you must make a phone call first to let us know. If you agree, then the money will be delivered to any account you want. Six million."

Martínez felt that the offer of money or death was being made because he was getting close to capturing Pablo. "Tell them you couldn't find me."

"But, my colonel, I can't do that."

"We never spoke." The colonel shut the door in his face.

Convinced he would eventually capture Pablo, he was concerned about his wife and children. At the age of 23, he'd fallen in love with Magdalena after his first year of police work in Bogotá. As he was about to be transferred to another station, his colleagues had organised a party for him. Seventeen-year-old Magdalena had attended the festivities. He had left with her phone number and had organised a date to the cinema. After a year, he was scheduled to be moved to another city, so he had consulted his father about Magdalena. The advice he received was to marry her if he loved her or to leave her if he didn't.

Martínez heard Pinina state in a phone call that he would be visiting a relative in Envigado, so the elite police stationed vehicles in the area. Pinina received another call that was intercepted:

"Hey, where are you?"

"Over here, arriving at the supermarket."

"Look, go back and pass by the side of the blue car, near the shoulder in the corner below. Those people are going to be *the* people." The caller had identified the police.

"If it turns out those people are, let's take them with us." Pinina started making calls and giving orders. Within ten minutes, sixty hit men had arrived with rifles.

Martínez scrambled for his radio. "They are mobilising against you! Change your location!"

After the police relocated, another call was intercepted: "They are in the upper corner. Let's shoot them."

"Evacuate immediately," Martínez said, saving his men.

For weeks, Pinina disappeared off the police's radar, but a raid on an apartment produced a notebook containing codes that identified cartel members. They traced him to a farm in Estrella, but a raid produced nothing as the property lacked even a phone. For three months, Martínez eavesdropped on his calls, but didn't have the equipment to pinpoint any locations. He learned that Pinina was using a rural service wave telephone adapted to turn it into a mobile phone. He only sent coded messages to beepers, never revealing numbers or addresses that would give away his location. However, the officers identified aliases, work areas and part of the structure of the organisation.

When the government first offered rewards on radio and TV, the traffickers suffered, as they were forced into hiding and away from family and friends. Whenever Pablo was in the company of Jorge Ochoa, and one of them needed to use the bathroom, the other guarded the door with a submachine gun.

With satellite photos and information from spy planes, Martínez learned about Pablo's hideout in the Envigado Mountains. It took forty-eight hours for the elite police to infiltrate the terrain. By 11 PM, they were camouflaged in the area, ready for the signal to raid the property.

At midnight, Martínez intercepted a call from Pinina: "Boss, they have located you and I'm told they're coming for you."

"Thank you very much. Let the other friends know."

At dawn, the police arrived at a small, empty house reinforced with an inner wall of stone and cement. They found information, accounts of war contributions, expenses, the names of important aliases …

Pablo infiltrated the Search Bloc headquarters. He learned that whenever the colonel was launching a raid, four convoys would be dispatched, only one on an actual mission, the rest as decoys. With an inside man hired by Pinina warning him about the actual target, he was always prepared. With him and his men always slipping away just before the troops arrived, Martínez grew suspicious.

Pablo ordered an inside man to assassinate the colonel or else he and his family would be killed. The assassin was ordered to poison the lunch soup served to forty Search Bloc troops, which would have killed all of them including Martínez. But on that day, the cook decided not to sequester the elite troops' food. Instead, he put enough food in the soup for 200 troops – the whole school – which diluted the poison. Troops who would have died ended up with diarrhoea, which they blamed on stale food.

Centra Spike sent Pablo's location to Martínez, who overheard a call from the headquarters to one of Pablo's men: "They're on their way. They're coming for you." A recording of the call was sent to Martínez, but he couldn't recognise the voice. He fired some of his men, but the warnings to Pablo continued. The implications were so grave that Martínez tendered his resignation on the grounds that he couldn't progress in such a hopeless situation that was out of his control. His resignation was refused.

The cartel ordered its inside man to shoot Martínez at his desk, during the evening when he was listening to the traffickers' calls. He smuggled a gun with a silencer into the compound. At night, he hid in the darkness outside of the colonel's window. Peeping through, he spotted Martínez, wearing headphones. Taking aim, he had doubts about the gun and its silencer. If the gun were defective and he failed, the colonel would return fire and kill him. He decided to assassinate the colonel the following night, after he had practised with the gun.

In the morning, Martínez called Colonel Aguilar and asked that some men be assigned to an operation at a shopping centre. Ten minutes later, he intercepted a call from Pinina: "Be careful, they're going to get someone at a shopping centre."

Fearful, Martínez rushed over to Colonel Aguilar. "How can the cartel know what I just told my second-in-command? It's either you or you need to find out who it is."

While investigating the leak, Aguilar realised that only one assistant had been in his office when the shopping centre instructions had been issued. It was a cadet who guarded the perimeter of the base, shined the officers' shoes and carved wooden figures of troops and vehicles. Hoping to trap him, Aguilar allowed him to overhear a conversation about him investigating a mole. Realising that his boss had identified him as the leak, the assistant broke down. "I'll tell you everything, but please don't hurt me."

Aguilar called Martínez: "We have him."

They interrogated the assistant, who said, "They paid me to kill you. I worked together with a second lieutenant who died in an operation against Escobar's men. The cartel has an apartment in front of the barracks, from where information is dispatched." The cadet confessed to accepting money to kill Martínez and divulged the attempts and that Pinina had recruited him. He ended up imprisoned.

The police intercepted a call from Pinina's maid to her boyfriend, whom the police located. Under interrogation, he revealed the address where his girlfriend worked. "I've accompanied her close by, but I don't know much about the building." They took him to the location, where his girlfriend took them by surprise by leaning out of a window and yelling, "Hello!"

"That's my girlfriend," he told the police. "They'll surely kill her now."

After withdrawing, Martínez positioned teams of police around the building, so that it would take less than five minutes to storm inside.

Meanwhile, the cartel targeted an elite policeman stationed in front of the El Poblado police station. A dynamite explosion killed multiple civilians, but the undercover policeman was saved because he had mistakenly parked elsewhere.

The next day, Pinina spoke on the phone, confirming his presence inside of the apartment that the police had under surveillance. Martínez authorised a raid. On the third floor, the police encountered an armoured door, which they blasted open with dynamite. They charged inside, but Pinina was absent. Outside of the building, he was spotted hanging from a window ledge. The police opened fire, and he dropped.

On June 14, 1990, the authorities announced the death of Pinina, who had been in charge of Pablo's military operations. As usual, his death was credited to a shootout with the authorities. An anonymous package received by Pablo told a different story. It contained pictures of armed undercover agents of the elite unit escorting Pinina, with a broken leg, from a building towards a grey Mazda.

In the Magdalena Medio jungle, in a wood and zinc hut, Pablo shrugged off the death – it was the normal fate of a warrior. Informants in the Armed Forces notified him of pending operations and raids. Based on their information, he rotated through safe houses.

In a plane, Martínez spotted a cabin on a small hill in the middle of the jungle. After hearing voices, he gave the order to fire and a machine gun rained down bullets. They landed and entered the cabin. It had solar panels, a refrigerator, a table, a box of mineral water and a microwave oven. It had even been built high enough for Pablo to obtain a television signal to watch the World Cup.

A cousin of Pablo's was at a farm with his family on vacation when the police showed up. After stating that he didn't know where Pablo was, he was hung upside down with his eyes covered, tortured by electricity and had needles inserted into his testicles. He died in front of his family. Friends, associates and bodyguards of Pablo received the same treatment. Teenage hit men continued to attack police stations with machine guns and bombs to claim thousands of dollars. In retaliation, the police death squads drove through the barrios, machine-gunning young people unlucky enough to be out after dark.

In June 1990, Pablo sent his son abroad to avoid the escalating danger. Using false travel documents and accompanied by bodyguards, Juan Pablo watched Colombia play in the World Cup in Italy. For extra disguise, Juan Pablo's face was painted the Colombian colours – red, blue and yellow. He wore sunglasses and wrapped a Colombian flag around his head.

At a hotel in Switzerland, Juan Pablo mostly stayed indoors playing cards with his bodyguards. The hotel staff grew suspicious and notified the police. The authorities waited until Juan Pablo and the bodyguards emerged to have lunch at a Chinese restaurant. Ten police grabbed them. More cars arrived with their sirens wailing. The restaurant was sequestered with yellow tape.

Transported to a secret-police house, Juan Pablo was strip-searched in a bulletproof glass cubicle. At another house, he was questioned. "Why is a teenager wearing a $10,000 Cartier watch?"

"My father is a wealthy Colombian rancher with 3,500 animals. He sold a few head of cattle to buy this watch."

Half a day later, Juan Pablo and the bodyguards were released.

"Where can we drop you off?" a policeman said.

"Back at the Chinese restaurant."

On June 23, 1990, the Cali Cartel sent a hit team to a nightclub in El Poblado, which some of Otto's hit men frequented. Travelling in black vans with tinted windows, the hit team was allowed through a checkpoint manned by the elite police. In the nightclub, they ordered the people to walk to the car park in a single file. Outside, the gunmen opened fire, killing nineteen people under 25 years old, and injuring fifty. Blamed for the mass murder, Pablo lost one man.

On June 30, Pablo wrote his son a letter, describing how much he missed and loved him. He intended to send Victoria and Manuela to join Juan Pablo for safety and because his son had asked to be with them. He reminded Juan Pablo to believe in the destiny of humans, some of whom are assigned joy and others suffering.

Having read a letter written by the son of the Argentinian president, criticising his father for corruption, cowardice and for ejecting his own family out of the presidential palace, Pablo wrote how it had unnerved him. It had motivated him to reread Juan Pablo's letters, which reassured him and made him proud. He wanted his son to find peace and happiness. The temporary family separation was essential because that was the way of life.

He urged his son to be confident and to consider Pablo's effort to encourage him to study to have a bright future. Being overseas provided an opportunity to study languages and cultures. He wanted his son to remain calm for the sake of Victoria and Manuela. As a teenager, Pablo had no worldly possessions, but he was always the happiest.

He cautioned his son not to do anything illegal or to listen to any bad advice. He should follow his conscience. Pablo was not just his father, but also his best friend. Bravery was not drinking shots of liquor in front of your friends. Bravery was not drinking at all. After apologising for philosophising, Pablo said he was working hard and making good progress. He was exposing the torture of the young people in Medellín by the authorities. He urged his son to write and send photos, to enjoy life and engage in sports, which is where happiness hides. He finished by telling his son he loved him "so so so much."

After the World Cup, Juan Pablo was reunited with his family in Frankfurt. He and his mother studied English at a language school in Switzerland.

On July 17, 1990, Juan Pablo received another letter. In high spirits, Pablo told his son that he was going to end the war with the government after the Gaviria administration took over. Gaviria had stated that he was not committed to extradition, and that its use would be determined by the public order situation. If he restored public order, Pablo expected extradition to be prohibited by an article written by the National Constituent Assembly. This would end the danger to his family, and they could all return from overseas.

CHAPTER 25
PRESIDENT GAVIRIA

While Pablo targeted politicians in favour of extradition, the Castaño brothers acted as the enforcement arm of a right-wing conspiracy to kill presidential candidates and politicians on the left. Moving away from Pablo, Fidel was offering his services to the military and oligarchs. After massacring people in rural locations, he controlled large areas in northern Colombia and had forged relations with sectors of the Armed Forces. His specialty was launching attacks with young hit men known as disposables, whom he trained at his farms with Ingram 380 submachine guns, which they fired at coconuts. People couldn't fathom why the disposables performed attacks that they couldn't survive. In most cases, they were deceived and brainwashed.

The Patriotic Union Party (UP) had been started by the FARC and the Communist Party in 1985, as part of the peace talks with President Betancur. The president of the UP, Bernardo Jaramillo, had visited Europe in early 1988 and witnessed the fall of Communism. Back in Colombia, he urged his movement to distance itself from the philosophy of the FARC. He urged the guerrillas not to kidnap or resort to war because it achieved nothing. Distancing himself from the guerrillas did not stop the paramilitaries from plotting to kill the senior members of the UP. At Bogotá's El Dorado airport, a hit man opened fire with an Ingram 380, killing UP leader José Antequera, who was meeting ex-president Ernesto Samper. Bullets ricocheting off the ground ended up lodged in Samper's torso, which he demonstrated to the media as proof that he was a victim of the traffickers to counter accusations that he had taken hot money.

A right-wing minister, Carlos Lemos Simmonds, claimed that the president of the UP was a spokesman for the FARC. Bernardo Jaramillo responded, "The minister has hung a tombstone on my neck." Jaramillo said in Congress, "They have even said that I am the guerrillas' candidate. Nothing could be less true and more irresponsible. Hopefully the president will realise that these fragile statements put my integrity more at risk. I am the people's candidate, the candidate of a large majority that feel the time has come to achieve a more just and equitable country for the working class."

A senator responded: "Mr Jaramillo, allow me to say that no matter what the result of the forthcoming election is, this debate is one more example, one more proof that the Colombian left-wing forces enjoy the privileges and guarantees to deal democratically with the other candidates, and that is thanks to this government."

"You are right, Senator," Jaramillo said. "And it is thanks to the peace efforts of the president that our movement is no longer a guerrilla group, but became a political force that will be present in the forthcoming elections with a mission of social equality, responsible development, but above all, peace and reconciliation in all of the nation's territory."

Walking down a hallway at the El Dorado airport, Jaramillo and his wife were confronted by a hit man with an Ingram 380. After Jaramillo fell from the force of the bullets, his wife threw herself over him. Bodyguards rushed the couple inside a car. "Hug me, I'm going to die," Jaramillo said. "These bastards killed me."

A radio presenter announced: "Breaking news. A few minutes ago, physicians from the National Police Clinic have confirmed the death of the Patriotic Union presidential candidate Bernardo Jaramillo, whom two hours before had been a victim of a criminal attempt at the airport of the Colombian capital. He was about to take a flight to the city of Santa Marta with his wife. These are the statements of General Maza, Director of the Security Department."

Maza attended a press conference. "This is a regrettable situation for Colombian democracy, and a demented act the whole society should condemn. This is the second presidential candidate that according to our investigation falls under the criminal bullets of the Medellín Cartel, headed by the worst assassin and criminal in the history of this country, Pablo Escobar Gaviria."

At the funeral, the president was besieged by journalists. "Mr President, does the government insist that Pablo Escobar killed Mr Bernardo Jaramillo?"

"That's what the intelligence agencies tell us."

"Mr President, when is your government going to admit that the public order situation got out of your hands?"

"Nothing has gotten out of our hands."

"Dead policemen appear every day in Medellín, Mr President. Newspapers and official buildings are blown up in Bogotá. Planes explode in the air and presidential candidates are killed in airports and public squares. Of course this got out of your hands."

The president's secretary took the question: "Look, the government can't be blamed for all those barbaric acts. If you want to look for the guilty ones, take a look at Medellín."

"Could this be retaliation on the part of the Extraditables Group due to the fact that the process on their so-called surrender was curtailed?"

"This is neither the place nor the moment to talk about those things," the president said.

A young man from Medellín was arrested for the murder of Jaramillo, and General Maza continued to blame Pablo. Due to his age, the minor was released after a few months and found dead in the trunk of a car.

Having signed a peace pact with the government to bring the M-19 into civilian life, Carlos Pizarro had become an extremely popular presidential candidate. The M-19 guerrillas had recently fired their weapons at the sky for the last time, burned their uniforms, abandoned their hideouts, turned in their rifles and machine guns to be melted down, and had started to transition to civilian life, confident that they had no great enemies. Now holding his wife, Pizarro paid respect to the corpse of Jaramillo.

Despite the danger, Pizarro decided to continue his campaign. On April 26, 1990, he boarded an Avianca plane destined for Barranquilla. Dressed in light-coloured clothes, he was accompanied by twelve bodyguards, one of whom was wearing his famous hat. After greeting the crew, he was told to go to row twenty-three at the back. Shortly after take-off, a dark-haired man in his early 20s, wearing a green sweater and grey trousers, went to the rear bathroom. Emerging with an Ingram 380, he aimed at Pizarro's head and opened fire. Responding slowly enough for Pizarro to die, a bodyguard killed the hit man.

The police announced, "The characteristics of the crime – a suicidal hit man who shoots his victim in front of a hundred people and then resigns himself to die under the bullets of the bodyguards – gives us the certainty that it is a drug trafficking job."

The Extraditables publicly denied any involvement in the murders of Bernardo Jaramillo and Carlos Pizarro. In a letter, Pablo blamed Fidel Castaño for the attacks on the left: "What happens is that killing a town counsellor is easy, or a leader of the left, when it is handled with money by the DAS who chooses the bodyguards."

Alejo from the M-19 asked Fidel if he had killed Pizarro. "Yes, but there were more people involved there." Fidel ended the conversation.

On a rainy day, Pizarro's funeral ceremony saw Bolivar Square adorned with blue, white and red M-19 flags and balloons. Red carnations and little pictures of the Holy Child decorated his coffin. After the tributes and a parade, he was buried in the Central Cemetery next to Luis Carlos Galán, Jaime Pardo Leal and Bernardo Jaramillo.

Continuing Galán's campaign, Gaviria had secured a 59.9 per cent majority in the primary election on March 11, 1990, which had launched him as the Liberal Party's choice. Railing against the traffickers had earned him non-stop threats. Fearful of public appearances since Galán's death, he had focused on using the TV to raise his campaign's profile. To thwart attacks, the streets surrounding his apartment had protective barrels, soldiers and sniffer dogs. His visitors were searched and checked with metal detectors.

"Thank you very much," Gaviria announced at a rally. "Tonight, the Colombian people have talked and elected me as the official representative of the Liberal Party to become the only candidate for the Presidency of the Republic of Colombia." While soaking up boisterous cheering, he swigged water from a plastic bottle. "Today is the first step. There will be elections in two months, and I need the Colombian people's support for us to honour the political and ideological legacy designed by Luis Carlos Galán." Gaviria displayed the peace sign, while his supporters waved red and white balloons and flags. He kissed his wife and they picked up their toddlers.

On May 12, 1990, two car bombs exploded in Bogotá. At one site, a female journalist reported: "Terror takes possession of the country's streets again. Today, the turn was for the Quiriguá neighbourhood in Bogotá, where a car bomb full of dynamite has just exploded. This place was full of innocent citizens who passed through the area without imagining that, in broad daylight, such an explosion was going to surprise them. I never thought about a bomb. An earthquake came to my mind because everything fell down, and at those moments you don't hear any explosion."

The news showed a Fiat 147 reduced to a heap of melted metal and unconscious people getting carried on stretchers, leaking blood; a row of cars that appeared to have survived a nuclear war, the paint stripped off and windows blown out; a grey high-rise with all its windows gone and rubble strewn everywhere. The female reporter said: "Counting the car bomb at Quiriguá and the one that has just exploded, twenty-six people have died so far, including five children and 180 wounded.

"Undoubtedly, these two terrorist actions are by narco-terrorists, who have simultaneously created innocent victims," the police announced.

Amid the turmoil and prior to the presidential election on May 27, 1990, the polls indicated that Gaviria would win by a strong margin, also confirmed by exit polls. He ended up with 48.2 per cent of the vote.

In a studio, the president was interviewed: "I'm not going to lie to you. The country's situation is very serious. We are living in turbulent and violent times. In less than a year, three presidential candidates have been killed, over 250 policemen were murdered in Medellín, and a car bomb was placed at the Elite Group commander's family – a car bomb that fortunately didn't explode."

"And what are we going to do to face this situation, Mr President? We Colombians, all Colombians, are afraid to go out on the street."

"And I understand you. That's exactly why I came to the booth to talk to you, for all your audience to listen to my call and help with information that allows us to find all of the Medellín Cartel people. There are 1 million pesos for each. Please denounce, report. Don't let some people end the peace for everyone in the country."

Fake callers flooded the police with false reports of sighting Pablo.

On August 7, 1990, Gaviria was sworn in as the president with a Colombian-flag-colours sash placed on his shoulders and around his back, in a plaza between the Congress building and the presidential palace. The security forces had cordoned off an area around the plaza. Attack helicopters buzzed overhead. Present were three South American presidents and the US vice president.

At a podium, holding papers, he read a speech. "Our nation finished the most difficult and violent election campaign in history. Violence threatened to devastate values and tutelary principles, our democracy and our freedom. We lost thousands of good Colombians, including our best and youngest leaders. Violence knocked at the doors of each Colombian and put the nation's character to test. But what the aggressors ignored was that the country grows in the face of adversity, that before death and pain, life and hope get bigger. In spite of bombs, Colombians went to the voting booths and expressed en masse for a democratic and peaceful country.

"Narco-terrorism is the principal threat against our democracy. We will face it without concessions … No nation in the history of humanity has paid as high a price as Colombia … for confronting the most powerful criminal organisations in memory." He cited extradition as a discretionary tool, and for the government to exercise discretion. "It is first required that the terror disappear and that we have a strengthened judicial system." He expressed support for an arrangement that would offer traffickers a Colombian trial instead of extradition if the war ended and the power of the court system restored by eradicating bribery. This required major reforms and extra protection for judges.

Afterwards, a journalist asked the US vice president whether America would stop aid to Colombia if extradition were abolished. He responded: "We anticipate that extradition will go forward, and we think it will. I have no reason to believe that it will not."

Hoping to end the war with the traffickers, Gaviria had long contemplated establishing a judicial option for them. In his acceptance speech, he pointed out that the war was a national problem with a national solution, whereas the illegal black market in drug trafficking was an international problem that needed an international solution. He felt that the best option was for them to surrender, but if the government had no evidence that they had committed crimes, then legally they could not be incarcerated.

To help resolve the issue, Gaviria consulted his security adviser, Rafael Pardo. Having negotiated with the guerrillas for the previous administration, and achieved an agreement with the M-19, Pardo hoped to repeat his success with the traffickers. The 38-year-old academic and economist was viewed as indispensable by Gaviria, as reflected by him receiving one of the first appointments in the new administration.

"Aren't you concerned that one of these guys will suddenly turn himself in and we won't have any charge to arrest him with?" Gaviria said to Pardo.

From his briefcase, the security adviser extracted his notes and read them. "The person surrendering will obtain a sentence reduction if he confesses to a crime that will allow the government to prosecute, and a second sentence reduction if he gives goods and money to the state."

As it dovetailed with his own ideas, Gaviria viewed the suggestion as the beginning of a solution. The judicial option would be the carrot, and extradition the stick. The traffickers would also need a guarantee of safety for their families.

After consulting his other advisers, the president authorised the Council of Ministers to sign Decree 2047 on September 5, 1990: Those who surrendered and confessed to their crimes could receive the right to not be extradited. Those who confessed and cooperated with the authorities would have their sentences reduced, up to a third for surrender and confession, up to a sixth for providing information – which equated to half of the sentence imposed for one or all the crimes for which extradition had been requested.

After examining the cases of six people, the Council of Ministers approved half of them to be extradited and rejected the rest, as if to show that Gaviria would maintain the stick while allowing the carrot for those judged as having earned it.

The Cali Cartel knew that Pablo would continue running his operation if he turned himself in, so its representative in the government, General Maza, didn't object to the decree, which he considered a fallacy of the times, but he did say, "This country won't be put right as long as Escobar is alive."

Finding the decree unacceptable – its wording did not guarantee non-extradition – Pablo issued a statement by the Extraditables. As the M-19 had been pardoned and accepted as a political party, surely the traffickers could receive a similar deal. The campaign for the Constituent Assembly included members of the M-19, and one former guerrilla had achieved a position as the minister of health. If the traffickers were incarcerated, how would their safety be guaranteed and that of their families and friends?

CHAPTER 26
APOCALYPSE 2

With the assassination of so many elite police, tension had skyrocketed at their headquarters. All of the troops feared that they might be next and the concern from their families increased their burden. As well as the bombs and hit men lurking in the shadows, informants in the police would notify the cartel about operations, enabling hit men to ambush them along their routes. Dynamite was even discovered in the car park outside of their headquarters. Despite these threats, the troops never refused to go on a mission.

On July 3, 1990, Henry Pérez delivered $1 million in contributions from friends to Pablo in the town of Aquitania, San Francisco, Antioquia. He offered his paramilitary forces as bodyguards. "You cannot rely on the guerrillas that we have fought so hard."

"Don't get involved in my war," El Patrón said.

After leaving, Pérez gave Pablo's location to Colonel Martínez, who planned an encirclement, which he called Apocalypse 2.

Bracing for the operation, the troops attended an early mass hosted by the chaplain of the barracks, who afterwards counselled several of them privately. Terrified but putting on brave faces, they were relying on God's protection to counteract their stress. Some spoke to their relatives as if it might be for the last time. The relatives insisted on them quitting or applying for a transfer. None of them quit or even expressed how afraid they were.

At 7 PM, a convoy headed out, with only Colonel Martínez and Colonel Aguilar aware of the destination. The trucks were stationed a couple of miles outside of Hacienda Nápoles. At 11

PM, 100 policemen and Henry Pérez travelled on foot in the darkness and rain towards the town of Aquitania.

"Twenty trucks full of police are on the way to the Magdalena Medio," a lookout notified Pablo at 3:30 AM. "They have just passed the Claro River." Pablo summoned his brother Roberto and his men to the living room. The lookout returned. "There are thirty trucks coming down the paved road from Bogotá to Medellín. They were last seen in Puerto Triunfo with even more trucks with armed civilians."

"It's the DAS and the DIJIN Reds," Pablo said. "They're raiding here. By 5 AM, helicopters will be circling overhead." Pablo instructed the nine men who knew about his secret hideout to accompany him, with as many arms as they could carry.

Closing in, the police encountered roadside bombs, but none of Pablo's men were around to activate them. Somehow, they circled off course and arrived at the wrong place at 5 AM.

"Pablo's close by. We have to take him down," Henry Pérez said.

Twenty minutes later, Pablo and his men entered the forest, and listened for helicopters for another twenty minutes, but there were none. "Carlos, go back to the house for a motorbike, so I can take the paved road and keep a lookout." Leaving his gun, Carlos headed for the house, making it too late for Pablo to rectify his mistake: if Carlos were caught, he would be tortured into revealing the hideout.

At 5:40 AM, a raid began with two helicopters and the task force shooting at the house. Pablo led his men away. The helicopters started to search the area, but when they arrived above Pablo and his men, the trees shielded them from their view. Five hours later, the men had just over an hour to get to the hideout, which was located by a stream. No helicopters could be heard. Although they were exhausted, resting was too dangerous.

At 11:50 AM, they arrived without Carlos, which worried Pablo. Not wanting to light a fire, they ate cold food from cans.

At 3:50 PM, a helicopter arrived. The men scattered into defensive positions.

"There's no doubt they are looking for the cabin," Pablo said. "Carlos must be with them." At night, Pablo told everyone to sleep soundly as the hideout couldn't be seen.

In the morning, the men established lookout posts in the area around the cabin. They were eating cold food when a helicopter started homing in on their location. "Carlos must have been taken prisoner. It seems he is cooperating with them." Pablo suspected Henry Pérez, the paramilitary leader whose best man had shot Galán, of reporting Carlos to the Search Bloc.

At 11 AM, two of Pablo's lookouts charged into the cabin. "Boss, they are coming by the water and there are too many of them."

Leaving behind two gunmen to delay their pursuers, Pablo and the rest fled. Assuming that Carlos would have informed the police that Pablo and his men were most likely to hide in the forest, Pablo took them to a mountain.

"Fly over the area and machine-gun the possible exit points!" General Martínez yelled.

Gunfire erupted at the hideout, and the police headed towards the mountain. Hiding in the trees, two gunmen shot at the police. Six helicopters rained down fire on the area. With shrapnel and tree parts flying everywhere, the men rushed for cover. Some big branches fell on the boss.

"Fire!" Pablo said as a helicopter descended, only to retreat after they had given away their position. "Advance everyone!" They ran from the area and stopped at a safe distance from the machine-gun noises of the helicopters. Otto was absent, so Pablo ordered two men to search for him.

In the cabin, the police found freshly cooked food. They searched three rooms. They believed that Pablo had slept in the main one, which had a bathroom. Under the bed was a dead snake that had been shot. They believed that Roberto and Otto had occupied the other two rooms and that the bodyguards had slept on boards. Surrounded by the sounds of the jungle, Colonel Martínez contemplated his enemy: Pablo was like a shadow or a ghost that never revealed his face or engaged in battle; he just ran from hideout to hideout. Such a powerful invisible enemy made the colonel feel ineffective and small.

"Let's go back to Aquitania," said a bodyguard. "The police would never expect us to return. Since they discovered the cabin, they think we'll only go further into the forest."

"Gentlemen, the forest will eat us alive if we allow it."

Otto returned with the two men sent to find him, followed by helicopters and a group of police. Shooting at the troops kept them at bay while the men fled under the cover of trees. Weighed down by equipment, the police fell back, while Pablo, who knew his way through the forest, guided his men to a resting spot.

With a man missing, Pablo said, "Has anybody seen him?"

"He took another path through the forest on his own."

"He must have disliked the idea of going to Aquitania," Pablo said, before ordering the men to proceed.

By darkness, they had not rested, and there was no sign of the police. The safest route to Aquitania was the lengthiest one, so they continued until everyone was exhausted. Eventually, Pablo ordered that they stop in a dark, calm area. With no gunfire or helicopter noises, the men relaxed. They proceeded to a cabin called the Super Secret, in the jungle at the base of a ravine called La Cristalina, under dense trees called Cartagenan ceibas, which blocked an aerial view. They had mattresses, radios, TV, food, an ideal stream of water for bathing and a pond for fishing. While lookouts guarded the access roads in the jungle, Pablo slept.

The next day, Pablo told a teenager, "Get back on the road on a motorbike to see if there are cops coming this way. If you don't come back in an hour, you'll no longer find us here." After the teenager never returned, the men hid everything and loaded a mule with food and clothes. "Boys, we have the lead," Pablo said. "The police have been up all night. They have worn themselves out. We are going to cross Aquitania's main road and continue on to the Clara River." After taking time to chat and make jokes about the missing man who had forged a path of his own, Pablo picked up a small lantern, which he fixed to his trousers. "This light shining on the ground will guide us outside the forest. We are going to walk through cattle fields. The area will be crawling with cops, and a big light would give us away."

The teenager on the motorbike had been hung by his feet and interrogated by the police. He divulged the first two safe houses, and led the police to them. Ten planes, forty helicopters and 5,000 troops were searching the area.

Pablo turned on the radio: "Pablo Escobar is completely surrounded in the Magdalena Medio. It's only a matter of time until he falls. The Search Bloc raided the gangster's main hideout earlier today, and the police have located him in the forest." Laughing, Pablo turned off the radio.

With their weapons ready, the men proceeded silently. After forty-five minutes, fires at the police camps were visible. Another twenty minutes brought them to a road. "Come on. Let's cross," Pablo said confidently.

They walked until 10 PM and rested 100 yards from the road. In a small gorge, they slept on the grass, holding their guns, protected only by darkness. At 4:30 AM, they rose to no police in the area.

"Leave your mini-Uzi," Pablo told one of his men. "Go to one of the stores on the road, and buy us bread, sausages and sodas."

Knocking on a door, Pablo's man woke up a shopkeeper and returned with supplies. While eating, Pablo turned on his radio: "Pablo Escobar is surrounded by 1,500 policemen at La Danta in the Magdalena Medio. He has fled with a small group of men. At night in Medellín, four policemen were assassinated by Mafia gunmen."

"Great, boys," Pablo said. "Let's move."

Travelling over the road brought them to the River Claro. Its massive boulders obstructed their path. At a safe distance from the noise of police helicopters, they zigzagged slowly along the river's edge. In the afternoon, bombarded by rain, they found a sheltered area to rest. They were so exhausted that their hunger wasn't even registering. With the rain continuing into the night, they fell asleep under the cover of banana leaves, shivering in the cold yet soothed by the river's sounds.

"Let's get close to combine the warmth of all three of us," Pablo said.

While Roberto slept, Otto pulled more leaves over himself and vice versa, so they spent the entire night readjusting leaves. Before dawn, the area shook and a massive black shadow travelled overhead. They assumed it was a military aircraft until the rising sun revealed that a boulder had detached itself from the mountain and skimmed off the tip of the rock they had slept under.

Sunlight woke them with wet clothes stuck to their bodies. Encountering snakes, anteaters, sloths, poisonous frogs, venomous vipers and other rare animals, they headed along the river until 11 AM, when they took a route through cattle ranches. At 3:20 PM, they arrived at a cottage of an old woman, whom Pablo greeted.

"Good afternoon, friends. Come in," she said, familiar with traffickers moving around her area and aware from her radio that she had just invited Pablo Escobar into her cottage.

"Thank you," Pablo said. "Do you have any food to sell us?"

"I'll make some. You boys rest."

The men hung their clothes to dry in the sun and took baths. Discussing Carlos selling them out dampened their spirits, which the smell of cooking restored.

The radio announced: "Pablo is hungry and totally surrounded. He is fleeing with Otto, Popeye and five more men. A thousand more policemen are on their way to the area. Two policemen in Medellín died at the hands of a cartel killer. A group of young people were massacred in the Santa Cruz district. The killers are unknown. Four more young people fell under the bullets of strangers."

"Not all the Reds are after us," Pablo said, pleased by the death toll of policemen.

"No need to run anymore, boys," the woman said. "Go up that little hill, and I'll bring you food and take care of you."

After feasting on chicken and resting, Pablo ordered everyone to leave.

"You should rest on the hill," the woman said.

"Sorry, but we have to keep going." Pablo gave cash to the woman.

"Goodbye, friends."

Four hours later, they arrived at a cattle ranch, where the owners knew two of Pablo's men. Welcomed by a farmer and his wife, the men rested. At 6:30 PM, three sons of the farmer greeted the men. Two were farmers. One was dressed in city clothes and was well spoken. After eating, they all went to sleep without any night lookout. While they ate breakfast, work around the farm began.

"Tell us about your escape from the police," one of the sons said.

Hearing the story, the son from the city showed the most interest.

"For helping us, I promise to get you a purebred bull," Roberto said.

"The nearest small village is ten hours away," Pablo said to one of his men. "I need you to go there, and call for transport. It's the only place with telephones near our escape route." He gave directions. "Stay in the village and wait for us there." Noticing the absence of the son from the city, Pablo asked one of his men familiar with the family, "Who is the young man in blue jeans and where is he?"

"He is the brother of the farmer's other two sons. He is a student at the University of Antioquia. He's on break. He went to get an axe from a neighbouring farm."

El Patrón got up and walked to the farmer's woodpile, where he found an axe. Remaining silent about his suspicions, he said, "Are there any other telephones in the area?" He learned there was a telephone four hours away by horse, at a Corona station. Away from the family, Pablo told his men to collect their belongings and to meet on a hill twenty minutes from the house. He ordered one of his men to investigate the missing son. After an hour, the man returned and said that nobody at the house knew his whereabouts. "Let's eat quickly and leave for another hideout before the police are notified."

At 3 PM, Pablo and his men positioned themselves at a safe distance with a view of the farm. At 3:30 PM, the missing son arrived on a horse, scanning the area frantically for the traffickers. Helicopters approached. By landing on a bridge, three helicopters prevented Pablo and his men from leaving the area. About 100 policemen started searching around the farm. At a shack, one of the bodyguards knew a fisherman, who could help them cross the powerful river, which required swimming while holding a rope.

"Will you help us cross the river if we pay you?" a bodyguard asked.

"No," he said, frightened.

"You help us or die," Pablo said.

For a few seconds, the armed men waited for the command to kill the fisherman. Sensing the danger, he agreed to help. With a rope, he escorted the men to the riverbank, while helicopters buzzed above the forest. Amid water crashing violently against rocks, he threw himself into the river, which he barely managed to cross. On the other side, he tied the rope to a tree. After returning to Pablo's men, he watched them cross with difficulty as the water slammed into their guns and bodies, attempting to drag them away. After everybody had crossed, Pablo sliced the rope and ordered the fisherman to escort them.

The gradient of the mountain increased, slowing down everybody's ascent. Near the top, darkness came and the helicopters retired for the night. The police remained near the farm as the area on the other side of the mountain was considered dangerous and under the control of traffickers.

At 11 PM, they arrived at a small country house and knocked on the door. "Sir, open the door."

"Who are you?"
"We are the guerrillas."
"No."
"Yes. Open up!"

The door opened and a peasant said, "Ah, you are Pablo Escobar's entourage. What do you want?"

"For you to make us a meal, with chicken or whatever."

"OK." The peasant slaughtered a chicken and made a stew with yuccas and bananas. They ate fast. Afterwards, they attempted to sleep in a corridor, until they resumed their journey.

Guided by a flashlight, the men walked until dawn, when Pablo decided to rest. With helicopters approaching, he remained eerily calm, which inspired his band of exhausted men in wet clothes. After two hours, he decided to head for a village. At 2:40 PM, the men arrived near the village, but stayed hidden in the jungle. One of the men left, and returned with good news: three covered trucks were on the way to pick everybody up outside the village.

Pablo ordered everybody up. After fifteen minutes, they found the trucks. He told two of his men familiar with the area, "Get out of here. Bury the guns and equipment. Take the fisherman with you. When everything calms down, we'll see each other again."

"Boss, we'll be here for you always. Don't worry about us. We have friends in the village."

After saying goodbye, the rest of the men got in the back of the truck, which had its top down. Pablo sat next to the driver. Travelling along dirt roads, they arrived at Otto's lakeside farm by 10 PM, where everybody ate and collapsed. The next day, they ate, washed their clothes and applied medicine to their cuts and bruises. The news claimed that Pablo and his men were trapped because the bridge with the helicopters was under constant surveillance. Footage of the secret hideout was broadcast.

As his exhaustion faded, Pablo plotted to kill Gacha's former paramilitary business partner, Henry Pérez (for volunteering information to the Search Bloc), his own man Carlos (for giving up the secret hideout) and the farmer's son from the city (for bringing the helicopters in an attempt to claim the multimillion-dollar reward on their lives).

Two days later, three cars arrived to transport the men to Medellín. Separating from the group, Pablo and Popeye went to Prisco's hideout in the mountains north of Medellín, where lookouts with radios protected the area. Pablo learned the fate of the bodyguard who had not accompanied them to Aquitania. Having travelled in the opposite direction, he had managed to escape by finding a highway and getting a bus to Medellín.

Every time Pablo ate, he vomited, rendering him so weak he ended up bedbound, and unable to even use the bathroom. Sweating constantly, he suffered various symptoms including headaches. Medicine didn't work and he couldn't even hold down water. Keeping his gun handy, he was wary of the many criminal visitors to Prisco's house. At his bedside, Popeye protected him and mopped the sweat from his forehead.

At 8:30 PM, Pablo was too weak to speak when a doctor arrived. "Popeye," the doctor asked, "in the jungle, did you drink unfiltered water?"

"All the time."

The doctor left with a blood sample. Throughout the night, Popeye and Prisco tried to reduce Pablo's fever with cold water and a towel. They administered the doctor's medicine, but Pablo threw it up. Hallucinating, he saw his wife, children and mother – proud and beautiful Hermilda – strolling in Bolivar Square while an important politician was cheered by a crowd. He saw himself playing like a child in the mountains of Envigado; and sometimes, helpless, embraced to his mother's protective belly.

With helicopters in the area the next day, the doctor arrived with an injection for malaria and medicine. Exhausted, Popeye slept until 5 PM and gave Pablo water and two tablets. Remaining silent, Pablo looked at his gun and Popeye's rifle.

"I don't think it's a good idea to have so many people coming and going around the hideout," Popeye said.

"All of the men who come here are trustworthy," Prisco said.

Popeye remembered that Pablo had once said, "It's those you trust the most who sell you out."

Two days later, Pablo was able to eat chicken soup and egg broth. He had lost a lot of weight. His sweating ceased and he devoured water. The next day, he could walk. He had a bath and changed his clothes. "Can I get rice with eggs?" he asked Prisco's cook.

"Popeye, get me out of here," Pablo said, a few days later. He thanked Prisco, and said he would send him cash. With his gun over his back, Popeye grabbed the medicine and two bottles of water. They travelled on a horse, with Popeye behind Pablo, who finished off the water. At a paved road, three cars arrived with bodyguards to take Pablo to a solitary farmhouse in Rionegro, surrounded by meadows.

At 9 PM, a cook arrived with food. Pablo learned that eleven workers from Hacienda Nápoles had been arrested. Alive and free, Carlos claimed that he had refused to cooperate even though the police had dangled him from a helicopter.

"He lies. Kill him." Pablo sent an order to the two men he had left behind at the village to kill the farmer's son who studied in the city. He wrote a war note to Henry Pérez, whom he had learned was going around with twenty bodyguards at all times. Medicine and plenty of sleep restored Pablo. Three days after issuing the order, he learned that Carlos was dead. After ten more days, he requested the company of an ex-girlfriend in Envigado. After she arrived, he locked his door and sweated out the last of his illness.

A young man told Pablo, "I will kill Henry Pérez if you give my mother 100 million pesos when the job is done." After murdering Henry Pérez, the young man was shot dead by bodyguards and Pablo paid his mother 100 million pesos. The assassination ended his paramilitary support. Unable to hide in the jungles of the Magdalena Medio, he felt that the safest place for him was Medellín, where he had the most support.

CHAPTER 27
DEATH OF GUSTAVO

In August 1990, President Gaviria called for a reduction in the demand for cocaine from the consumer countries, which was viewed as a peace offering to the traffickers. Although he had staunchly defended extradition during his presidential campaign, he tried to defuse the war by offering the traffickers a way to avoid extradition. Any traffickers who surrendered and confessed to crimes would be eligible for non-extradition.

Gaviria announced: "The declaration of the state of siege expressly empowers the judges of the republic to process criminals who surrender to justice. If they confess their crimes, they will get the benefits included in the decree, which are the reduction of the sentence for surrendering and confession, plus an additional reduction if they denounce their accomplices. Additionally, criminals that willingly give in to justice will get the government warranty that they won't be extradited to the US."

Although some of the Extraditables such as the Ochoa brothers were pleased by the non-extradition option, Pablo didn't trust the government. His lawyers demanded that non-extradition be made unconditional, that confession and indictment were not obligatory, that the traffickers' prison would be invulnerable to attack and that their families and associates would be protected.

While the president attempted to broker a deal, the National Police continued to pursue the traffickers. To combat the state's elusive enemies, Colonel Martínez concentrated on intercepting calls, gathering intelligence and developing informants. Listening to a call, he heard a cartel member referred to as Mister, which implied a senior ranking. The suspect said, "Look, we need to send some mail to Cartagena," and the following day, a bomb exploded there. The suspect made decisions on trafficking logistics and quotas for cocaine shipments. Familiar with Pablo's voice, Colonel Martínez realised that the suspect was Gustavo Gaviria. Operating through third parties, aliases and codes, Pablo's cousin refused to meet people and never disclosed his phone number. Having tracked him down, Martínez ordered an immediate raid of a bunker in Envigado, a centre of operations, but nobody was present. Half a mile away, the police found a house with a cordless phone, from where they assumed that Gustavo had escaped.

Following the raid, Pablo changed his codes, telephones, names and aliases, which set the police technicians back six months until they heard Gustavo's familiar voice and his underlings addressing him as Mister. A telephone company revealed an address, but the raid failed because it was a fake location fed to the police by cartel insiders.

Disguised as Mafioso, the police bribed workers at the telephone company. With uniforms, ladders, helmets and company workers, the undercover officers and technicians went out to search for the cartel's telephone line. On Holy Thursday, they arrived at the front of Gustavo's cove in the Laureles neighbourhood. For several days, they monitored the location, and determined that there were no external bodyguards or security in surrounding houses. They noticed that only one woman went in and out.

On Sunday, August 12, at 2 PM, Gustavo spoke, verifying his presence, so Martínez ordered a raid. The noise alerted Pablo's cousin, who called the police for help.

"Yes, sir. Who is speaking?" the operator asked.

"No, look, look! It's that … they're gonna kill me! There's a lot of people around my house and they're gonna kill me. They're gonna kill me!"

"Give me the address, sir."

The police broke a fence and exploded open a door.

"I'm unarmed! Don't kill me!" Gustavo yelled before they shot him.

At the scene, a female journalist reported: "When he had just taken office as President of the Republic, Mr César Gaviria surprised the country with the killing of Gustavo Gaviria … by the Police Elite Force in Medellín. Gustavo Gaviria was Escobar's cousin and one of the most important members of the Medellín Cartel and the so-called Extraditables."

The police reported that Gustavo had confronted them with a gun, but Pablo learned the truth and with great sadness he had a lawyer file a criminal complaint against the police.

At the small funeral, a mariachi played songs. His son Gustavito, who had studied in Europe, spoke several languages, and had attempted to become a TV presenter, pledged to avenge his father's death. Inheriting the cocaine empire, he lacked his father's skills, which created liquidity problems for Pablo.

Any hope of peace was off. Pablo went berserk, blaming Gaviria. Devastated by the loss of his right-hand man, he started to torture and kill people inside his organisation whom he felt were cooperating with the authorities. He unleashed more terrorism on the country, and plotted to kidnap elite family members, journalists and politicians.

CHAPTER 28
ATTACKING CALI

On September 25, 1990, Pacho Herrera – the youngest of the Cali godfathers – was playing soccer with his brother and bodyguards at a personal ranch called The Coconuts, on a remote piece of land surrounded by sugarcane fields. Holding cans of beer and soda, about fifty men were sat on the grass and rows of wooden benches cheering at the players in sports uniforms on a pitch illuminated better than any stadium in Colombia. Directing one of the teams was a former pro footballer, which added to the excitement. The Tuesday-evening game had attracted an increasing number of spectators, including workers from the neighbouring farms such as cane cutters, who relished cooling off. Despite the threat from the rival Medellín Cartel, Pacho's security was lax.

In the preceding days, twenty assassins – sent by Pablo – had drifted into the area. Travelling by bus, either alone or in small units, they had arrived unnoticed. Mostly in their late teens, they had rendezvoused at a farmhouse near the village of Santander.

Locals tended to report the arrival of strangers to the Cali Cartel, which paid taxi drivers and others to be its eyes and ears. Anyone protecting outsiders ran the risk of torture, death and the massacre of their families. But Pablo had outsmarted Cali by sending young, unarmed men covertly and renting an assembly point from a farmer known to keep quiet for the right price.

Deliveries arrived at the farmhouse: a variety of military uniforms, two trucks and AR-15 automatic rifles capable of spraying a crowd with bullets in a matter of seconds. On the night of the game, Pablo's men dressed, grabbed guns and got into two trucks with sky-blue cabins. Brown canvas over the rear of the trucks concealed them. They drove for about twenty minutes.

Clean-shaven and in excellent shape, Pacho was focused on the game when the first truck parked at around 7 PM. The play continued as armed men in uniforms emerged from the darkness. As the local authorities worked for the Cali Cartel, everyone assumed that the soldiers were friendly. No one noticed the hodgepodge of uniforms and that the soldiers were mostly wearing sneakers not boots. As the soccer players were unarmed, the assassins initially aimed their guns at those in charge of surveillance and the rows of spectators.

Bam-bam-bam-bam-bam-bam …

The AR-15s fired so fast that the shots were impossible to count. They sounded like firecrackers sped up three or four times. The players stopped chasing the ball. Their gaze swung to the slaughter of the spectators, some of whom flopped down in pools of blood. Those unharmed stampeded as the guns began to cut down some of the players. A lady in the kitchen heard the shots and abandoned the food that she had been preparing.

Pacho, his brother and others sprinted over the field into the darkness. When they felt they had gone a safe distance, they hid among thick crops. Eventually, the shots ended, suggesting that the assassins had fled. Warily, Pacho and the survivors returned to The Coconuts. Yelling in Spanish, they rushed to almost twenty corpses of relatives and friends; others leaking blood, writhing, moaning and begging for help. With fire in his eyes, Pacho pledged to kill Pablo.

In green military garb, police with rifles arrived, rushed around and questioned the survivors, who were dazed, injured or angry. Corpses were loaded onto a truck and transported to the morgue.

Eager to earn extra money from the Cali Cartel, the police combed the area. Two young men were discovered on a remote road. The police grew suspicious after the men claimed that they had been staying with friends and were trying to get a bus to Medellín, yet were walking in the wrong direction. In jail, interrogated by a representative of the Cali Cartel, they detailed the entire plot, including the farmhouse they had stayed at.

At the farm, the police found uniforms, weapons and vehicles. The farmer's siblings claimed that their brother had vanished without telling them anything. A week later, two of the farmer's brothers and his sister were found shot in the head.

Pacho ordered the execution of the two hit men in the local jail, which prisoners handled with homemade knives. He dispatched his own assassins to find the farmer, who remained elusive. It took two and a half years for the cartel to catch him. A helicopter transported him to a ranch belonging to Pacho. The cartel men studied the man with a bruised face sat at a table in a stable, holding a cigarette. They knew his fate.

The two senior godfathers arrived last. Everyone hushed. Displaying little emotion, Gilberto and Miguel studied the farmer. With an air of command, Gilberto told the captive that he was in big trouble. The farmer stared at the ground, nonchalant. Gilberto said that the farmer was delusional to have thought that he could have gotten away with it, and that the farmer must have believed that he was so smart and they were so stupid. Remaining silent, the farmer smoked.

"Why did you help Pablo?"

In a calm way that startled his captors, the farmer looked at Gilberto and admitted that he had made a mistake. He had taken money to accommodate visitors, who had left him in the dark about their intentions. Gilberto asked if the farmer knew what was going to happen to him. The farmer gazed down.

The godfathers departed except for Pacho, who had a fierce expression. Cartel men removed the farmer's boots and shirt. He flailed as his legs were tied to the back of a truck and his arms attached to another. Men kicked and spat on him. After the farmer was securely attached to both vehicles, their engines revved and they slowly moved away from each other. As his arms and legs stretched to an abnormal length and eventually popped out of their sockets, the farmer urinated on himself and screamed like an animal getting slaughtered. For half an hour, what remained of the farmer was reattached to the trucks, which moved forward and backward to torture him for as long as possible until he stopped breathing.

Fleeing from the pitch, Pacho had dropped his notebook. Reading it, Pablo laughed at the measly amounts of pay Pacho had given his employees and how Pacho had recorded even miniscule expenses. The war between the cartels was three years old, and Pablo had destroyed approximately fifty of Cali's drugstores. Pablo's men poured over phone-call lists provided by phone-company employees. People in regular contact with the Cali bosses were kidnapped by Pablo's men. Driving around Medellín with a license plate from Cali was an invitation to be abducted.

In November 1990, Pablo sent a message to his family about the president, who had promised him heaven and earth before Gustavo's assassination. He said that Gaviria had asked him to call, and he had even received a letter from Gaviria's wife. In response, Pablo's representative had spoken to Gaviria for a few hours, but Pablo had dismissed the government's response as nonsense. They mistakenly thought that killing Gustavo would have wounded Pablo so badly that he would have been unable to recover, but now he had the government scared by kidnapping more elites and everything would be resolved.

In December, Pablo's family members were visiting a supermarket when they detected two men following them. Everywhere they went, the men trailed along. Worried that Cali had located them, Pablo moved his family into a big seventh-floor apartment in Medellín. With the curtains permanently closed, they played board games with the bodyguards, including Popeye and Shooter. For updates on the negotiations with the government, Pablo obsessively watched the news at 7 PM, 9 PM and midnight. After his family complained about the boring news broadcasts and his constant channel surfing, Pablo invested in a split screen TV, which displayed multiple channels.

According to the Colombian National Police, there were

25,000 murders in Colombia in 1990. They included judges, politicians, three presidential candidates and many of Pablo's associates, friends and family. With George HW Bush and the US military stepping up actions against him, he needed a new strategy to emerge unscathed. It didn't take long for him to come up with one: El Patrón would build his own prison.

REFERENCES

Bowden, Mark. *Killing Pablo*. Atlantic Books, 2001.

Bowen, Russell. *The Immaculate Deception*. America West Publishers, 1991.

Castaño, Carlos. *My Confession*. Oveja Negra, 2001.

Caycedo, Germán Castro. *In Secret*. Planeta, 1996.

Chepesiuk, Ron. *Crazy Charlie*. Strategic Media Books, 2016.

Chepesiuk, Ron. *Drug Lords: The Rise and Fall of the Cali Cartel*. Milo Books, 2003.

Chepesiuk, Ron. *Escobar vs Cali: The War of the Cartels*. Strategic Media, 2013.

Cockburn, Leslie. *Out of Control*. Bloomsbury, 1988.

Cockburn and Clair. *Whiteout*. Verso, 1998.

Don Berna. *Killing the Boss*. ICONO, 2013.

Escobar, Juan Pablo. *Pablo Escobar: My Father*. Ebury Press, 2014.

Escobar, Roberto. *Escobar*. Hodder & Stoughton, 2009.

Grillo, Joan. *El Narco*. Bloomsbury, 2012.

Gugliotta and Leen. *Kings of Cocaine*. Harper and Row, 1989.

Hari, Johann. *Chasing the Scream*. Bloomsbury, 2015.

Hopsicker, Daniel. *Barry and the Boys*. MadCow Press, 2001.

Leveritt, Mara. *The Boys on the Tracks*. Bird Call Press, 2007.

Levine, Michael. *The Big White Lie*. Thunder's Mouth Press, 1993.

MacQuarrie, Kim. *Life and Death in the Andes*. Simon & Schuster, 2016.

Márquez, Gabriel García. *News of a Kidnapping*. Penguin, 1996.

Martínez, Astrid María Legarda. *The True Life of Pablo Escobar*. Ediciones y Distribuciones Dipon Ltda, 2017.

Massing, Michael. *The Fix*. Simon & Schuster, 1998.

McAleese, Peter. *No Mean Soldier*. Cassell Military Paperbacks, 2000.

McCoy, Alfred. *The Politics of Heroin in Southeast Asia*. Harper and Row, 1972.

Mollison, James. *The Memory of Pablo Escobar*. Chris Boot, 2009.

Morris, Roger. *Partners in Power*. Henry Holt, 1996.

Noriega, Manuel. *The Memoirs of Manuel Noriega*. Random House, 1997.

North, Oliver. *Under Fire*. Harper Collins, 1991.

Paley, Dawn. *Drug War Capitalism*. AK Press, 2014.

Porter, Bruce. *Blow*. St Martin's Press, 1993.

Reed, Terry. *Compromised*. Clandestine Publishing, 1995.

Rempel, William. *At the Devil's Table: Inside the Fall of the Cali Cartel, the World's Biggest Crime Syndicate*. Random House, 2011.

Ross, Rick. *Freeway Rick Ross*. Freeway Studios, 2014.

Ruppert, Michael. *Crossing the Rubicon*. New Society Publishers, 2004.

Salazar, Alonso. *The Words of Pablo*. Planeta, 2001.

Salazar, Alonso. *Born to Die in Medellín*. Latin America Bureau, 1992.

Saviano, Roberto. *Zero Zero Zero*. Penguin Random House UK, 2013.

Schou, Nick. *Kill the Messenger*. Nation Books, 2006.

Shannon, Elaine. *Desperados*. Penguin, 1988.

Stich, Rodney. *Defrauding America* 3rd Ed. Diablo Western Press, 1998.

Stich, Rodney. *Drugging America* 2nd Ed. Silverpeak, 2006.

Stokes, Doug. *America's Other War: Terrorizing Colombia*. Zed Books, 2005.

Stone, Roger. *The Clintons' War on Women*. Skyhorse, 2015.

Stone, Roger. *Jeb and the Bush Crime Family*. Skyhorse, 2016.

Streatfield, Dominic. *Cocaine*. Virgin Publishing, 2001.

Tarpley and Chaitkin. *George Bush*. Progressive Press, 2004.

Tomkins, David. *Dirty Combat*. Mainstream Publishing, 2008.

Valentine, Douglas. *The Strength of the Pack*. Trine Day LLC, 2009.

Vallejo, Virginia. *Loving Pablo, Hating Escobar*. Vintage, 2018.

Velásquez Vásquez, Jhon Jairo. *Surviving Pablo Escobar*. Ediciones y Distribuciones Dipon Ltda, 2017.

Woods, Neil. *Good Cop Bad War*. Ebury Press, 2016.

GET A FREE BOOK: JOIN SHAUN'S NEWSLETTER SIGN UP PAGE

SHAUN'S BOOKS

English Shaun Trilogy
Party Time
Hard Time
Prison Time

War on Drugs Series
Pablo Escobar: Beyond Narcos
American Made: Who Killed Barry Seal?
Pablo Escobar or George HW Bush
The Cali Cartel: Beyond Narcos
We Are Being Lied To: The War on Drugs (Expected 2020)
The War Against Weed (Expected 2020)

Un-Making a Murderer: The Framing of Steven Avery and Brendan Dassey
The Mafia Philosopher: Two Tonys
Life Lessons

Pablo Escobar's Story (4-Book Series)
T-Bone (Expected 2022)

SOCIAL-MEDIA LINKS

Email: attwood.shaun@hotmail.co.uk
YouTube: Shaun Attwood

Blog: Jon's Jail Journal
Website: shaunattwood.com
Instagram: @shaunattwood

Twitter: @shaunattwood
LinkedIn: Shaun Attwood
Goodreads: Shaun Attwood
Facebook: Shaun Attwood, Jon's Jail Journal,
T-Bone Appreciation Society

Shaun welcomes feedback on any of his
books and YouTube videos.

Thank you for the Amazon and Goodreads reviews and to all of the people who have subscribed to Shaun's YouTube channel!

SHAUN'S JAIL JOURNEY STARTS IN HARD TIME NEW EDITION

Chapter 1

Sleep deprived and scanning for danger, I enter a dark cell on the second floor of the maximum-security Madison Street jail in Phoenix, Arizona, where guards and gang members are murdering prisoners. Behind me, the metal door slams heavily. Light slants into the cell through oblong gaps in the door, illuminating a prisoner cocooned in a white sheet, snoring lightly on the top bunk about two thirds of the way up the back wall. Relieved there is no immediate threat, I place my mattress on the grimy floor. Desperate to rest, I notice movement on the cement-block walls. *Am I hallucinating?* I blink several times. The walls appear to ripple. Stepping closer, I see the walls are alive with insects. I flinch. So many are swarming, I wonder if they're a colony of ants on the move. To get a better look, I put my eyes right up to them. They are mostly the size of almonds and have antennae. American cockroaches. I've seen them in the holding cells downstairs in smaller numbers, but nothing like this. A chill spread over my body. I back away.

Something alive falls from the ceiling and bounces off the base of my neck. I jump. With my night vision improving, I spot cockroaches weaving in and out of the base of the fluorescent strip light. Every so often one drops onto the concrete and resumes crawling. Examining the bottom bunk, I realise why my cellmate is sleeping at a higher elevation: cockroaches are pouring from gaps in the decrepit wall at the level of my bunk. The area is thick with them. Placing my mattress on the bottom bunk scatters them. I walk towards the toilet, crunching a few under my shower sandals. I urinate and grab the toilet roll. A cockroach darts from the centre of the roll onto my hand, tickling my fingers. My arm jerks as if it has a mind of its own, losing the cockroach and the toilet roll. Using a towel, I wipe the bulk of them off the bottom bunk, stopping only to shake the odd one off my hand. I unroll my mattress. They begin to regroup and inhabit my mattress. My adrenaline is pumping so much, I lose my fatigue.

Nauseated, I sit on a tiny metal stool bolted to the wall. *How will I sleep? How's my cellmate sleeping through the infestation and my arrival?* Copying his technique, I cocoon myself in a sheet and lie down, crushing more cockroaches. The only way they can access me now is through the breathing hole I've left in the sheet by the lower half of my face. Inhaling their strange musty odour, I close my eyes. I can't sleep. I feel them crawling on the sheet around my feet. *Am I imagining things?* Frightened of them infiltrating my breathing hole, I keep opening my eyes. Cramps cause me to rotate onto my other side. Facing the wall, I'm repulsed by so many of them just inches away. I return to my original side.

The sheet traps the heat of the Sonoran Desert to my body, soaking me in sweat. Sweat tickles my body, tricking my mind into thinking the cockroaches are infiltrating and crawling on me. The trapped heat aggravates my bleeding skin infections and bedsores. I want to scratch myself, but I know better. The outer layers of my skin have turned soggy from sweating constantly in this concrete oven. Squirming on the bunk fails to stop the relentless itchiness of my skin. Eventually, I scratch myself. Clumps of moist skin detach under my nails. Every now and then I become so uncomfortable, I must open my cocoon to waft the heat out, which allows the cockroaches in. It takes hours to drift to sleep. I only manage a few hours. I awake stuck to the soaked sheet, disgusted by the cockroach carcasses compressed against the mattress.

The cockroaches plague my new home until dawn appears

at the dots in the metal grid over a begrimed strip of four-inch-thick bullet-proof glass at the top of the back wall – the cell's only source of outdoor light. They disappear into the cracks in the walls, like vampire mist retreating from sunlight. But not all of them. There were so many on the night shift that even their vastly reduced number is too many to dispose of. And they act like they know it. They roam around my feet with attitude, as if to make it clear that I'm trespassing on their turf.

My next set of challenges will arise not from the insect world, but from my neighbours. I'm the new arrival, subject to scrutiny about my charges just like when I'd run into the Aryan Brotherhood prison gang on my first day at the medium-security Towers jail a year ago. I wish my cellmate would wake up, brief me on the mood of the locals and introduce me to the head of the white gang. No such luck. Chow is announced over a speaker system in a crackly robotic voice, but he doesn't stir.

I emerge into the day room for breakfast. Prisoners in black-and-white bee-striped uniforms gather under the metal-grid stairs and tip dead cockroaches into a trash bin from plastic peanut-butter containers they'd set as traps during the night. All eyes are on me in the chow line. Watching who sits where, I hold my head up, put on a solid stare and pretend to be as at home in this environment as the cockroaches. It's all an act. I'm lonely and afraid. I loathe having to explain myself to the head of the white race, who I assume is the toughest murderer. I've been in jail long enough to know that taking my breakfast to my cell will imply that I have something to hide.

The gang punishes criminals with certain charges. The most serious are sex offenders, who are KOS: Kill On Sight. Other charges are punishable by SOS – Smash On Sight – such as drive-by shootings because women and kids sometimes get killed. It's called convict justice. Gang members are constantly looking for people to beat up because that's how they earn their reputations and tattoos. The most serious acts of violence earn the highest-ranking tattoos. To be a full gang member requires murder. I've observed the body language and techniques inmates trying to integrate employ. An inmate with a spring in his step and an air of confidence is likely to be accepted. A person who avoids eye contact and fails to introduce himself to the gang is likely to be preyed on. Some of the failed attempts I saw ended up with heads getting cracked against toilets, a sound I've grown familiar with. I've seen prisoners being extracted on stretchers who looked dead – one had yellow fluid leaking from his head. The constant violence gives me nightmares, but the reality is that I put myself in here, so I force myself to accept it as a part of my punishment.

It's time to apply my knowledge. With a self-assured stride, I take my breakfast bag to the table of white inmates covered in neo-Nazi tattoos, allowing them to question me.

"Mind if I sit with you guys?" I ask, glad exhaustion has deepened my voice.

"These seats are taken. But you can stand at the corner of the table."

The man who answered is probably the head of the gang. I size him up. Cropped brown hair. A dangerous glint in Nordic-blue eyes. Tiny pupils that suggest he's on heroin. Weightlifter-type veins bulging from a sturdy neck. Political ink on arms crisscrossed with scars. About the same age as me, thirty-three.

"Thanks. I'm Shaun from England." I volunteer my origin to show I'm different from them but not in a way that might get me smashed.

"I'm Bullet, the head of the whites." He offers me his fist to bump. "Where you roll in from, wood?"

Addressing me as wood is a good sign. It's what white gang members on a friendly basis call each other.

"Towers jail. They increased my bond and re-classified me to maximum security."

"What's your bond at?"

"I've got two $750,000 bonds," I say in a monotone. This is no place to brag about bonds.

"How many people you kill, brother?" His eyes drill into mine, checking whether my body language supports my story. My body language so far is spot on.

"None. I threw rave parties. They got us talking about drugs on wiretaps." Discussing drugs on the phone does not warrant a $1.5 million bond. I know and beat him to his next question. "Here's my charges." I show him my charge sheet, which includes conspiracy and leading a crime syndicate – both from running an Ecstasy ring.

Bullet snatches the paper and scrutinises it. Attempting to pre-empt his verdict, the other whites study his face. On edge, I wait for him to respond. Whatever he says next will determine whether I'll be accepted or victimised.

"Are you some kind of jailhouse attorney?" Bullet asks. "I want someone to read through my case paperwork." During our few minutes of conversation, Bullet has seen through my act and concluded that I'm educated – a possible resource to him.

I appreciate that he'll accept me if I take the time to read his case. "I'm no jailhouse attorney, but I'll look through it and help you however I can."

"Good. I'll stop by your cell later on, wood."

After breakfast, I seal as many of the cracks in the walls as I can with toothpaste. The cell smells minty, but the cockroaches still find their way in. Their day shift appears to be collecting information on the brown paper bags under my bunk, containing a few items of food that I purchased from the commissary; bags that I tied off with rubber bands in the hope of keeping the cockroaches out. Relentlessly, the cockroaches explore the bags for entry points, pausing over and probing the most worn and vulnerable regions. *Will the nightly swarm eat right through the paper?* I read all morning, wondering whether my cellmate has died in his cocoon, his occasional breathing sounds reassuring me.

Bullet stops by late afternoon and drops his case paperwork off. He's been charged with Class 3 felonies and less, not serious crimes, but is facing a double-digit sentence because of his prior convictions and Security Threat Group status in the prison system. The proposed sentencing range seems disproportionate. I'll advise him to reject the plea bargain – on the assumption he already knows to do so, but is just seeking the comfort of a second opinion, like many un-sentenced inmates. When he returns for his paperwork, our conversation disturbs my cellmate – the cocoon shuffles – so we go upstairs to his cell. I tell Bullet what I think. He is excitable, a different man from earlier, his pupils almost non-existent.

"This case ain't shit. But my prosecutor knows I done other shit, all kinds of heavy shit, but can't prove it. I'd do anything to get that sorry bitch off my fucking ass. She's asking for something bad to happen to her. Man, if I ever get bonded out, I'm gonna chop that bitch into pieces. Kill her slowly though. Like to work her over with a blowtorch."

Such talk can get us both charged with conspiring to murder a prosecutor, so I try to steer him elsewhere. "It's crazy how they can catch you doing one thing, yet try to sentence you for all of the things they think you've ever done."

"Done plenty. Shot some dude in the stomach once. Rolled him up in a blanket and threw him in a dumpster."

Discussing past murders is as unsettling as future ones. "So, what's all your tattoos mean, Bullet? Like that eagle on your chest?"

"Why you wanna know?" Bullet's eyes probe mine.

My eyes hold their ground. "Just curious."

"It's a war bird. The AB patch."

"AB patch?"

"What the Aryan Brotherhood gives you when you've put enough work in."

"How long does it take to earn a patch?"

"Depends how quickly you put your work in. You have to earn your lightning bolts first."

"Why you got red and black lightning bolts?"

"You get SS bolts for beating someone down or for being an

enforcer for the family. Red lightning bolts for killing someone. I was sent down as a youngster. They gave me steel and told me who to handle and I handled it. You don't ask questions. You just get blood on your steel. Dudes who get these tats without putting work in are told to cover them up or leave the yard."

"What if they refuse?"

"They're held down and we carve the ink off them."

Imagining them carving a chunk of flesh to remove a tattoo, I cringe. He's really enjoying telling me this now. His volatile nature is clear and frightening. *He's accepted me too much. He's trying to impress me before making demands.*

At night, I'm unable to sleep. Cocooned in heat, surrounded by cockroaches, I hear the swamp-cooler vent – a metal grid at the top of a wall – hissing out tepid air. Giving up on sleep, I put my earphones on and tune into National Public Radio. Listening to a Vivaldi violin concerto, I close my eyes and press my tailbone down to straighten my back as if I'm doing a yogic relaxation. The playful allegro thrills me, lifting my spirits, but the wistful adagio provokes sad emotions and tears. I open my eyes and gaze into the gloom. Due to lack of sleep, I start hallucinating and hearing voices over the music whispering threats. I'm at breaking point. Although I have accepted that I committed crimes and deserve to be punished, no one should have to live like this. I'm furious at myself for making the series of reckless decisions that put me in here and for losing absolutely everything. As violins crescendo in my ears, I remember what my life used to be like.

SHAUN'S INCARCERATION CONCLUDES IN PRISON TIME

Chapter 1

"I've got a padlock in a sock. I can smash your brains in while you're asleep. I can kill you whenever I want." My new cellmate sizes me up with no trace of human feeling in his eyes. Muscular and pot-bellied, he's caked in prison ink, including six snakes on his skull, slithering side by side. The top of his right ear is missing in a semi-circle.

The waves of fear are overwhelming. After being in transportation all day, I can feel my bladder hurting. "I'm not looking to cause any trouble. I'm the quietest cellmate you'll ever have. All I do is read and write."

Scowling, he shakes his head. "Why've they put a fish in with me?" He swaggers close enough for me to smell his cigarette breath. "Us convicts don't get along with fresh fish."

"Should I ask to move then?" I say, hoping he'll agree if he hates new prisoners so much.

"No! They'll think I threatened you!"

In the eight by twelve feet slab of space, I swerve around him and place my property box on the top bunk.

He pushes me aside and grabs the box. "You just put that on my artwork! I ought to fucking smash you, fish!"

"Sorry, I didn't see it."

"You need to be more aware of your fucking surroundings! What you in for anyway, fish?"

I explain my charges, Ecstasy dealing and how I spent twenty-six months fighting my case.

"How come the cops were so hard-core after you?" he asks, squinting.

"It was a big case, a multi-million dollar investigation. They raided over a hundred people and didn't find any drugs. They were pretty pissed off. I'd stopped dealing by the time they caught up with me, but I'd done plenty over the years, so I accept my punishment."

"Throwing raves," he says, staring at the ceiling as if remembering something. "Were you partying with underage girls?" he asks, his voice slow, coaxing.

Being called a sex offender is the worst insult in prison. Into my third year of incarceration, I'm conditioned to react. "What you trying to say?" I yell angrily, brow clenched.

"Were you fucking underage girls?" Flexing his body, he shakes both fists as if about to punch me.

"Hey, I'm no child molester, and I'd prefer you didn't say shit like that!"

"My buddy next door is doing twenty-five to life for murdering a child molester. How do I know Ecstasy dealing ain't your cover story?" He inhales loudly, nostrils flaring.

"You want to see my fucking paperwork?"

A stocky prisoner walks in. Short hair. Dark eyes. Powerful neck. On one arm: a tattoo of a man in handcuffs above the word OMERTA – the Mafia code of silence towards law enforcement. "What the fuck's going on in here, Bud?" asks Junior Bull – the son of "Sammy the Bull" Gravano, the Mafia mass murderer who was my biggest competitor in the Ecstasy market.

Relieved to see a familiar face, I say, "How're you doing?"

Shaking my hand, he says in a New York Italian accent, "I'm doing alright. I read that shit in the newspaper about you starting a blog in Sheriff Joe Arpaio's jail."

"The blog's been bringing media heat on the conditions."

"You know him?" Bud asks.

"Yeah, from Towers jail. He's a good dude. He's in for dealing Ecstasy like me."

"It's a good job you said that 'cause I was about to smash his ass," Bud says.

"It's a good job Wild Man ain't here 'cause you'd a got your ass thrown off the balcony," Junior Bull says.

I laugh. The presence of my best friend, Wild Man, was partly the reason I never took a beating at the county jail, but with Wild Man in a different prison, I feel vulnerable. When Bud casts a death stare on me, my smile fades.

"What the fuck you guys on about?" Bud asks.

"Let's go talk downstairs." Junior Bull leads Bud out.

I rush to a stainless steel sink/toilet bolted to a cement-block wall by the front of the cell, unbutton my orange jumpsuit and crane my neck to watch the upper-tier walkway in case Bud returns. I bask in relief as my bladder deflates. After flushing, I take stock of my new home, grateful for the slight improvement in the conditions versus what I'd grown accustomed to in Sheriff Joe Arpaio's jail. No cockroaches. No blood stains. A working swamp cooler. Something I've never seen in a cell before: shelves. The steel table bolted to the wall is slightly larger, too. *But how will I concentrate on writing with Bud around?* There's a mixture of smells in the room. Cleaning chemicals. Aftershave. Tobacco. A vinegar-like odour. The slit of a window at the back overlooks gravel in a no-man's-land before the next building with gleaming curls of razor wire around its roof.

From the doorway upstairs, I'm facing two storeys of cells overlooking a day room with shower cubicles at the end of both tiers. At two white plastic circular tables, prisoners are playing dominoes, cards, chess and Scrabble, some concentrating, others yelling obscenities, contributing to a brain-scraping din that I hope to block out by purchasing a Walkman. In a raised box-shaped Plexiglas control tower, two guards are monitoring the prisoners.

Bud returns. My pulse jumps. Not wanting to feel like I'm stuck in a kennel with a rabid dog, I grab a notepad and pen and head for the day room.

Focussed on my body language, not wanting to signal any weakness, I'm striding along the upper tier, head and chest elevated, when two hands appear from a doorway and grab me. I drop the pad. The pen clinks against grid-metal and tumbles to the day room as I'm pulled into a cell reeking of backside sweat and masturbation, a cheese-tinted funk.

"I'm Booga. Let's fuck," says a squat man in urine-stained boxers, with WHITE TRASH tattooed on his torso below a mobile home, and an arm sleeved with the Virgin Mary.

Shocked, I brace to flee or fight to preserve my anal virginity. I can't believe my eyes when he drops his boxers and waggles his penis.

Dancing to music playing through a speaker he has rigged up, Booga smiles in a sexy way. "Come on," he says in a husky voice. "Drop your pants. Let's fuck." He pulls pornography faces. I question his sanity. He moves closer. "If I let you fart in my mouth, can I fart in yours?"

"You can fuck off," I say, springing towards the doorway.

He grabs me. We scuffle. Every time I make progress towards the doorway, he clings to my clothes, dragging me back in. When I feel his penis rub against my leg, my adrenalin kicks in so forcefully I experience a burst of strength and wriggle free. I bolt out as fast as my shower sandals will allow, and snatch my pad. Looking over my shoulder, I see him stood calmly in the doorway, smiling. He points at me. "You have to walk past my door every day. We're gonna get together. I'll lick your ass and you can fart in my mouth." Booga blows a kiss and disappears.

I rush downstairs. With my back to a wall, I pause to steady my thoughts and breathing. In survival mode, I think, *What's going to come at me next?* In the hope of reducing my tension, I borrow a pen to do what helps me stay sane: writing. With the details fresh in my mind, I document my journey to the prison for my blog readers, keeping an eye out in case anyone else wants to test the new prisoner. The more I write, the more I fill with a sense of purpose. Jon's Jail Journal is a connection to the outside world that I cherish.

Someone yells, "One time!" The din lowers. A door rumbles open. A guard does a security walk, his every move scrutinised by dozens of scornful eyes staring from cells. When he exits, the din resumes, and the prisoners return to injecting drugs to escape from reality, including the length of their sentences. This continues all day with "Two times!" signifying two approaching guards, and "Three times!" three and so on. Every now and then an announcement by a guard over the speakers briefly lowers the din.

Before lockdown, I join the line for a shower, holding bars of soap in a towel that I aim to swing at the head of the next person to try me. With boisterous inmates a few feet away, yelling at the men in the showers to "Stop jerking off," and "Hurry the fuck up," I get in a cubicle that reeks of bleach and mildew. With every nerve strained, I undress and rinse fast.

At night, despite the desert heat, I cocoon myself in a blanket from head to toe and turn towards the wall, making my face more difficult to strike. I leave a hole for air, but the warm cement block inches from my mouth returns each exhalation to my face as if it's breathing on me, creating a feeling of suffocation. For hours, my heart drums so hard against the thin mattress I feel as if I'm moving even though I'm still. I try to sleep, but my eyes keep springing open and my head turning towards the cell as I try to penetrate the darkness, searching for Bud swinging a padlock in a sock at my head.

OTHER BOOKS BY SHAUN ATTWOOD

Pablo Escobar: Beyond Narcos
War on Drugs Series Book 1

The mind-blowing true story of Pablo Escobar and the Medellín Cartel beyond their portrayal on Netflix.

Colombian drug lord Pablo Escobar was a devoted family man and a psychopathic killer; a terrible enemy, yet a wonderful friend. While donating millions to the poor, he bombed and tortured his enemies – some had their eyeballs removed with hot spoons. Through ruthless cunning and America's insatiable appetite for cocaine, he became a multi-billionaire, who lived in a $100-million house with its own zoo.

Pablo Escobar: Beyond Narcos demolishes the standard good versus evil telling of his story. The authorities were not hunting Pablo down to stop his cocaine business. They were taking over it.

American Made: Who Killed Barry Seal?
Pablo Escobar or George HW Bush
War on Drugs Series Book 2

Set in a world where crime and government coexist, *American Made* is the jaw-dropping true story of CIA pilot Barry Seal that the Hollywood movie starring Tom Cruise is afraid to tell.

Barry Seal flew cocaine and weapons worth billions of dollars into and out of America in the 1980s. After he became a government informant, Pablo Escobar's Medellin Cartel offered a million for him alive and half a million dead. But his real trouble began after he threatened to expose the dirty dealings of George HW Bush.

American Made rips the roof off Bush and Clinton's complicity in cocaine trafficking in Mena, Arkansas.

"A conspiracy of the grandest magnitude." Congressman Bill Alexander on the Mena affair.

We Are Being Lied To: The War on Drugs
War on Drugs Series Book 3

A collection of harrowing, action-packed and interlinked true stories that demonstrate the devastating consequences of drug prohibition.

The Cali Cartel: Beyond Narcos
War on Drugs Series Book 4

An electrifying account of the Cali Cartel beyond its portrayal on Netflix.

From the ashes of Pablo Escobar's empire rose an even bigger and more malevolent cartel. A new breed of sophisticated mobsters became the kings of cocaine. Their leader was Gilberto Rodríguez Orejuela – known as the Chess Player due to his foresight and calculated cunning.

Gilberto and his terrifying brother, Miguel, ran a multi-billion-dollar drug empire like a corporation. They employed a politically astute brand of thuggery and spent $10 million to put a president in power. Although the godfathers from Cali preferred bribery over violence, their many loyal torturers and hit men were never idle.

The Mafia Philosopher

"A fast-paced true-crime memoir with all of
the action of Goodfellas" – UNILAD

"Sopranos v Sons of Anarchy with an Alaskan-snow backdrop"
– True Geordie Podcast

Breaking bones, burying bodies and planting bombs became second nature to Two Tonys while working for the Bonanno Crime Family, whose exploits inspired The Godfather.

After a dispute with an outlaw motorcycle club, Two Tonys left a trail of corpses from Arizona to Alaska. On the run, he was pursued by bikers and a neo-Nazi gang blood-thirsty for revenge, while a homicide detective launched a nationwide manhunt.

As the mist from his smoking gun fades, readers are left with an unexpected portrait of a stoic philosopher with a wealth of charm, a glorious turn of phrase and a fanatical devotion to his daughter.

Hard Time New Edition

"Makes the Shawshank Redemption look like a holiday camp"
– NOTW

After a SWAT team smashed down stock-market millionaire Shaun Attwood's door, he found himself inside of Arizona's deadliest jail and locked into a brutal struggle for survival.
Shaun's hope of living the American Dream turned into a nightmare of violence and chaos, when he had a run-in with Sammy the Bull Gravano, an Italian Mafia mass murderer.
In jail, Shaun was forced to endure cockroaches crawling in his ears at night, dead rats in the food and the sound of skulls getting cracked against toilets. He meticulously documented the conditions and smuggled out his message.
Join Shaun on a harrowing voyage into the darkest recesses of human existence.

Hard Time provides a revealing glimpse into the tragedy, brutality, dark comedy and eccentricity of prison life.

Featured worldwide on Nat Geo Channel's Locked-Up/Banged-Up Abroad Raving Arizona.

Prison Time

Sentenced to 9½ years in Arizona's state prison for distributing Ecstasy, Shaun finds himself living among gang members, sexual predators and drug-crazed psychopaths. After being attacked by a Californian biker in for stabbing a girlfriend, Shaun writes about the prisoners who befriend, protect and inspire him. They include T-Bone, a massive African American ex-Marine who risks his life saving vulnerable inmates from rape, and Two Tonys, an old-school Mafia murderer who left the corpses of his rivals from Arizona to Alaska. They teach Shaun how to turn incarceration to his advantage, and to learn from his mistakes.

Shaun is no stranger to love and lust in the heterosexual world, but the tables are turned on him inside. Sexual advances come at him from all directions, some cleverly disguised, others more sinister – making Shaun question his sexual identity.

Resigned to living alongside violent, mentally-ill and drug-addicted inmates, Shaun immerses himself in psychology and philosophy to try to make sense of his past behaviour, and begins applying what he learns as he adapts to prison life. Encouraged by Two Tonys to explore fiction as well, Shaun reads over 1000 books which, with support from a brilliant psychotherapist, Dr Owen, speed along his personal development. As his ability to deflect daily threats improves, Shaun begins to look forward to his release with optimism and a new love waiting for him. Yet the words of Aristotle from one of Shaun's books will prove prophetic: "We cannot learn without pain."

Un-Making a Murderer: The Framing of Steven Avery and Brendan Dassey

Innocent people do go to jail. Sometimes mistakes are made. But even more terrifying is when the authorities conspire to frame them. That's what happened to Steven Avery and Brendan Dassey, who were convicted of murder and are serving life sentences.

Un-Making a Murderer is an explosive book which uncovers the illegal, devious and covert tactics used by Wisconsin officials, including:
- **Concealing Other Suspects**
- **Paying Expert Witnesses to Lie**
- **Planting Evidence**
- **Jury Tampering**

The art of framing innocent people has been in practice for centuries and will continue until the perpetrators are held accountable. Turning conventional assumptions and beliefs in the justice system upside down, *Un-Making a Murderer* takes you on that journey.

The profits from this book are going to Steven and Brendan and to donate free books to schools and prisons. In the last three years, Shaun Attwood has donated 20,000 books.

ABOUT SHAUN ATTWOOD

Shaun Attwood is a former stock-market millionaire and Ecstasy supplier turned YouTuber, public speaker, author and activist, who is banned from America for life. His story was featured worldwide on National Geographic Channel as an episode of Locked Up/Banged Up Abroad called Raving Arizona.

Shaun's writing – smuggled out of the jail with the highest death rate in America run by Sheriff Joe Arpaio – attracted international media attention to the human rights violations: murders by guards and gang members, dead rats in the food, cockroach infestations…

While incarcerated, Shaun was forced to reappraise his life. He read over 1,000 books in just under six years. By studying original texts in psychology and philosophy, he sought to better understand himself and his past behaviour. He credits books as being the lifeblood of his rehabilitation.

Shaun tells his story to schools to dissuade young people from drugs and crime. He campaigns against injustice via his books and blog, Jon's Jail Journal. He has appeared on the BBC, Sky News and TV worldwide to talk about issues affecting prisoners' rights.

As a best-selling true-crime author, Shaun is presently writing a series of action-packed books exposing the War on Drugs, which feature Pablo Escobar and the cocaine Mafia. On his weekly true-crime podcast on YouTube, Shaun interviews people with hard-hitting stories and harrowing prison experiences.

Printed in Great Britain
by Amazon